What Literary Studies Could Be, And What It Is

Bruce Fleming

University Press of America,® Inc.
Lanham · Boulder · New York · Toronto · Plymouth, UK

University Press of America
4501 Forbes Boulevard
Suite 200
Lanham, Maryland 20706
UPA Acquisitions Department (301) 459-3366

Estover Road
Plymouth PL6 7PY
United Kingdom

Library of Congress Control Number: 2008931038
ISBN-13: 978-0-7618-4160-9 (paperback : alk. paper)
ISBN-10: 0-7618-4160-1 (paperback : alk. paper)
eISBN-13: 978-0-7618-4266-8
eISBN-10: 0-7618-4266-7

Contents

Preface

TAKING A LITERATURE CLASS IN COLLEGE could be a life-changing experience. Books give us an up-close and personal look at what people do, and let us think about why they did it. Because we're both close up to them and distanced from them (they're not real: they can't see us), we can look at them with an intensity comparable to the way we look at fish in an aquarium: they're right there, going about their business inches from our eyes. Literature is so important because we rarely get this kind of view of human actions in the real world: we're not allowed to stare at real people, and they don't like being talked about. Neither of these is an issue with literature: in fact, it's made to be started at. Literature can help us give names to feelings and situations that didn't have names, allows us to understand what's happened and what's happening to us so we can move forward. It could help us understand ourselves, other people, and ultimately, the course of history.

This is all that literary studies could be. Nowadays it rarely is. In the last fifty years or so the professorate has developed a new animal: literary studies. The point of reading is no longer to help students process their world. Instead professionalized literary studies is about the professors, not the students. Literature is now regarded not as an end in itself, something that students are meant to use for understanding their own lives, but rather as part of a quasi-scientific body of works (usually we call them "texts") that has to be interpreted for students by the priestly class, the professorate, who Explain It All To Them. The classroom frequently becomes little more than a theater for the exercise of professorial power. Students come to the professors, who give them the point of view they're selling, and grade them on how well they've adopted the particular point of view of that course. It's not about helping students achieve freedom from the limitations of their own viewpoints or their own youth; instead it's about control.

In graduate school, professors learn to specialize, for which the justification is that we're contributing our bit to the realm of Knowledge about literature that literary studies constructs. It's been noted that students rarely share our passion for the tiny bit of the field we cultivate; this has led to the widely-perceived gulf between graduate studies, on one hand, and undergraduate courses on the other. Only graduate students, whom we can turn into versions of ourselves, Understand Us. Undergraduates are the unwashed masses. The way universities have bridged this gulf between two groups of readers is by giving the undergraduate courses to the younger, less professionalized people (of course they're students themselves, and cost the universities less): full professors at many institutions rank out of undergraduates, certainly freshmen. The clash of world-views between those who are looking for ways literature can help them with their lives, and the professorate that lives in a world where literature is the whole of life is attenuated because we largely avoid the clash: they go one direction, we another. (Nowadays literature professors make claims for literature that seem ludicrous to those outside: all power is textual, for example—but what of armies and jailors, the students wonder?) But of course the younger people who do teach courses to the young largely themselves lack any context for the literature, any way to make clear their larger issues, the things that might actually be of some use to undergraduates. And they're learning the jargonized speech of the priestly class too, or have just learned it themselves, fresh out of graduate school: they tend to try it out on their even younger charges, who look about in puzzlement—this isn't what literature is about, they're pretty sure, but then again, maybe it is. They leave no clearer about their lives, typically, than when they went in.

Literary studies has moved Heaven and Earth in the last decades to re-make itself in the image of science. Now it does "research" with jargon that would make a nuclear scientist envious (or more likely, roll her eyes), presents findings at just as many conferences as any science, has its "breaking news discoveries"—we have to rush home to apply Benjamin's *Arcades Project* to our own personal writer, as it seems everyone else is applying it to his or her own "subject"—and sees itself as transmitting this exciting new world of "discoveries" to young men and women who, like as not, are more concerned with their own much more fundamental discoveries: the complexity of sexuality, the strangeness of human relations, and the oddness of adults, among other things.

This notion that literature forms a coherent objective whole that individual "researchers" develop bits of has harmed students. If you sit for a whole semester while a wild-haired Assistant Professor Explains It All To You, most typically nowadays through a political filter, you most likely feel resigned at best, but more likely resentful or even outraged. Studying literature isn't a way to make discoveries about the world you could actually use: it's another body of dry "objective" knowledge you have to master. You might as well have taken engineering classes: at least you'd be more employable when you graduate. But whom are you going to grumble to? The graduate assistant has the power of the grade (if you are the graduate assistant, the professor has the power of the grade), and the professor is interested in getting others to see things his or her way; the Dean, for his or her part, dare not meddle with the professors, or question their scientific pretensions, since that's so fundamental nowadays to their self-image, and indeed the basis on which methodology-heavy literary studies has been built.

In fact there is no objective manifold of literature, unless we adopt the circular definition that this manifold is what we're "working on." Books come to be or not, stay around or not, are read or not, depending on many factors, including Acts of God like earthquakes (which destroy libraries), politics (which makes their countries more or less accessible to the industrialized West), intellectual fashions (which makes one author "hot" this year), and academic gamesmanship (whom do I have to suck up to in my department?). There's no objective manifold of literature, no Platonic Idea of the Great Library in the Sky. Literature is highly personal (subjective) in its production, and it's highly personal (subjective) in the uses to which it's put. Books come to be or not, are written or not, are read or not, like the evanescent patterns of clouds that drift overhead on a summer's day. It may not actually matter which books we read with our students—certainly it doesn't matter as much as the defenders of one particular author, politics, sexual orientation, or ethnicity seem to think it does: nowadays we seem to think the only big decisions have to do with syllabi and hiring. Getting that "right" is going to solve all our problems: no. What matters is whether or not the books help students think about fundamental issues.

Trial and error has shown that the books that stay around as "classics" do address fundamental issues. Of course a "classic" can fail to do this for a number of reasons, including a clueless professor: there's no intrinsic value in having read (but not been able to apply) 100 Greatest Whatevers. Similarly, nothing says that Bahamian Lesbian students have to read works by Bahamian Lesbians to be about to understand their world. If this were so, then the converse would likely be true too: straight white males can't get anything from works by (or about) Bahamian Lesbians. Since the number of Bahamian Lesbian students is likely to be less than that of straight white men, it seems we should stick with white males of verifiably heterosexual tendencies for our reading lists.

All of this is of course nonsense: I, though male, and white, can understand life through the work of a black female writer; so too can the black female reader understand life through the work of a white male. In fact the obsession of the 1980s and 1990s with syllabi was only another expression of the classroom as a forum for power—and a pretty pitiful power platform at that, though it could make students miserable for a while.

It's a truly odd notion, this conviction that we "work on" or "make progress on" something as liquid as what comes to be as literature, the notion that literature is a manifold that can be studied, just the way science studies the objective world. Still, the belief that such a manifold exists grew naturally from the Modernist notion, which the Modernists took over from their progenitors the Romantics, that art would redeem us in a way that other things had failed to do. The Modernists thought had to go to artists to get a true perception of the world: artists would explain the world to you. In the professorial re-casting of this view, you have to go to professors to understand the "deep meaning" (a phrase my students think pleases the professor) of the literature. You don't understand the world, you understand literature. The difference is, literature has broken off from the world as its own self-enclosed manifold: that's all we understand when we understand. To many people this doesn't seem like enough—but it is the logical end result of conflating reading literature with something we think of as literary studies.

Most professors nowadays don't see themselves as doing a power number on their students (it's typically only the students who are very aware of that). Instead they're likely to be outraged if it's suggested that they are out for anything so crass as worldly influence. Most, instead, see themselves as underpaid toilers in the vineyards of Knowledge, working for years to add their little bit to the edifice of literary studies, sweating long hours to find a crack in the stone where they can attach their own roots.

What if it turns out, as I'm suggesting here, that the whole notion of an edifice is wrong-headed, a misconception? What if it turns out that there's no "there there" (to mis-use a phrase of Gertrude Stein), no edifice at all of literary studies? What if reading literature is more comparable to consuming food? We eat to get the energy to live, but nobody says we're doing anything remotely objective by figuring out ways to grow, cook, or serve it, beyond nourishing and, if we're lucky, pleasing people. It is. Nothing is gained by writing "the definitive article" on anybody: like as not, the next generation won't even read the Anybody, or wants to make its own discoveries. And there are only so many hours in the day: they're going to read the Anybody, who helps them comes to terms with their own lives, not our article about the Anybody. At most, writing about literature serves as a sort of intellectual diary for the writer: but unfortunately, even this is rare—usually it's something done because the writers think they have to. They don't. It doesn't help the world one bit.

In fact literature doesn't need to be "studied," only read and reflected on. That makes it normal, not abnormal. More of the world fails to be amenable to study than lends itself to it. The patterns of passing clouds aren't amenable to study, merely to observation. The tones of voice we use in a single conversation aren't amenable to cataloguing, much less those in all the conversations in the world: they're too numerous, slippery, too imprecise, too context-bound. Sure, we can analyze a single conversation, and might well learn a good deal from doing so. Similarly, we can analyze a work of literature, and learn about ourselves by doing so. But we don't add anything to an external objective manifold of Knowledge About Literature, because there is no such thing. There is such a manifold for science because science takes as its manifold the whole world. The manifold of science is All That There Is: we define this from within, not from without. What sense does it make to separate off a sub-folder from the whole, and then use the same terminology on this sub-folder? How can we hope to communicate with people on the outside?

Literary studies has created its own internalized world in the last fifty years or so. It makes perfect sense to those inside it: people are trained to carry it on, and do so daily. It's just that from the outside, it looks quaint, and odd, and pointless, none of which it seems to those inside. Or perhaps it does: there are some suggestions that literature professors might just be getting as disaffected as their students. Surely the younger, more exploited ones are; perhaps even the tenured ones are as well.

This book is written for those at all levels—students, graduate assistants, younger professors, older ones, college presidents, cultural commentators—who sense, perhaps only vaguely, that there's something dry about analyzing texts, coherent and self-contained to be sure, but as pointless as counting the grass blades on my front lawn. Sure we can do it, but why? So many people go into literature to find great world-changing ideas, and find instead the repetitive stamp, stamp, stamp of the boots of all the well-regimented students, marching in ranks. They become officers, thinking that someday they'll outrank all this; what they discover is the tedium of shining those boots, the eye-rolling boredom of inspections, the sycophancy necessary for promotion. The literary profession, in short, ends up being quite similar to the military, whose officers-in-training I've taught for more than two decades, where you really have to work to remember the lofty goals of duty, honor, and country that brought you there to begin with.

Most of the students are gone or going through the motions; many of the professors are discontented; those who run university presses roll their eyes at the tedium of what they publish, which in any event fewer and fewer people read. The time has come to understand how we came to this pass, and what we can do to get out. For we can get out: beyond literary studies lies literature. Beyond a conception of professors as priests giving Truth we can aim at a conception of the professor as a kind of intellectual coach in the classroom, there to organize the motion, give the students a workout, and strengthen and make more agile their minds. We're teaching skills in the classroom, or can once again do so, not facts. And we have to be humble: in most cases we work in a void, never aware of whether or not the students get anything from what we have to say. Perhaps even those who do only get this benefit years later. And only rarely do they come back to tell us about it. It's all the loneliness of the long-distance professor. But if you wanted immediate feedback, you should have gone into business.

There are reasons for reading literature in the academy (in brief: it's the only spot where most people will read literature at all, and we can help them see the point). But we can't keep on with things they way they are: it's a big waste of time at best, and at worst, turns students off to the very things that could be helping them deal with their lives. The only people who gain from the way things are is a small percentage of the professorate with secure jobs (harder and harder to get), who get to feel that they're doing something just like the big boys and girls in the science departments. They're not, and the pretense that they are is much worse than admitting cheerfully that they're not, and then explaining what they *are* doing.

Every person discovers the world anew, comes to problems as if for the first time. Literature can help them see that others have done the same before them, and give them ways to make their own decisions, live their own lives. Professors can be the coaches on this so-momentous undertaking, guiding, showing, encouraging, challenging. This is a profession we could be proud to belong to.

Soon, with luck, we may be able to cry: Literary Studies is dead! Long Live Literature!

Annapolis, Maryland
1 May 2008

Introduction

Pyrrhic Victory

THE STUDY OF LITERATURE HAS BECOME professionalized. That's the good news: the rules of what it means to study or teach literature became well codified in the second half of the twentieth century. That's also the bad news. It's a Pyrrhic victory. (The Greek leader Pyrrhus is supposed to have said, as translated into English from Plutarch, "Another victory like this and we are lost.") We've given literary studies a solid basis as a discipline, but at the cost of cutting it off from the rest of the world.

It's time to leave "literary studies." What we'll end up with again is the contact sport of the classroom, just what we had before we English professors decided we wanted to play at being scientists. The teacher will once again be seen in his or her proper role as the coach: we lead the workout, hope to make the students better in the game of making sense of literature by helping them do it, react to their games (their written and oral work) and call it a day when it's over.

Professionalization, what we've effected in literary studies, emphasizes the ritual of the profession rather than what it's a profession of. The academic study of literature nowadays has almost nothing to do with the sweaty world of literature, wrung from the living, breathing world outside. On one side of the desk it's, well, academic, all about what to teach (which is to say: syllabi) and who "owns" what literature (hiring decisions). On the other side of the desk, it's no less academic. Students in the age of "literary studies" are told that literature is most essentially about other works of literature and about the expression of power rather than having any more direct relation with life.

In a climate where marginalized groups were clambering to have "their" works read instead of others, "their" members hired before others, the real issues in departments of literature seemed reduced to those of syllabi and faculty composition, as if literature were not in fact about the large, messy, smelly, but oh-so-interesting world the university had apparently forgotten it existed to serve, but instead about questions of courses and makeup of university departments. Surely the most important question facing us as human beings in a troubled world can't be whether we teach a book by a Dead White Male or by (say) a living Bahamian lesbian? Both, after all, are books, discussed as part of a group three times a week from 9 to 9:50 a.m. Maybe, given those similarities, differences between particular texts don't matter?

Gerald Graff tried to put an end to the controversy about what to teach by telling us to "teach the controversy"—which means, teach the arguments between professors, in the time allotted to teaching the work of literature: all literature exists to end as part of literary study.[1] All literature is "texts," ceaselessly referring to each other: cut free of their moorings to anything else, these formed the objective manifold that literary study was then free to focus on, the givens of the literary world just as the physical universe is the basis of science. Because the world of literature is conceived of like the objective physical world, it's worth pointing out our subjectivity in its perception, as Norman Holland emphasized the variability of memory in reading, the way we apparently read what we want to read.[2]

Scholastic philosophy was very interested in questions like the age souls/angels would be in heaven, whether they would be male or female, and whether they had extension (bulk, weight: how many angels could dance on the head of a pin?). Answers were provided, somewhat arbitrarily, to many such questions (we'd all be 33 in Heaven, like Jesus at His death; we wouldn't have gender, and we wouldn't have extension, so an infinity of angels can dance on the head of a pin). Nowadays we just don't care about these questions. That's not a factor of the questions; it's a factor of the way periods in intellectual history get played out: we simply lose interest, and walk away. The time of literary studies is played out; some people have begun to walk, and I think many others are thinking about it. In any case we lost most of the students many years ago—unsurprising, as the phase in intellectual history wasn't about them at all, but about establishing what the professors did as a quasi-scientific enterprise, a topic uninteresting to all those who aren't literature professors.

I think many more people will walk if they're reassured that that's the way we show that questions no longer hold our interest. We can walk away with a much weaker justification than we might think: it's enough to say how deadly dull most contemporary literary studies has become in a world full of much more interesting things. "I'd rather not" is, it turns out, a pretty good justification for not doing something.

Soldiers and snowflakes

It's true that everything we read is a "text." But that's as trivial as saying that all people are *homo sapiens*. What then? Are there no differences between them that matter, no fundamental distinctions to be made at more than a secondary level? Instead, let's say: of course they're texts; now let's talk about how an individual text relates to something outside of it. Wouldn't that be much more interesting? It merely shows a lack of imagination to assume that the relation of a work of literature with the world has to be the one we inherited from the pre-Romantic world, the notion of mimesis, or of mirroring the world. That particular notion of the relation of texts to the world led us down all sorts of dead ends, such as trying to convince ourselves that little black squiggles on paper, say those in *War and Peace*, really are the same as Napoleonic soldiers and snowflakes. We know they're not, so for some people, the only alternative is the conclusion that they're the opposite of real things, merely signs without meaning except by relation to each other, texts talking to texts. This, by and large, has been the conclusion of the later twentieth century, the time that gave us professionalized literary studies.

But merely because *War and Peace* doesn't contain real soldiers and snow, this doesn't mean the book has *no* relationship to the world. It just means it doesn't have a *predictable* relationship to the world. We're not limited to the two choices offered in M.H. Abrams's celebrated contrast of pre-Romantic and Romantic tropes, literature either as the mirror of nature or the lamp of the author's genius.[3] The relationship of literature with the world isn't through something we can establish once and for all, but through something that's much more dependent on the situation: the effect it has on the reader's life, something that may only become clear decades down the line, if then.

Reading, say, *Anna Karenina* can change our life. Surely this is not just the result of its portraying what we personally do: probably we're not involved in an adulterous relationships, and by definition we haven't committed suicide. Do we see ourselves? In which character(s)? Do we see things we do? Things we might do? What we're in danger of doing? None of us lived in nineteenth-century Russia, and many readers aren't female. Perhaps we only need identify with the characters, not be identical to them. But how literal does the identification have to be? What does "identification" mean? What effect does it have on us if we *do* identify with someone? We can't say beforehand where we'll find a place to latch on, or if we will. Attempts to ensure a link with a piece of literature are futile; we can't even say what the nature of the link is. All we can do is describe the sense of looking up from a page full of these little black and white squiggles with the feeling that suddenly we understand our own lives, that names have been given to things that lacked them, and that the iron filings that hitherto were scattered about have configured into a clear pattern. Things are now different, somehow. Maybe that will cause us to act differently; maybe not. It's not really something that is amenable to prediction and in many cases not even to description (or at least, simply isn't described)—which means it can't be part of a process of professionalization, which requires more dependable processes.

Since the Romantic era we haven't talked much about the mirror. More recently, we've rejected the lamp: authors aren't "creative" any more. Literature nowadays is neither the mirror of nature nor the lamp of authorial inspiration: it just is, apparently produced in an airless room by machines working through permutations of keys on the computer, our twenty-first century version of the monkeys on typewriters. We've re-made our vision of literature to make it amenable to the teaching situation, pedagogy calling the shots.

Waves crash elsewhere

Our greatest victory is to have made literary studies something that can, and has been, professionalized. That's also our greatest defeat. Literary study nowadays is secure and self-contained; but at the same time completely sidelined from the mainstream. It's a methodology, of course, with its way of doing things and its unquestioned presuppositions. So we can do it forever. But in exchange for that, we've ensured the placidity of the undertaking, which is to say its irrelevance. The waves crash elsewhere; we're in the quiet tide pools. SomFe of the animals that flourish within the tide pools and the backwaters undoubtedly think things are fine. Others may yearn, if only secretly, for the open sea. In fact, I think many of the people caught in the backwater of professionalized literary studies nowadays harbor fantasies of riding really big waves.

The study of literature, in order to be a separable enterprise, has to be regulated and predictable, with change kept within bounds. We've attained that: the changes are all rung on the same pattern of bells. The problem is, nobody has ever shown the bells serve any other purpose than themselves, or that there's an external point in this particular regulated and predictable enterprise. So there's no clear gain. The loss, by contrast, *is* clear: literature in universities, where most people contact it (and where the contact frequently ends) is now something to feed the process of teaching literature—rather than something that can change the lives of those who read it.

We don't need this kind of literary studies, any more than it turned out we really needed Scholastic philosophy, whose questions now seem to us so dry and uninteresting, though none of them have actually been answered.

Air Pump

My focus here isn't politics, nor the economic nature of American higher education, nor how unappreciated American intellectuals are. The sun goes up and goes down each day in the humanities; students write dissertations, professors write articles and books—and then yet more articles, yet more books. (Yes, this is a book too.) Yet it all seems peculiarly and increasingly airless, like the environment of the bird in the famous painting "Experiment on a Bird in the Air Pump" of Joseph Wright of Derby, in the National Gallery, London, where an amateur scientist is demonstrating the effect of a vacuum on a bird in a bell jar to his simultaneously fascinated and horrified family.

At least the bird struggles, aware of the threat to its life (it's unclear whether the experiment has to end with its death, or whether the jar will be lifted). American academia contains many people who are proud of being where they are, doing what they do, and are unaware that there's anything wrong. An outsider, or even an insider with contacts to the outside world, might well notice that the provisions have now diminished to close to zero, and no one inside seems concerned. Vaguely uneasy, probably—but not fundamentally concerned, as if they hadn't quite managed to connect the dots and figure out where their feeling of turning a prayer wheel was coming from. The only way to change things is to lift the bell jar so the bird can breathe, break the glass tubes of the elaborate apparatus we've constructed in which rarified gases circulate over and over.

We need to transcend the sense of satisfaction we get from turning our profession into something with its own methodology, its own justification, and its own jargon, and its emphasis on the stage and the canvas rather than what's portrayed on the stage or on the canvas, its insistence that the only thing that counts in the world is language, written if possible, and that all texts do is endlessly refer to each other. This gives us a reason for doing what we do, and it strengthens our power position over those who submit to its givens. But it's not good for the students. I don't even think it's good for professors. It makes us strangely defensive creatures, craven for respect from the world and furious that we don't get it. Besides, if we demanded less power in the classroom, we might have a fighting chance at getting it in the world outside. What we should want is for our students to say: Oh yes, Prof. X. She really made me work, but she was there cheering when I made it across the finish line. Or, Ah, Prof. Y. He really opened my eyes to the possibilities of the world. If your students say that about you, you get into heaven. But of how many of us won't they say instead, if they say anything at all: Yes, that Bastard Prof. Z. Always carrying on about his own views, and wouldn't let anybody who disagreed with him get a word in edgewise.

The pretense of studying literature as a systematic undertaking is hollow, so we gain little from it. Insisting on this hollow pretense, however, also makes it impossible for us to study literature as an unsystematic guide to life. We lose both ways. Paradoxically, it's having had for twenty years students at the United States Naval Academy who do literally march to the same drummer on the parade field that has convinced me that we have to give this up if we're to serve the literature and thus our students, rather than using both to serve ourselves. It's not about us, it's about them. Coaches can't play the game for the students, nor should they want to. In professionalizing literary studies, we've made it all about us. No wonder students feel left out in the cold.

Letters and spaces

So why aren't more people in open rebellion? The answer is that any way of doing things quickly becomes its own end, because it has the virtue of familiarity. We might call it "the inertia of the known." We can't, after all, question everything, as Descartes discovered. So some things are going to continue to be done simply because they're done. Besides, literary studies does have its positive side: it gives the professors a profession, so of course they're the ones who defend it.

Any study that had this virtue would be defended in the same way and for the same reasons. We can postulate an alternative world where students arrive prepared to talk about the number of letters on each page, the pattern of spaces between words, and the texture of the paper. If this sort of study has become well entrenched, those in charge of it would almost invariably be nonplussed, and probably also furious, at someone suggesting there are other things to do with books than this. To the outsider, this seems to miss the point. To those doing it, it *is* the point, because it's something codifiable, something that can be transmitted. It's got something to do with literature, so it's "literary study." That's its justification in the university. It can be turned off and on easily, like water from a faucet—which after all is the primary requirement of doing this "on call" in a scheduled situation for which people are paying money.

I'd say that the meticulous "research" a graduate professor of mine was engaged in on applying Claude Lévi-Strauss's "semiotic square" (paired opposites) to first one text and then another made fully as much sense as counting letters, and for the same reasons.[4] His application of these now otherwise forgotten "semiotic squares" to yet another text, and making his students do it too, opened a practically inexhaustible vein. It had many virtues, starting with the fact that it gave him a career. Too, it could be packaged easily: he could start doing it on call and stop on call; people could be tested on whether they could apply the squares, and so on. It was, in short, made for the university.

Indeed, most all our literary study today is made for the university, in the same way most of our art is made for the museum. Most art works are too large, too ugly, or too self-referential to "work" in a personal living space, which perhaps as a result is denigrated as bourgeois and domestic, beneath the notice of true artists. That keeps the riff-raff out. Most literary study involves too much apparatus and is too impersonal to have any chance of life with individuals trying to do it on their own.

This is the source of both the strength and the weakness of literary studies. (It's also the source of both the strength and weakness of most contemporary art.) When we're within them, they seem to make sense, as counting letters surely makes sense to those who do it. From the outside, however, they seems only another of the countless futile pastimes people have invented for themselves, from solitaire to video games. The more cumbersome the academic analysis becomes, the more it seems both to justify and be justified by the university—the way the huge trumpet-like sculpture that hung in the former power plant turned into Tate Modern, an artwork larger than a blue whale, both required this gargantuan space and was created to fill it.

Shrink wrap

Literary study requires something to "study," which means, something we simply presuppose, a science starts with the natural world. The more "scientific" we become in talking about literature, the more we presuppose the works without asking where they come from. This means, we fail, or resolutely refuse, to consider the relationship of works to the world outside: we assume they merely *are*, like stones. Nowadays we teach humanities as if we were giving a tour of a grocery store to Martians: we explain the vegetable section, the dairy section, the meat section, note similarities and differences, variations of texture and color, the fact that there's no milk where the applesauce is, and perhaps the fact (which we bemoan) that there are no papayas. We don't presuppose visitors know anything about where the things on display came from; if they do, it's because we told them—that can be our work too, speaking of the world before it ended up in the grocery store. But we're the ones who decide whether or not to include this, and how much.

Our work is on drawing distinctions and connections between the carrots and the aubergines—or if we're daring, between the pork chops and the celery. To be really avant-garde (a by now tired artistic concept that's found new life in the scholarly world), we introduce a new vegetable and insist that it be given shelf space. Not that we necessarily deny the origins of what's in the store: it's just that we include it as footnote to the store, to be passed out in little leaflets to store-goers, rather than as something with importance in its own right. Some of our colleagues think themselves daring for doing "field work" on a dairy farm, where they live with the farmers and report on how that milk actually gets to the store. We write biographies of authors, hoping to track down the sources of the works. These reports become part of the same air-conditioned world in which everything has a place, order reigns supreme, and we are in charge. What we don't want is anybody realizing that the world of the store occupies only a tiny place in the world, that the world as a whole is actually is far more disordered than ordered, or that they can dispense with the grocery store altogether. We're in charge of the grocery store, after all, and we want them to come to us to get their food.

I admire the astonishing and revelatory consistency of the tenets of professional literary studies, the numerous ways in which the self-sufficiency, and hence ultimately the irrelevance, of the discipline were created. It's all consistent. That's the problem: it's too consistent. Those inside won't be able to say what's missing: to them everything is inside the store. It's only those outside who can explain what's still outside, because they're the only ones who see it.

The Mutiny

The state of the humanities in America is comparable to the state of the luckless inhabitants of the (only slight fictional) British Residency in J.G.

Farrell's novel about the so-called Mutiny of 1857 in India, *The Siege of Krishnapour*—who, besieged by the Indians they are purportedly there to serve, gradually run out of provisions, go mad, or starve to death; it also shows elements of the situation in Edgar Allan Poe's lurid somehow-parable "The Masque of the Red Death" about people who decide to party to escape the plague and find Death at the center of their revels.[5] There's no outside, it seems, to care about what's going on inside: those outside the ivory tower have long since ceased besieging the gates, if in fact they ever did. The danger is within.

At least, this last phrase has a nice ring. It may however be over-dramatized to say "the danger is within," since the situation isn't even so colorful and dramatic as the appearance of Death in the innermost, scarlet room of Poe's closed-off site of revels. It isn't dramatic danger that's done in the humanities, it's the slow passage of time—in this like the simple diminution of provisions in Farrell's novel, as those besieged eat first one set of things hitherto thought inedible and then the even more inedible; sacrificing possessions and furniture that only days before had seemed indispensable—and having the sacrifice be for naught.

Professional literary studies as currently constituted wipes from the table the process of life turning into books, declared irrelevant to its nature, and constructs a universe out of words. No wonder, for several decades, one of literary study's most-read story/parables was Borges's "The Library of Babel," the world become vast library. And no wonder professors tried to eliminate the inconvenient fact that individual writers, responding to their own reality, had had to make these micro-worlds from the raw stuff of the world as a whole, smaller worlds that then became nothing but the mosaic tiles in a greater picture, that of literary studies. Usually this took the form of the assertion that artists weren't "creative" in any way that critics weren't: that notion, of couse, was part of the nonsense of the Romantics. The argument would have been more convincing had critics not themselves been claiming the same creativity for themselves they were denying to artists: it wasn't an attack on the commodity, only on who owned it.

This book is not a defense of artists against critics, though most artists don't waste the time to read critics—the scorn between artists and literary professors is mutual. Susan Sontag's much-discussed essay "Against Interpretation" (whose most famous line was that "interpretation is the revenge of the intellect upon art") was a useful bromide, but it doesn't really touch the problem I'm addressing—that the study has become the victim of its own success.[6] What could the practitioners of professional literary studies do in the face of such blanket rejection as hers but soldier on as before? They think in fact they've taken over the role of the artist; how are artists supposed to react save with frustrated fury? My point is a bit more oblique than Sontag's. It's that literary studies has been successful; its almost total irrelevance is the result of that success. We can't merely attack that success, we must concede it. And then point out the price at which it was procured.

Aboutir à un livre

One Modernist giant, the poet Stephane Mallarmé, wrote that "everything in the world exists to end in a book."[7] Literary studies nowadays acts as if this were an axiom of literary studies in general: the books are primary; everything else leads to them. Thus the study of literature is not the study of literature by chance: we need consider nothing outside them at all, and if we do consider the world outside, it can be as much or as little as we choose. Our point of departure is that books grow on library shelves the way city children are said to believe that hamburgers grow in supermarket freezers. If we choose to add any information about this world, this is gravy, and we can control what we add: we, the literature professor, are in charge of the world.

The easiest way to object to this notion that literature grows in libraries is to point out the most obvious factor behind the literature that's not in the library: the author. Those who object to this self-involved way of doing things have thus tended to be defenders of that now-faded notion of "authorial intention." Disciples of Michel Foucault, who announced the "death of the author," got to feel daring.[8] The old guard, led by E.D. Hirsch, Jr., came on with a strong defense of the author—to the point where insisting that we should read to get "authorial intention" is nowadays the sign that you're right-wing.[9]

It's a good impulse to insist that there's a whole world outside of the library. However "authorial intention" is not the way to indicate this; the right-wing needs to let this one go. Anyone who reads can brush this one aside with no problem: of course we're never going to get at the author's intention. The author is usually dead, and even living authors are famously gnomic, unhelpful, or downright mendacious when it comes to their own works—not to mention frequently far from the best people to analyze them. If we concede that we'll never get at the author's "intention" then, according to the methodology of literary studies, we have to allow the world of literary scholars to go back to its rustling discourse of interpretation.

If speaking of "authorial intention" is the most logical means of insisting that there really is a world outside of the library, the next most logical means is to talk about the facts of the world that produced it, such as the marketing system and tastes of the times. This however usually has the disadvantage of losing the focus on the particular work: there's no reason, it seems, to read or discuss this work rather than any other typical work. If what we say about the world outside the work has independent validity, it renders a focus on any particular work arbitrary. So we don't read works, we read types. Only we don't read types: we read individuals. All the specificity comes out in the wash.

Marxist analysis of socioeconomic conditions at the time a work was produced doesn't help us understand *that* work, merely works of that type. (Of course what we can learn is precisely that this individual work *is* a work of a certain type.) I'm proposing that we can help clarify the connections of a specific work to the world without losing the particularity of the specific work. We ask: how does this work relate to our world? The world? The world of here and now? Other worlds? To what you know? To what I know? We can, indeed must, use generally valid facts to express these connections. But unless we train them on the work, we're not doing literary analysis, we're doing sociology. There's nothing wrong with that, only it's simply wrong to say they're the same things, any more than statistical analyses of the population variations in a small town has anything to do with the individuals who lived there.

The trick in balancing text with context is to be able to focus on the work without asserting or implying that the rest of the world fails to exist: this focus on the work allows us to choose from the whole world outside, using our knowledge of that world to comment on this work. We don't assert or imply that we have thereby used up the world, merely picked and chosen from it to better understand this work. This isn't "literary study," it's spending time with literature, and making the rest of the world our trove of ways to link it to things outside of itself.

The seminar room may be the venue where talking about literature is most effective. Yet even at the opposite end of the spectrum, where a professor stands at a lectern and speaks impersonally to hundreds, it's possible to have this kind of interaction with literature, even if the students don't speak up. If the professor engages their attention and says things that get them thinking, they can do their interaction silently: not all classrooms require immediate articulation of ideas. Nor should we conclude that fewer students in the room is always better. It's possible to have too few students as well as too many, as most students have flashes of insight, rather than continuous ones, and they combine to create a viable collective.

Supermen

For decades in the late twentieth century, students and professors of literature gleefully quoted Jacques Derrida's flip *"il n'y a pas de hors-texte"*—there's no realm outside the text.[10] Writing, according to the impish Derrida (but how unimpishly, how earnestly, his doctrine was preached for so many decades!), holds primacy over oral transmission, while presence—held by Western philosophy to be more real in some sense than absence—is really a subsidiary of absence. Writing therefore trumps talk, being ontologically primary. And if there's nothing outside writing, so the highest form of life is—the envelope please... —the professor of written texts! There, wasn't that easy? Suddenly literature professors, caricatured for so long as hollow-chested pipe-smoking pedants, could see themselves as Superman, or Wonder Woman. Their narrow corner of the carpet turns out to be the whole carpet, or at least the only part that matters. We've all but convinced others, and assert as a matter of course for ourselves, that processed food is the only kind there is, that literature can't exist in any other form except as a part of literary study as it's practiced nowadays.

Literary studies nowadays offers the equivalent of a meal of instant mashed potatoes, breaded fish sticks, ketchup, and Twinkies. Everything has been ground up and re-formed, and bears little resemblance to anything you might see running around or growing in the ground. And then we tell those we feed on this fare that that's okay: this is food, that stuff outside isn't. Don't even think of catching your own.

No one seems to have noticed that more processing of the material isn't necessarily better, any more than the beautifully pure white bread of the New World, that immigrants raised (and made hardy) on brown bread learned to prefer to the peasant fare of the Old, is in fact better. It's more processed, to be sure. It's always the same, and it's now sliced so beautifully, and comes in a plastic bag, and keeps forever.

Sitting in the dark

Literary studies since the professionalization of literary study isn't about literature, it's about the study, like an art history class from the 1950s. The students sit in the dark. The assistant manipulates a slide projector and the professor talks: "Notice the symmetry of this composition, a standard Renaissance nativity. Note the classical arches over the crib. Next slide please. Note the way this Venetian Madonna and child is off-center, incorporating landscape in the area that before Bellini would have been relegated to the side. Now it's much more central. Compare with the landscape in 'La Giaconda,' the 'Mona Lisa' which is considerably more peripheral. Next slide please." Now, with the computer, the professor doesn't have to ask for the next slide. But s/he is still using the individual works to construct a larger whole.

What's being taught is not the works, it's the connections between the works. The assumption may be that the students already know the works and are paying tuition for the connections. But this is not an assumption that anyone lays out; if we did we'd certainly note that few of the students in the class have ever looked at these works independently of the class that focuses on connections. The professor thinks s/he is earning his/her pay by saying something new; only graduate students already in the world of the professor can appreciate this small amount of extra added value and understand its difference from what it's being added to. But what attempt does the system make to ensure that they can differentiate between the added value and what the value is added to? What's taught to students at every level is only the connections, the patterns between works.

A class visit to an art museum can be frustrating for someone who's never been to this museum before and wants to look at the works, make discoveries on his or her own. If the professor is earning his or her pay, there's always an agenda: the class is going to look at certain works and not others, stay as long before each one as the professor sees fit, and file dutifully on to the next one when the professor says so. You're supposed to look at the shading, or the landscape, or the shading and the landscape. Not, certainly, the whole picture. "How beautiful!" isn't the desired response.

To be sure, many first-time visitors don't know what to look at, or how they're to react, so they are glad to be told all this. They exit "knowing" things about the artworks. Or at least thinking they do: is there anything more horrible than listening to two American girls on a semester in Florence talking to each other in the Uffizi about the paintings? This is the simulacrum of knowledge without the substance: perhaps nothing at all would be better, after all.

People reading works for the first time don't want to focus on connections, they want to focus on the things being connected. We've scotched that one by insisting, by and large, that there is no way to focus directly on the things without their connections; the literary work slips away when we focus our attention on it, being nothing but the sum of various readings. If there's no way to access the thing without the connections, that leaves us professors free to focus on what's most congenial with the professionalization of the study. It's too like the way, in a patriarchal society, any other point of view than that of the person in the power position (usually the *paterfamilias*) was dismissed as irrelevant, secondary, childish, or female. Instead of a tyranny of the father, we now have a tyranny of the institution. It amounts to the same.

This is the reason why major universities neglect undergraduate literary education: undergraduate needs do not fit with the needs of literary study. Thus in an indirect way, this book is a defense of undergraduate teaching as opposed to research. It's not that teaching is legitimate and scholarship isn't, because scholarship feeds into teaching. And we don't know when that might be, so there's a point in keeping scholarship around, stockpiling it (so to say) in places we call libraries. But its only point is in use, in the way it may one day help the person in the institutional middle between reader and book—the professor—to make the book more meaningful to the reader. Of course, the act of scholarship may also be deeply satisfying to the person who pursues it (though my impression is that this is a distinct minority of the professorate). But so too is my enjoyment of a good chardonnay deeply satisfying: it has no objective point outside of that. I can't claim that the world is a better or more fact-filled place because I've enjoyed drinking the wine.

Learning more

We need to walk away from, give up, literary studies—at least, literary studies as we've constructed them in the last fifty or so years. Giving up literary studies means giving up the notion that we can "learn more" in any absolute sense about literature. We only learn more with respect to the last increment: we study two books by Joyce, not one. So in that sense we do know more. But while we are studying Joyce, what have we forgotten about Chaucer? What have we failed to learn about someone else who, by definition, remains that much less well understood than Chaucer? Oh, we say: I personally need not know more about Chaucer. "Literary studies" knows more about Chaucer. But what does this mean? More articles are published? Fine. But which of these are actually read? Of what's read, what's understood? What transmitted to others? Perhaps more produces less: what if we write so much about X, or read it, that we become heartily sick of X, or of writing about X, and want only to read Y? Is this knowing more about X or knowing less? It's all like making sand castles, that are swept away by the next wave. If we concentrate only on making this castle, or the next, our life seems to have a point. If we pull back our gaze, however, we lose our sense of urgency. Why make yet another sand castle if it's only going to be washed away? If the point isn't simply the making of the sand castle, the exercise has no point.

Girly

The point of engaging in literature is to help students learn about themselves, not help them see the professor's "take" on the work. Yet in far too many classrooms since the institutionalization of literary studies, the classroom exists to end in a certain content, a bill of goods the professor is selling. Both the particular content of this bill of goods and the fact that students are expected to sign on the dotted line for any content at all can be deeply alienating to many students. Many men, in particular, come into literature courses with some degree of suspicion: literature, in the popular mind, is "girly." Reading is something well-mannered people do inside, when in fact what they want to do is make noise outside. In courses run by the methods of professionalized literary studies, the men find these prejudices confirmed. They discover that literature courses are run with the intention of getting them to sign off on things they're not so sure they want to sign off on, and run by someone who's going to ram his or her point of view down their throat—and punish them with a bad grade if they balk. They find their negative feelings about literature confirmed, and simply vote with their feet, abandoning the humanities departments of the university. Of course the pay is better with an engineering degree too, but if the study itself were more congenial to them, they might be willing to follow their heart, rather than their pocketbook. As it is, their heart says no—and so does their pocketbook. Why stick around?

Young men especially are deeply invested in their own pride: literary studies takes no account of this, and insists that its point of view is something they must bow to. If instead it's offered merely as something interesting, something that could be of use to them, they would probably be more inclined to want it. Nobody wants to be controlled, and young men drunk on their own testosterone least of all. If we had set out to make a discipline unappealing to men, we couldn't have done a better job than we've done in making professionalized literary studies. If literature were presented less objectively, less as something they have to "learn" (which it isn't), but more as something they might like, I'd guess that more men would stay in literature classes.

This book is critical of what many students are offered in college and graduate school courses. But it lacks the political agenda that deforms many other such criticisms. This book isn't about politics; it's about the crying shame of teaching literary works as if they were footnotes to footnotes, murmurings of the eternal stream of words, when in fact they could be life-changing for the people who read them. In professionalizing literary studies the way we have, turning it into its own end, we've cut literature off from its connection to the world. Instead of being acknowledged as the great unpredictable animals they are, works of literature have been tamed and turned into house pets, or at best put behind bars in the zoo. It's time we let them loose again, if only on the game preserves of universities. (Perhaps libraries are the wild: anything goes.) We owe it to ourselves, and to the students who in many cases are our own children. We need to do better by them than we're doing.

What is literature?

In order to get back to books, we have to understand how books are related to, yet different from, face-to-face social interactions with people. Books have been written by people, yet the people have gone away, indeed are perhaps long dead. We have the sense of seeing the traces they left behind, walking through the maze they constructed, without the immediacy of speaking to real people. So books, and indeed all human products, are in this sense abandoned constructions we happen upon. And yet books are, at the same time, more "here" before us than any person could be. We hold them in our hands, read them on our own time, and can put them down or even throw them away. We hold them in our power, as they in theirs. Books in this sense are more immediate than would be the social ballet of speaking to someone face to face—not to mention the fact that the probability would be against our ever meeting this person at all, or having him or her accessible to us, even if we are contemporaries in the same general location. Books are both more immediate than people, and less.

This status as neither fish nor fowl is the source of their power: they bear the traces of people, but belong to us, or can, with an intensity that no other person can. But we can equally well walk away from them: books have no honor to defend, and no one will call us ill-mannered for walking away. We don't even have to smile ruefully, or say "no thank you." We don't have to say anything, in fact, at all.

Because books are so, in a way, defenseless, we can take them to our hearts in a way we rarely do with other people, who after all have their own lives to live, and probably compete with us for resources. The power of books is, paradoxically, their powerlessness: they demand nothing from us, so we can choose to give them more. Too, we come upon books as surprises, as we don't very often come upon people who surprises us. Most of the people we meet are part of our daily round. We're used to them, we expect them, they no longer surprise us. Books allow us the equivalent of getting out of our rut: suddenly something new! That's undoubtedly what Emily Dickinson meant by comparing a book to a ship: "there is no frigate like a boat, to take us lands away."[11] Literature lets us be continual tourists: they're not part of the daily round. This is the reason they can jolt us so in a way that is much rarer with experiences in the rest of the world: having an experience in life that changes us requires more (so to say) raw material than reading a book. We have to go on vacation, or have someone dear to us die, or have a major life change. It's not impossible to use real world experiences to re-order our lives, but we can't control them, and they're comparatively rare. Books, by contrast, are all over. All we have to do is read them.

Many people understand that literature occupies a half-and-half midway position between real people and stones. For some people, call them "(wo)men of action," this fact is negative: they correctly see that art is neither human nor not-human. (Wo)men of action like the world divided into two neat categories: subjective and objective. Every object is either a stone or a person, and you can use the stone to affect the person (usually negatively). Action is action with brute objects among other human beings.

That's why business(wo)men typically don't see the point of art, at least not since the Romantic era, when so many artists felt so alienated from the rising bourgeoisie of the nineteenth century. People of action see correctly that art is neither objective nor subjective, so they tend to think it pointless. The problem is, nobody has ever explained that of course art is precisely this thing, that's neither completely subjective nor completely objective: they can't object to it being what it is, or claiming that art is illegitimate by being between objective and subjective when that's precisely what makes it art. All that shows is that their map of the world contains nothing in this spot; others' maps may well do so.

The notion of something so weak (as literature is weak) that it can end up being more powerful is a notion that has to be explained to everyone. I think most people of action would understand this if it were explained, but typically it isn't. They note correctly that they can walk away from the work without opening it. Nobody explains to them what they might be giving up by doing so; nobody points out to them that they have to be pro-active about understanding their lives, as they are pro-active about changing them.

So if people of action don't "get" literature and books, as is so frequently the case, the fault is with poor teaching. The first step has to be to acknowledge that people of action are completely, utterly, right: literature has no claim on us. We have to reach out to it; it won't reach out to us. This is why it can matter so much to us: we feel as if we've discovered it, not that it's forcing itself on us. That's something that people of action can understand easily: only projects they adopt as their own will ever come to fruition. The weakness of literature has to be acknowledged, not denied.

In fact modern literary studies have gone in precisely the wrong direction, in the direction of denying this weakness. If literature can be made part of a power play, a teaching situation where professors hold the power of the grade over students so that they have to read these things and come to these conclusions, then (so apparently the thinking of those who constructed literary studies) literature can be made to matter in the world. But in fact this is precisely what people of action will reject: they're good at fending off attacks, and literature as part of modern literary studies is felt as merely another attack.

Aesop's fable of the sun and the wind is appropriate here. Both saw a cloaked man down below; the wind asserted it could get the man to take off his cloak. The sun demurred. The wind then blew its hardest; the man merely wrapped his cloak the tighter. The sun then took its turn: as the man became overheated, he took off his cloak. People only resist literature if it's made into something that has to be learned. If it's made into something that can be discovered, people—even people of action—may want it.

In the pre-Modern age, a platitude was to say that reading books was like having conversations with the great men and women of the past. As people realized how insufficient this notion was, they paved the way for the opposite extreme in which we now find ourselves: that books are merely the rustling flow of words, with no human touch at all. What's in the middle is called literature. That's not a list of works, it's a space in the world, a type of thing. We needn't ever know what works belong there, or how many there are, to understand the nature of literature. Literature isn't a list of individual works, it's a type of object. As Plato pointed out, we can understand the notion of "chair" without making a list of all the chairs that have been, are, or could ever be. We know one when we see one.[12]

Shock

What's been lost in institutionalizing and codifying literary study is the shock a book can have on a reader. Books can, somehow, change our lives. If they do so, we can usually say, at least haltingly, how this was so. "It made me think about how I'm going to die," we might say. Or: "suddenly I realized I didn't have to suffer through a bad marriage." Or: "I realized I had to be nicer to my mother because of all she went through with me."

The power of literature on us, when it has this power, is precisely that we've decided to let it in. We don't get our backs up; our fur isn't spiky, nor our eyes red with fury, nor blinded by the sense that "you're not going to tell me what to do." We don't have to negotiate the social situation of someone forcing something on us: it's just us and the book, and nobody cares what happens. So why not let it happen? Literature removes itself from the fact that all human relationships happen in the social sphere.

This is its disadvantage in the here and now: we can't insure it will have any effect right now, much less a particular one. However it's some compensation that literature has no statue of limitations on how long it's "allowed" before its possible effects kick in. It can take years before we "get" a certain book, or before its relevance to our life is clear. Or perhaps there's never a moment where we "get it." Not all books affect us, any more than we are interested in everything we see. Only some things catch our eye.

Nor is there any way to predict what aspect of which book will, if any does, alter us: we might assume that a book about a black woman (or is it: *by* a black woman?) will prove engaging for a black woman reader, but in fact it might be a white male character who causes such a reader to suddenly understand, say, her mother. Certainly the mere fact that a character (or writer) is a white male doesn't endear him to white male readers; it's been the fallacy of thinking that like is endearing to like, and lack of like is a deal-breaker, that's led to such a tempest in a teapot in literary-critical circles, the "canon wars" of the 1980s and 1990s. These turn on the mistaken notion that the reason a fill-in-the-blank reader has failed to be engaged by a work of literature X is that it is neither contains nor is by a fill-in-the-blank person, a member of the same "blank" group. In fact most people fail to be moved by most works, whomever they're by. The failure rate for the goal of being engaged by literature is very high. We don't know what causes the connect, when it happens. And we don't know when it will happen.

These facts make things difficult for those who think institutionally—which is to say, professors of literature and the universities in which they are at home. How, we will certainly say in exasperation, can we run an airline given all these variables? If only (pick a number from a hat) 40% of students in a classroom have any kind of electric connection with a given work, we can't predict which aspect of the book will provide this connection, and we can't say that it won't happen (if it does) until years after, then how the Sam Hill can we go on with the daily work of discussing, testing, issuing grades, giving credits?

The answer is clear: we can't. Or at least, that's not what we focus on. We simply shift gears and find aspects of the literature that are more predictable, can be packaged better, turned off and on, and finished up by the end of the semester. Those can be talking about the patterns of letters, or using invented technical terms to discuss the expression of power by the author. The fact that we're using the technical terms gives apparent validity to what we're doing, and facts about the "text" can be turned off an on at will, like faucets.

Any institutionalized study of literature will tend to block out, insofar as it's given its head, the unpredictable intensities of private engagement with literature. That's what it means to institutionalize an undertaking: we sacrifice the individual to the predictable. Trains are supposed to run at a certain time whatever the people on them are thinking.

Some of this is a given whatever the institution: grade probably have to come in, and tuition must be paid. Still, we're not condemned to this particularly intense institutionalization of literary studies that we've invented for ourselves. We can be alive to the requirements of institutionalization without saying that more of them is more, or that if we accept a few we should ask for more. What we have now is more like the neat rows of the absolutely silent authoritarian classroom of the Prussian nineteenth century, the students in identical clothes all staring down at their books, the boys ruthlessly squashed at any expression of energy, bathroom calls discouraged, self-expression not desirable. The alternative is something more like a Montessori classroom, where the teacher knows that kids need to move around sometimes, that going to the bathroom is a natural right, and that games are a valid way of learning. This doesn't change anything about the fact of it being a school with rules (don't hit other kids, don't swear): it just acknowledges the fact that people are unpredictable, and sometimes need to do their own thing before coming back to the collective.

Eating brain

Professors of artworks—all artworks, but especially literature, as that's the art form where it's easiest to make this mistake, since the literature too is in words—need to give up the pretense that somehow they take on the power of the work by teaching it. It's as ghoulish as the pre-modern (once we would have said "primitive") belief that one ingested the strength of one's prey or enemy by killing him and eating his heart or brain. People who debunk powerful literature don't thereby become powerful. Boy, have we done a number on them! We've taken fill-in-the-blank (Tolstoy, Proust, Chaucer) down a peg! The only people such debunkers don't shred are the ones they've discovered, the ones who "belong: to them. Look at our own private author who's been denied her rightful place! The bad guys here are the authors currently in place who have to be resisted. The real "anxiety of influence," to use Harold Bloom's so-popular-in-the-1980s concept, is not between writers, but between professors and the writers they teach.[13] Professors seem the perennially unsure-of-themselves sons of famous fathers.

But we don't need to lose ourselves in this fruitless agon, to use one of Bloom's favorite words. Nobody else expects us to compete with the works; we professors are the only ones who said we should. We should say to ourselves: "There's no contest. I'm the living one, and I'm the one who gets to interact with living people." So interact! Help them to see something. Acknowledge the situation and use it wisely.

Some critics of academia-as-we-know-it insist professors should be more concerned for the students. Others say, they should be more concerned with the works. Both are right. Let's focus on where students interact with works. We get to coach from the sidelines, but the real action is on the field. Our satisfaction is that we get to help make it happen, and give the students a real workout so that, with any luck, they leave the field sweaty and smiling.

The problem is not that literary study is too hot to handle, though those who practice it still insist this is so: they are *too* mad, bad, and dangerous to know. In fact they're none of these things. The reason people resist literary study as we've codified it isn't because it's too dangerous, it's that it's reduced literature to wallpaper. It can keep people busy forever. But to what end?

Chapter One

100 Views of Mount Fuji

THE MOST ELEMENTARY (AND ALSO MOST IMPORTANT) thing to say about academic, classroom, study of the humanities—literature, philosophy, and their offshoots—is that it's something specific, something different than what those outside it are doing: tilling the soil, washing windows, or making clothes, umbrellas, or roofing tiles. Studying literature, like doing any one thing, is a precise undertaking. This was so in Socrates' time, though students walked rather than sat; it was true in the Scholastic universities of the Middle Ages; it was true in Victorian England when students parsed Greek and Roman classics. And it's true for literary studies in the early twenty-first century.

Until the second half of the twentieth century, however, this difference was merely an accepted fact of the situation: if talking about literature is what you want, a classroom is the place you go, as a hat shop is where you go if you want a hat. Yet in the last half-century, something new has happened: nowadays the divergence with the world outside is written into the justification of the undertaking. What happens in a classroom isn't just specific, it's all there is, at least according to the by now unquestioned methodology of the humanities—methodology being the patterns for what we do that lie so deep in the enterprise they're part of how we do business.

Linguistic Turn

With what Richard Rorty and countless other thinkers have called the twentieth-century's "linguistic turn" in philosophy (this phrase was the title of Rorty's edited collection of essays by many philosophers on twentieth-century language philosophy), emphasis was suddenly on the surface of signification, the words—not on what they represent.[14] This was so whether we were saying, with the early Wittgenstein, the author of the *Tractatus*, that words showed their meaning in a sort of mimesis (the so-called "picture theory of meaning"), or whether we were saying, with the late Wittgenstein, author of the *Philosophical Investigations*, that meaning was produced by use. In either case fundamental questions are questions about words, whatever we ultimately decide they do. The question of how words mean becomes central to philosophy, and literary study devotes itself to the medium rather than the message.

Whether you decide words gain meaning from an intrinsic relationship with the world or through use, you've answered the question once and for all: changes are minor compared to the unvarying and unchangeable Big Question you've answered. What won't work, if your goal is making a methodologically tight study, professionalizing your undertaking, is leaving open the relationship with the world, as I'm suggesting we have to with literature. That's why literary studies has come to focus on what's here in front of us, the text. If there's one concept contemporary humanities rejects with a shudder, it's the notion that language is something that has to be looked through in order to see what's on the other side. For contemporary humanities, books are about the process of representing rather than about the things represented. Windows aren't windows *to* anything—which is what the people in the houses probably would have said they were. Instead they're all about the glass in them, what the glazier who replaces the glass and who can measure and gauge thickness and quality sees. The twentieth century demanded we all become glaziers.

This point of view was first espoused by early twentieth-century Modernism, itself echoing the Romanticism of a century before. With the same gleeful abandon with which Lytton Strachey tore aside what he saw as the pious veil of Victorian hagiographic biography meant to teach and serve as models, other forms of Modernism happily tossed aside the notion that the arts, and study of the arts, were primarily models to behavior expressed in a mimetic garb, something those outside the arts could recognize as related to their world.[15] Suddenly, paintings were about their painted surfaces, music about its tones, sculpture about the possibilities of the material.

Modernism took a century to use up its intellectual capital, whose centerpiece was the assertion that there is nothing outside the X, where X was first the artwork and then later on, the study of the artwork. In the late 1990s, almost a century after the English aesthetes of the "art for art's sake" movement, some of the first proto-Modernists, I heard a "docent" in the Hirshhorn Museum carry on for five minutes about the paint application in one of Clyfford Still's boringly repetitive paintings, in which only the shade and pattern of the sponge-painting-like blotches (sometimes all over, sometimes upper right, sometimes clustered like climbing vines) altered over dozens and dozens of paintings. "Look at that red!" she exclaimed to a group of baffled museum-goers trying, I gathered, to see the profundity she was insisting on—and failing. I imagine they knew, but could not yet articulate, the fact that there's more to life, and art, than a shade of red and what corner of the canvas the splotches are on.

From the initially heady refusal of the Russian Formalists to use literature as yet another illustration of high-minded biographical principles, to the "semiotic squares" of the structuralists, to Derridean deconstructionists who waited for people to fall silent and then showed them what they hadn't done, to the Foucauldians who insisted that all texts are about power (whose illegitimate but widespread corollary was, all power is textual), humanities in general and literary studies in particular have justified their enterprise by insisting not that they serve a legitimate purpose in the world, but in fact *are* the world. It's quite an achievement for those in literary studies, this re-centering on one's self—one that in purely intellectual terms deserves our admiration.

I do admire it. Yet at the same time my attitude toward this achievement is: Yes, but. That's the Pyrrhic victory of literary studies. It's become a profession, but at the cost of stifling the literature.

Anna Karenina

Most professors aren't as interesting as, say, Tolstoy. So if what's taught is the professor's take on *Anna Karenina*—the more that consists of professor and the less it consists of *Anna Karenina*—the less interesting the experience becomes. And in all probability, that's the only experience of *Anna Karenina* the students are going to get. They don't even have another class with another perspective on *Anna Karenina*: whatever this was, they've had it, "done" Tolstoy. When did they ever get the "standard" reading? (A "standard" reading isn't a value-neutral or "objective" reading, it's just a standard one; see below.) Ideally they'd have the time and leisure to read *Anna Karenina*—and then take one course with a stimulating professor, and another on this same topic with another professor, and another. But that's not the way literary studies is structured. Indeed nowadays few people read the works outside the classroom at all.

The people running the culture of processed food we've developed aren't likely to be the ones to overhaul it. Plus, why should it occur to them they should? The professor isn't likely to see him- or herself as giving insights to help students experience the "text" if the theory and methodology s/he ingested in graduate school and continues to espouse insists that a) there's no such thing as the objective world at all (and hence, presumably, no reading outside the classroom experience), b) all texts are re-invented by their readers, and c) texts are only about other texts, part of the endless rustling flow of words responding to other words, if not that d) all texts are merely texts and, therefore, equivalent to each other: they might as well have been reading the Manhattan phone book as reading Tolstoy.

How many decades of bored and inattentive students, a captive audience going through the motions because they think these are the only motions to go through, will it take before the people professing literature realize this: nobody but them is interested in books as books? Most people are interested in books as adjuncts to life. Most people go to a library to get a book and take it home, not to live in the library. Nowadays we teach as if we live in a library. No wonder the students' attention strays.

What about other issues in *Anna Karenina*?: like the power of love, the way life rarely goes the way we think it will, the way marriage sometimes just doesn't work out, the strange quality of life that it can be soaked up by a single wild passion, and/or the way motherhood doesn't replace womanhood (Anna has a little boy but kills herself anyway)—just for starters. The professor could spend his or her time talking about these things, showing how the specifics of the book (these people, this setting) which by definition make them seem alien to all readers, who by definition are who they are, right here right now, can be generalized.

This is an alternative to our current acceptance of the odd notion that what we should be doing in a university classroom is "studying literature" rather than using literature as a way to conceptualize life. Most students need help stripping away the level of specifics to see the patterns underneath; it's only through patterns that they can see relationships between their own worlds and that of the literature, and most people aren't too good at seeing patterns. Professors typically are much better, having read many books, dealt with many students, and having (typically) lived longer than the students. They're needed to show what's general about Madame Bovary's situation: nobody reading about her will be exactly like her, if only because this isn't 1830s France.

One hugely high hurdle for the young in understanding the point of a work is their own youth: for them this is the most basic definer of who they are. It's therefore difficult for them to see any of themselves in older characters. Here a professor, somewhat older him- or herself, can make connections that simply would not have occurred to the young: that an old man in a novel is a young man plus time and experience, for instance. It's strange how odd this notion appears to so many of the young: we can see them in us, but typically they can't see us in them.

A lot of what professors can productively do seems to them like stating the obvious: how Madame Bovary being carried away by reading her romances is like an adolescent male sitting enraptured in a movie theater watching an action hero, for example, or how sexual fantasy always gives us what we want, as that's the nature of fantasy. Most people can't get past the envelope of their own particularity on their own; that's what the outsider is there for. But once this outsider, the professor, has articulated the similarity, it may well seem evident to the student.

Nor does everything the professor says have to be something the student has already felt or lived. Perhaps s/he hasn't felt the intensity of Anna Karenina's passion: it's useful information to be told that merely knowing a passion is unwise doesn't mean people cease to feel it. The professor knows this fact to be true, which is why s/he can articulate it: s/he adds the ability to contextualize what happens in a work, saying, This is true, or This seems exceptional to me, or This is what adolescents think but most adults don't find it so. The professor is free to comment on the book as s/he sees things, and to encourage the students to do the same—not with any hope of ever arriving at scientific conclusions, but merely so as to have something articulated that the student can later come back to, perhaps to revise, perhaps to reject utterly.

Let's say the professor gets the student to articulate his or her belief that Anna is simply immoral, beyond the pale. Perhaps this person, twenty years down the pike, will have changed his or her mind. Perhaps the professor never knows this (how many students look up professors to tell them how wrong they were?). But the student, now an adult, may remember his or her reaction twenty years before, and be able to use it as a way to reflect. This will by definition be clearly the professor's experience talking, not a claim to objective knowledge, say about a text. It's an "in my experience, here's what's true" for the student to think about, the way the student would think about the view of any older person giving a reaction. Students don't have to believe these things, but if they respect the person who says it, they'll probably file it away for later possible use.

100 Views of Mt. Fuji

Professors today are hired and get tenure, lifetime employment, because they have a quirky or "different" view of the works, not necessarily because they're good at relating the works to life. Sometimes this quirky view is a result of being from a "different" group of people. Frequently, however, the assumption is the converse: that if they're from a different group, they'll have a different point of view. Someone from India, let's say, will have a view of Indian literature that someone from the United States—or Bolivia—won't. Of course this isn't necessarily so, but many of our hiring decisions are based on the assumption that it is. An African-American will have a peculiarly African-American view of, say, Melville, or Molière. The Bolivian, even if s/he was educated in Paris, is assumed to speak for Hispanics. Nor do we make distinctions within a nation-state: the white Spanish Bolivian can be a spokeswoman for mixed-race Hispanics outside Bolivia, even if inside Bolivia she is regarded as an oppressor of the indigenous Indian people. The "wheaten" Bengali Brahmin (India has many words to describe pale skin colors, the desired tone), who is one of the aristocracy at home, becomes, through an astonishing process of transformation, a spokeswoman for the oppressed Third World once in the West.

Literary study in the classroom offers views of the work of literature rather like the views of Mt. Fuji in Hokusai's celebrated "100 Views of Mt. Fuji" series. In each print, the mountain, while present, is frequently tiny and in a corner, viewed (in the most famous print) beyond the crest of a wave whose foam seems to make fingers at the edges, or (in another striking work) through a hoop that a barrel-maker is shaping for his barrel. People are hired specifically to offer views of the literature that are clever in this way, rather than offering the front-and-center shots of a postcard. "Artsy" shots of famous monuments are always such shots: the famous building seen in part, or reflected in a puddle, or seen through a keyhole, or looking sharp up at it, or down on it. They are in their way as predictable as the postcard or archival shot, front and center.

Of course it's true that there's no such thing as a complete lack of style, or an absolutely neutral treatment: the postcard shot is a specific treatment. This is a point much beloved of the proponents of "artsy" shots. But at least the postcard shot is what we agree to call neutral, and the thing closest to a common base we'll ever have. This in turn means that individuals can depart from this standard on their own. It's much more difficult to depart from a specific individualized treatment because it's so specific: it's new, it's individual, and we're meant to be aware of this. We're far more conscious of the treatment of Mt. Fuji in an "artsy" Hokusai print than we are in a postcard shot. It requires a much greater effort on the part of the viewer to remove the mountain mentally from the Hokusai and give another treatment of it than it does to start with the postcard shot and do something else with it.

The pre-Modern (nineteenth century) classroom never denied that each individual student might be making his or her individual "View of Mt. Fuji" from the postcard shot the professor was supposed to be presenting, views that related to that person's life. But they were individual, and no claims were made for them beyond this. At some point, perhaps about the same point we as a culture became addicted to daytime television chewing over personal scandals for all the world to see, we've decided that such personal views have to be made the social. Now, the professor gets to give his or her personal "View of Mt. Fuji." This, we hear over and over, is really the same thing as the postcard shot: there is, after all, no such thing as true neutrality.

No, we should say wearily to all those thousands of classrooms where a wild-haired Assistant Professor is busy debunking the myths of old: you're so right; the postcard shot isn't neutral either. But in fact, that's not the issue. The issue is how conscious we are of the treatment. In the postcard shot, the treatment isn't the "dominant," to use a word of Roman Jakobson, so we can depart more easily from the given for ourselves.[16] It's easy to get beyond a postcard shot for our own point of view because it's so expected, so formulaic. That's its virtue, in fact. But how do you get beyond a shot of Mt. Fuji through a barrel? You don't.

The power of the professor who gets to claim that his or her View of Mt. Fuji *is* Mt. Fuji is thus exponentially greater than the professor who purported (or purports: this kind of teaching is after all possible today as well) to be offering the straight-on, front and center postcard view of Mr. Fuji so students can take it and do with it as they chose. We expose students to Mt. Fuji, usually for the first time, through a person selling a specific "View of Mt. Fuji." That person is in charge of the classroom, and of grades. Guess whose view of Mt.

Fuji the students are going to adopt, or at least play at adopting? And it's the artsy view of Mt. Fuji that's the star of the show; not the ability to use Mt. Fuji to understand other things.

Perhaps the problem is, most of us aren't in Japan: those in the classroom are seeing their first view of Mt. Fuji from this professor, they haven't grown up with it. They read *Anna Karenina* for the first time in a class: most of them are very young and haven't read much anyway. If they had grown up with it, or came to this study as adults who'd read on their own, they'd have something with which to compare the individual "take" they're getting. Instead they get the individual "take," justified not as a take on an objective entity the students have some access to on their own, but instead as a contribution to the sum of knowledge. Literary studies, both theory and practice makes clear to them, doesn't elucidate something outside of itself; it contributes to an ever-burgeoning sum of literary studies. The view is of Mt. Fuji. What the contemporary professor is offering is a view of this work (novel, poem, play), not: using this work to offer a view of life. Who cares about views of a work when we could have views of life? The gruel that's being served is, by objective standards, pretty thin. Even those who sense that the gruel is thin don't know they're allowed to complain, or even that there's a point. They don't know there's an alternative.

Literary studies nowadays thus seems to presuppose that people nowadays have a view of Mt. Fuji they bring in the classroom, that can then be "challenged" or "decentered." In fact, they're not likely to have any view at all. What the classroom offers them *is* the decentered view; they have no other. They should be offered a centered view not because this is what they should end up with, but because the centered view is the only thing they can effectively decenter on their own—and doing it themselves is the only way that the decentering has any value for them, have for them the charge of individual discovery.

Literary studies nowadays has lost the realization that individuals are capable of individual decentering: if the professor doesn't do it for you, we think nowadays, it isn't going to be done. That's part of the assumption that literary studies is its own world: nothing goes on outside the classroom, so what goes on inside it is of paramount importance. Too, the decentering—personalization, we might say—of the professor is the only one. Where are the decenterings of this? This person is the one teaching the course and giving the grade.

The people in charge of contemporary classrooms see themselves as overthrowing prejudices, fiercely challenging the status quo. In fact, for the purposes of literary studies, they *are* the status quo. The sooner we acknowledge that nowadays classroom literary study is the only exposure to these works most students are going to get, the sooner we can address the insularity of contemporary literary studies.

Mad keen

Why are we so mad keen on professorial originality? Who honestly cares whether Professor X has a ground-breaking view of Y? Paradoxically, professorial originality is where the Romantic, and later Modernist, insistence on artistic originality and creativity has ended up: artists don't say it so much any more, instead we mostly hear it from professors—"X's brilliant insight," "Y's trenchant observation." I think professors got tired of being told they were second-raters, servants of their masters the "creative" artists. We can be creative too, they began to insist; it's as simple as saying we are. But that means, the difference between art and scholarship has to be blurred, and if possible the axis shifted: art exists only to make scholarship, not scholarship to serve art.

The alternative to the way we now do things is to acknowledge, rather than deny, the fact that what we're serving is processed food—and then try to make stew rather than slurry, fence in the power aspect of things. We can leave at home the artsy view of Mt. Fuji, and work on articulating postcard versions instead: things that each individual student can then do something with, if s/he chooses, on his or her own. We acknowledge that people will get a grade and are taking a course for academic credit for which they're paying, respect these givens, make conditions for grades clear, and then move beyond them. The trick is simply to acknowledge the givens of the situation so we can turn our attention to other things, not submerge them in presuppositions nobody articulates, and so which nobody questions.

Of course the classroom situation relies on talk: say this. Of course it presupposes the power of the professor: say this too. Once this is acknowledged, we can relax and go on to the literature: a postcard view that we're not ashamed of, not thinking (as the professor) that we have to show how clever we are by offering an "artsy" view that we have the students mimic. And then add on to that as much of the admittedly secondary scholarship as seems necessary to tailor the work to this group, whose knowledge and presuppositions we have to "feel out" for ourselves.

The purpose of scholarship is to maximize relations of students with literature in cases where they need maximizing, add yet other arrows to the professor's quiver to help the students get a personal reaction to the postcard view that's being discussed. Have you thought of this? What about that? Essays in learned journals about the work, or about other things entirely, can give professors more ways to keep students thinking. So for that matter can paying attention to everyday things, and human relations. None of these things, in any objective sense, advances knowledge, any more than the countless words we use each day to get through our social situations. We take none of it with us, and it's of no use to anyone outside of the situation of personal transmission. But at least it can help us help others while we're here.

Academic hunger strike

In about the mid twentieth century, I'm arguing, intellectual life in America—at least that led by professional thinkers in departments of humanities—began to starve itself to death, putting itself on the path to a suicide it has now largely attained. To be sure, it may have seemed to those who took the steps that led to current state of affairs that they were doing what was necessary to save intellectual life rather than kill it. Still, the steps that were taken put things on the path to the situation we now face: intellectuals in America have withdrawn into the ivory tower, perhaps initially to save themselves from the barbarians outside, and now have used up all their provisions.

At one point in the 1970s and 1980s, those outside seemed intensely irritated at the methodology of things inside: all these people with guaranteed jobs, the (in fact relatively few) tenured professors, were issuing what seemed incendiary statements to the effect that reality didn't exist and all power in the world was textual (which seemed to leave out those who acted rather than wrote about books). This time period saw the publication of Roger Kimball's *Tenured Radicals: How Politics Has Corrupted Our Higher Education*, first cousin to books by Alan Bloom (*The Closing of the American Mind*) and E.D. Hirsch, Jr. (*Cultural Literacy*), as well as a slew of other works pointing out the economic basis of higher education (more students = more $ for the universities), the fact that most freshmen are nowadays taught by graduate assistants, and the fact that most of what is called "research" in the humanities doesn't seem to have much of a connection with the world outside and doesn't actually seem to lead to anything—unlike research on, say, cancer. [17]

Now the people outside the tower seem uninterested in any issue but politics; about things like methodology, they just don't really care any more. The issues they object to in college professors, if the blogosphere is to be believed, seem to be the same things they object to in a political figure on the other side of the aisle. For this reason they miss a good many things that both can and should be changed about the teaching situation, things particular to the classroom and not shared with politics at all.

No politics as usual

It's a shame that criticism of academia has been so political in nature, because a number of the critics' points deserve to be considered outside of a political context: they're true for either side, but are expressed as if true only of one. One of the points, made by the critic David Horowitz and others, is the potential for abuse of the power situation of the classroom—more fundamentally, the fact that it is a power situation. [18] This tends to be presented as a problem whose solution is more right-leaning professors. It isn't. The problem has nothing intrinsically to do with politics and can be solved in a nonpolitical way. The problem, at least in theory, can also be solved by an easy-going professor who makes no secret of his, say, liberal politics but doesn't push them on students. A comparable situation might be a humane, easy-going professor who makes no secret of the fact that he's gay but doesn't talk about it unduly or suggest that others should be gay too. But this kind of solution is apparently not what the right wing wants. They want somebody who looks, and talks, like them: it seems unlikely to me they'd be as upset about an aggressive right-wing professor: s/he'd merely, in their view, be correct.

In a column for the web magazine FrontPage, Horowitz tells a story he says will make readers' "blood boil." [19] It's about a ROTC-member undergraduate at a state university who found himself in a course on the Vietnam War. As Horowitz tells the story: "The professor turned out to be a '60s leftist who regarded America as an imperialist monster and the Viet Nam War an expression of America's inherent racism and capitalist greed." Most of us would say this is neither here nor there; certainly the professor isn't the first to take this view. However the next idea in the article about the professor (there's a sentence explaining that the student had to wear his uniform to class because those days were ROTC days) takes a jump to the following: "Of course, a professor who regards his classroom as a political platform for indoctrination is not likely to respect the rights of students who disagree with his point of view and this professor was no exception. Having discovered a member of the military he hated sitting in his classroom, he could not resist the temptation to single out the uniform-clad student as a symbol of the imperialist enemy he was lecturing about." It's unclear how Horowitz gets from summarizing the professor's political views, which I think we'd all agree he's entitled to, to the next issue, logically unrelated, of seeing the classroom "as a political platform for indoctrination."

The rest of the piece explains how the professor hounded the student; the student even tried to withdraw but wasn't allowed to—no explanation of why, but I'd guess it was beyond some deadline—and the piece ends with the implication that the reason the student failed (and so couldn't graduate) was that he disagreed with this Simon Legree of a professor.

Regardless of the professor's politics, and whether or not this particular professor hounded this particular student (we have only Horowitz's version of things), it's true that the classroom is a power situation. Nowadays we know this cuts both ways. In the early 1990s David Mamet's play *Oleanna* garnered such attention, I'm willing to bet, because it turned the professor-controls-student power relationship on its head. [20] The female student who accuses her professor of sexual harassment grows more powerful as the play continues, the male professor less powerful. We're more conscious of power when we see it against the grain: we may not blink at the power parents have over children, thinking it the inevitable way of things (which it may in fact be). But a play about a powerful child becomes an exercise in the diabolical, from *The Exorcist* to the *Omen* films. Many people conclude that the play is telling us that education, perhaps because it can never be disassociated from power, is a swindle. The title, after all, refers to a land swindle perpetrated, according to folk tales, by a man named Ole and his wife named Anna, and hence referred to as the Oleanna Swindle. So nowadays the threat of misuse of power seems a two-sided one, with the possibility of student complaints of whatever nature—sexual harassment is perhaps more common than political insensitivity.

As for the fact of college professors being mostly liberals, I've suggested in *Why Liberals and Conservatives Clash* that that's simply something conservatives have to live with if they want to have anything to do with colleges.[21] Liberal and conservative politics aren't lists of beliefs, they're the result of deep-seated ways of approaching the world: they tend to cluster. Believing that discussing ideas has a virtue in itself is an intrinsically liberal notion, according to *Why Liberals and Conservatives Clash*. Conservatives focus on lists of actions they're supposed to do, goals to be achieved. You don't discuss the goals themselves. "Let's discuss this" is what liberals say. "Let's do it" is what conservatives say. So of course universities, devoted to the notion that mere discussion of points of view has value, will be overwhelmingly liberal, especially in the humanities and social sciences. They discuss options, and question received opinion. For conservatives, accepting received opinion is the name of the game, so this constant putting into question of (liberal) professors goes beyond irritating: it denies the central premise of the conservative world-view, which is that the actions we are to aim at are unvarying and universal.

Conservatives have been right to set up their own dogmatic institutions if they object to the liberal emphasis on questioning presuppositions. The particular flavor of a conservative institution will vary, from Catholic to Baptist to anti-sexual to Mormon. They may well fail to get along with each other, each laying down a different absolutism that may not be contravened. But all of them are alternatives to the liberal arts university devoted to questioning presuppositions: the presuppositions in a dogmatic institution, by contrast, must be reiterated, not questioned. Liberals who insist that universities are value-neutral are wrong, and conservatives who point this out are right. It's just that this is a situation that can't be changed without altering the fundamental nature of what this sort of institution is meant to do.

Class angle

There's a class angle as well to the professionalization of literary studies: only at the elite schools is this kind of rarification of what we do with literature even remotely thinkable, in the same way that useless but fun luxury goods tend to make more sense for the rich whose more fundamental needs are already taken care of. Yet because these schools set the tone, this "discourse" filters down the ranks, quickly becoming nothing but silly. What seems interesting at an Ivy seems simply strange in a cow college. Yet if that's the only vocabulary available to teach about literature in, that's what people use. I think of the description of the hardscrabble inner-city campus of Rutgers University that the narrator of Philip Roth's still-wildly-funny-after-all-these-years *Goodbye Columbus* goes to, adult education at night to exhausted workers.[22] (The academic class war of this book is, for me, the most trenchant part: Radcliffe and Bennington leave Rutgers-Camden in the dust.) That's nowadays more nearly the reality of people in the profession than (say) the so-intellectual Yale-Hopkins deconstructionism of the 1980s and 1990s. Still, it's the top schools which create the vocabulary and set the tone, which takes a decade or two to trickle down.

Not to mention, to trickle out. In 2005 I lectured for the summer at the University of Hyderabad, in Andra Pradesh, India. One lecture was a seminar with the students and professors of the small Comparative Literature program, run by a stylish and frighteningly articulate Bengali woman in a turquoise sari. I suggested—I'm sure I was just showing my wishful thinking—that the usefulness of Foucault for conceiving of post-colonial discourse had dropped in the so-called First World. She looked at me, hesitated as if weighing her options on how to annihilate me without offending me, gave a dazzling smile, and check-mated me by saying (what is so devastating about the educated Indo-English intonation?): "Well, he's still quite useful to us, here." And that was that.

Nowadays the once-Third World expresses its relationship to the First World in vocabulary developed in the First World to express its relation to the Third. Developed by the colonial powers, in the industrialized world, it's transferred to a world that has nothing to do with this—much as Marx's theories of industrial development were imposed on the egregiously non-industrial Russia. India (to take only one example) takes its image of itself in part from Hollywood, the mirror echoing the mirrored, using the only vocabulary going— a self-reflexive vocabulary of the mainstream to articulate the marginalized. This transference is similar to how the celebrated movie theorist Laura Mulvey suggested that women viewers of male-oriented films take on the point of view of the male protagonist, having to see themselves being seen as he sees them.[23] There may not actually be much connection between the reality of life as an underpaid Assistant Professor of English at a Midwestern State University and the high-falutin' assertion of "discourse" that only seems even remotely plausible in the ivy-draped halls of the major universities. I'm arguing, of course, that it isn't a good idea even there: the students there have read more, perhaps, than those at the lesser universities—but this is a big "perhaps." And in any case, their lives aren't substantially different, so the literature means the same sort of thing to them as it does to others. But if that's the celebrity product, or indeed all there is, that's what everybody is going to use.

That shouldn't be all there is. It's silly out of the ivory tower, and pernicious within, because it cuts literature off from the rest of life. It's not true that the only way to read literature in a public forum is as part of a homogenized "study of literature" that largely usurps the place of the literature itself. It's time to admit—no: assert—no: shout from the rooftops—that the intensely personal nature of literature means that we, the professor, can at best provide a forum for this to play out, not get our students marching in the classroom to the same drummer—which inevitably means, us.

Paying the piper

Those outside who reacted more than a decade ago to what the humanities were up to were largely upset by the provocations that at the time were still being thrown over the battlements by those within, streams of invective dumped like vats of boiling oil. These usually took the form of variations on the assertion that there is no such thing as facts (usually written as "facts"). If this had been offered in a classroom with a quiet explanation of the technical sense in which this was to be understood, it would hardly have caused the stir it did. Those on the inside could have explained why this wasn't an outlandish position. If the point being made had been left at merely the insistence of the subjective nature of all communication, those outside undoubtedly would not have been able to care less (though they might well have said they "could care less").

Throwing as a taunt the assertion that "there are no facts" was designed precisely to make a stir, like yelling the sky is falling. If the sky is an acorn, we're not upset. But if someone had said merely that an acorn had fallen, how much of a reaction would the doom-sayer have gotten? Clearly such statements issuing from academia were meant to provoke howls of rage. The joke on those issuing them nowadays is that people have long since stopped listening for nuances as small as how the humanities approach things: now criticism has focused on questions like, Do professors support a right-wing president's military policies? Those inside the ivory tower react to such criticism by turning away.

Nowadays many outside, those who don't write books at all, whether pro or con, seem not only unconcerned by the refusal of those in the tower to participate in the world outside, but delighted: now they can do what they want. Intellectuals spend all their time determining how many angels can dance on the head of a pin—or at least the modern equivalents of those Scholastic questions we've ceased to ask—rather than using their analytical abilities to influence public life, which many outside regard as their own private fiefdom. The results of this lack of involvement in the world outside by intellectuals have not been pretty. Lacking the reflection that those used to more complex reasoning could have helped them to, those outside the tower have largely given in to an orgy of action, now separated off from the pure thought of those in the tower.

Some of the blame for this state of affairs is structural, not individual. I offer this definition of intellectuals: people who have enough thought left over from the actions of their lives that it plays an appreciable role in their lives as a separate entity. And in our world, these people go into academia, usually in the humanities and social sciences. Even if academics wanted to interact with the world outside, it's not clear how they'd do it. Slots in America for people who combine thought, or talk, and the action that typifies the world outside the academy, are few. What job even begins to approach a fusion between thought and action? Perhaps some of the most cerebral of upper-level military officers approach this fusion, though my nearly twenty years on the fringes of the military suggest to me that these people are the exception rather than the rule. Perhaps dedicated public servants who can serve many political administrations fall into this category; perhaps too some of the most imaginative of lawyers, professors in public policy programs or law schools. But the political appointees ultimately have to toe the party line, and the influence of professors is muted, or secondary, unless they themselves write op-ed columns, where the pressure is to take a political side.

Probably most people would say that science and technology currently attract many of the brightest minds: here at least it seems that real inroads into the world can be made with the use of brainpower. But only a few scientists are what we think of as intellectuals, with the excess of thought itself not soaked up by the action of doing. Nor are inventors who make things that change our lives, admirable though they are, the people I'm talking about. My focus is on people who think professionally.

Still, whatever the reasons for this state of affairs, it's not a good thing to funnel off the intellectuals and set them to discussing how many angels can dance on the head of a pin while the brutish warlords outside exploit the peasantry and wage fruitless wars whose only effect is to keep themselves in power. This of course better describes low periods of the Middle Ages than our stable democracy, and I don't foresee Apocalypse as a result of the way we teach literature nowadays: it's just not that important. Saying it is would be to perpetuate the exaggerations of those who currently do it. The effects of teaching literature are simply too hard to predict, and can't be codified. But it does seem clear that if our most gifted intellectuals are set comparing grains of sand rather than visualizing how to stabilize the beach, it can't be good for anyone—not for them, not for the rest of us.

Chapter Two

Why do They Hate Us?

TEACHING HUMANITIES NOWADAYS SEEMS LIKE so much energy and *tsoris* for so little result, and this at all levels of academia. Let's say you're a graduate student. You find a protector, someone with a "name" who will give you a topic for a Ph.D. dissertation, usually an application of his or her own work. You sweat late nights, after correcting the freshman composition papers you're responsible for as part of your fellowship, to apply his or her methodology to a couple of examples, put in references to many other thinkers to explain how forlorn and hopeless the world was until you came along, deal with the objections to the result of a handful of people who hold your fate in their hands—your doctoral committee—and then are the proud holder of a degree.

With the recommendation of your big-name professor, you apply for jobs that hundreds of freshly-minted Ph.D.s will apply for as well. The Holy Grail here is a "tenure-track" job that lets you go up for permanent employment after a period of five to six years during which you're supposed to have turned your dissertation into "the book." Most probably you won't get a "tenure-track" job, at least not right out of graduate school, which means a handful of years (if you're lucky, only a handful) being what's called a "gypsy," a semester here or a temporary year there on (in all probability) the opposite side of the country from your partner, grateful for whatever you get. After that, you hope to get a tenure-track job, but the chances have shrunk this time around, not increased: you're a bit shop-worn, and you're competing against all the other people who have gotten Ph.Ds since you too, in addition to your own group.

Let's say you hit the jackpot: you get a tenure-track job. You have virtually no control over where this might be geographically or as a situation. City or country, college or university, you take whatever you get. You teach your classes, correct your papers, serve on committees, and in your non-existent spare time, turn your dissertation into a book. For the sake of your own sanity, you shouldn't spend too much time worrying about all those articles on "The Crisis in Scholarly Publishing" you'll see (there are too many books and not enough readers, libraries buy fewer copies, they're checked out less and less often). Nor need you know that students do "research" nowadays by going online; nor that even university presses have to show a profit, so both the quantity and nature of what they print has changed radically in the last few years. It may not matter.

Nobody will review or even read the products of any but the few big-name presses anyway. Reviews rarely translate into sales, in any case. It's literary deflation: too few readers for too many books.

You spend your time cursing the papers you have to correct until, let's say, the miracle happens: you've been attentive to enough members of your department to be voted in, your book has been accepted somewhere (sales be damned)—you get your tenure and can breathe again. After that, many people lose their moorings, and spend their time playing computer solitaire. And all this for what? Oh yes, to contribute to mankind's knowledge of . . . Katherine Anne Porter's short stories? Katherine Mansfield's? Is it any better if it's someone no one's ever heard of but who's the Next Hot Thing in, say, Malaysian literature? What if someone has a more intense reaction to a Katherine Anne Porter short story reading it without all the scholarly accretions, the barnacles of who's said what about it? What if the story is so covered with barnacles the story's invisible? What if the reader spends all his or her time scraping away the barnacles to get at the story and finds it's not really what the doctor ordered at all? By then the reader is old. It all ends up sounding like "Before the Law," the Kafka parable of the man who comes to the door to the palace of justice to plead for entrance; he grows old interacting with the doorkeeper, "counting the fleas on his fur coat." When he dies, the doorkeeper informs him that now this door will be closed: it was made only for him.[24]

In Randall Jarrell's wickedly funny, if static and overwritten *Pictures From an Institution*, a series of vignettes set at a "progressive" college in the early 1950s, the narrator, a poet who seems to coincide with the author, makes fun of a pedantic professor who thinks she's doing a supremely generous thing by offering him, the shadowy poet narrator, bound volumes of the *PMLA*, the *Proceedings of the Modern Language Association*.[25] His disinterest in this dry fare is so evident as to be a source of a joke with the reader: we're never supposed to be in any doubt at his utter lack of connection with anything that might be in *PMLA*. And he gets to take a swing at another professor, an older unmarried woman (apparently to suggest sterility) who—he suggests delicately to his would-be benefactress—is by far the more appropriate recipient. "Oh," gasps the benefactress, "I'd assumed she had them already!" As in fact she does. It's a two-fer for Jarrell.

Too much thought probably isn't good for anybody in the profession these days, at any stage from Ph.D. candidate to tenured professor. What if it begins to dawn on you that there is no ever-accreting "knowledge" of any author in this sense, but only a series of reactions, like the tail on a kite that one day will drag it down if we insist on adding each new piece? What if you wake up one morning and decide you just don't even *like* Katherine Mansfield? People used to torture themselves that they'd never read Chaucer, or *Beowulf*. Then one day we heard that some hitherto unknown Palestinian is worth more than all the

Dead White Males combined. Does this make things better or worse? Let's say your "subject" *is* the Palestinian. But if writers go in and out of fashion (as we begin to suspect they do), who says the Palestinian will still be the flavor of the month by the time his supporters get tenure, much less by the time they're 50? Remember (we realize, panic gripping us) how just *everybody* was reading Wallace Stevens in the 1980s? (If you're new to the professorate, of course you don't remember: ignorance is bliss, and besides, you're not going to be like your parents.) Think how odd it seems when a die-hard Derridean deconstructionist is uncovered somewhere nowadays, like a Japanese soldier who's found still hunkered down in the brush ready to die for the Emperor decades after the war is over.

Last person out

Many people who do make it to tenured positions, after several years of sighing with relief, begin to notice signs that the intellectual capital that almost a century ago seemed inexhaustible—the development of a proto-scientific methodology to professionalize humanities and give them a structure and a justification—has now played out. Now we split ever-finer hairs, no longer reacting against the world outside, which, ironically, doesn't care. I think it produces many people who continue to turn the prayer wheel, but feel more and more discontented.

A much-discussed article by one-time college English professor Rebecca Steinitz suggests that her own unhappiness with being a tenured professor is general across the profession.[26] She writes that she bravely played the game, until one day she didn't. And she sketches the reaction she received from other professors: most were surprisingly sympathetic, confessing that they too had dreamed of leaving academia, but had been unable to carry out their plans for one reason or another. Their reaction to her decision to leave was admiration, not condemnation. As Steinitz puts it: "They said I was a role model and an inspiration. Just knowing that I had taken action made them feel better."

Steinitz thinks the malaise she herself felt and that she found echoed in her colleagues' reactions is in fact quite general: "There are an awful lot of people out there who live their lives in a constant state of low-level despondence." Her solution is to leave academia; this article is a sort of "Goodbye to All That." Many of her reasons—living in a not-fun place (she was in Ohio; subsequently she lived in Boston), too far from family—are specific ones that not everyone will share. I for example live with my wife and children, and quite close to two sets of grannies. Annapolis is an attractive place, both intrinsically and in its proximity to Washington, D.C., Baltimore, New York, and the beach. Besides, not many academics can just up and leave; apparently Steinertz can because her husband earns good money, and she writes for publications that pay.

Yet a lot of her points do seem generalizable to people whose situation isn't identical to hers. Steinitz suggests that academics are trapped by their own conception of themselves. She's trying to answer the question, If so many people she tells she's leaving academia are envious of her doing so, why don't more leave? Her answer is that whatever the price we pay in reality, we think it has to be worth it because this is the life we think we were meant to lead.

Here's Steinertz:

> We academics are deeply invested in our own significance. We were the smartest ones in the class. We believe the life of the mind is sacred and we are living it. Our ideas are our selves. When we come up against biased tenure committees or uncongenial locations or grinding teaching loads, we convince ourselves that this is the price we must pay for the greatness we are meant to achieve, and we suck it up, complaining all the way.

Greatness we are meant to achieve? That's the heart of the problem. That kind of attitude only comes from believing that literary studies is its own world: we're going to conquer it. Literary studies seems increasingly like what the French call a *pays d'operette*, a country from an operetta, one of those imaginary principalities whose eligible princes figure in romantic stage works of the escapist Victorian era. Intrinsic to the notion of a *pays d'operette* is the inverse relationship between intrinsic importance of the country and degree of pomp and circumstance within it: the first is very low indeed, and the second quite high.

Some of what makes academics unhappy comes with the territory, so we have to endure it. These include low pay, usually a lack of geographical choice, and oh-so-serious colleagues debating whether our article for, yes, the *PMLA* is really quite up to snuff. But the rest of what makes us unhappy doesn't come with the territory; it's something we've done to ourselves. By creating a world so airtight, but also closed off from the world, we've condemned ourselves to irrelevance. This airtight world lets us feel like the lords of our tiny realm—the problem is the small size of the realm, and the fact that our pomp and circumstance, our syllabi, our hiring decisions, and our endless discussions about the quality of others' scholarship, matter to no one but us.

Make it new

Novelty is something the Modernists, echoing the Romantics, told us was a good in itself. The "Imagist Manifesto" of Ezra Pound and F.S. Flint famously enjoined artists to "make it new."[27] The problem with Modernist theory, such as that of the Imagists and the Russian Formalist Victor Shklovsky, was that the justification for always having to have things new was the theory that if it wasn't new, it faded to the point where we couldn't even perceive it any more. In the famous words of Shklovsky, which echoes a conception of the poet Shelley a century before, "art makes the stone stoney": we only perceive the qualities of the world when someone, namely the artist, calls our attention to these qualities in art.[28] Without artists to constantly shake things up, the world becomes bland, lacking taste.

This was a self-serving theory for artists: its effect was that they were absolutely essential to something as fundamental as perception. Of course, it was too big an overreach with respect to the world outside, composed of people who had no intention of waiting around for an artist to let them perceive. What if the artists' works were unavailable? Must you spend your whole life shrouded in silence and darkness? Did the lights come on the day your eyes digested the markings on the page which allowed you suddenly to perceive?

Such over-reach is a paradigm that's been adopted by literary studies in the universities as scholars took over the pretensions of artists. In the arts, this insisting that "we've got everything all wrapped up, and you have to come to us" led to the gradually more bloodless post-Modernisms that plagued the late twentieth-century, presupposing as they did a knowledge of all the previous artistic steps: art was always about art. New art is learned art; you have to understand all the steps before in order to understand this one. Art isn't perceived, it has to be learned about. You had to be an insider to "get it."[29]

This is as self-referential as the binding of feet on Chinese ladies in the Qing Dynasty: bound feet were a sign of beauty, but partly because they showed the woman need never work—or walk. She had servants to hold her up. You could, and should, bind feet because they necessitated the props that women with unbound feet couldn't afford. In much the same way, art requires previous art for its comprehension, so you perceive art through the classroom: that's the only way you'll understand it. This is a comprehensible situation with works of art the current of time has almost taken away from us. How many people can read *Orlando Furioso* outside of the classroom? Now we've made new works that render the here-and-now equally strange, equally in need of explication. Is that progress? And what about the fact that many people have abandoned even contemporary literature for Barbie (doll) and Princess Di? Those seem like interesting topics, for sure: only here I thought this was an English department. When are they going to read the books?

Cutting edge

Colleges and universities now privilege the shock value that formerly was the claim to fame of bohemian artists: academics see themselves as the heirs of people who once changed the world. Only what's being changed is no longer the world outside, but the course of study inside. And the changes, strictly internal, have lost their oomph. Nowadays it isn't enough for the university to be a repository; they have to be the "cutting edge," a position we'd think uncomfortable, but is where current literary scholars aspire to be. Only it's a knife that isn't cutting anything at all.

To a degree, this hustle and bustle within the university, this push for hipness, is the result of the pressure of the market. Universities develop academic fields the way real estate developers do their work: they develop the most obvious lots first, and only later the less promising ones, which they have to sell as being, in fact, the latest "hot" thing, better really than the more evident ones, and in any case newer. The way a university makes waves, at least in humanities, is apparently to buy up all the plots on what used to be thought of as the fringes and develop the heck out of them so they become the hot part of town.

A story on the web site www.insidehighered.com about Vanderbilt University shows how.[30] We read that "Vanderbilt University has been on a faculty hiring spree and is about to officially announce a series of moves that have been rumored in recent weeks in literary and black studies circles as extremely significant." The article then lists two professors at name universities, each of whom is "each considered a leading figure in black literary studies nationally," and each of whom is exchanging one endowed chair for another. The wife of one, in women's studies, is also being hired, as is "an expert on African American and Caribbean literature," as is the author of a parody, from the black perspective, of Margaret Mitchell's *Gone With the Wind*.

The article then comments:

> The round of hires that will be announced in the next week build on recruitment over the last few years in both black studies and the English department that is seen as a repositioning of the university. . . . In English, once seen as a traditional department best known for Southern literature, hires in recent years have included . . . a specialist in Caribbean social and literary history; . . . another scholar of the Caribbean and also of Latin America and the intersection of cultures across the Americas . . . ; and [a professor] whose work focuses on colonial literature and race and gender theory. . . . multiculturalism and interdisciplinarity have been key qualities that the university has been seeking out.

The university has appropriated the doctrines of bohemia. New is good, perhaps even necessary. If you just read the same old people, you don't read at all, or you've missed the boat, or you're hopelessly out of date—with literary studies anyhow, and literary studies is what it's all about, not literature. You don't perceive at all, at least not what's worth perceiving. Nowadays it's not the artist who's necessary to perception, but the professor. Without the professor to give his or her take on literature you probably haven't heard of, you're not on the "cutting edge." It's as self-referential too as fashion in clothes: you have to get this year's styles. If you don't have them, you don't have them: you're not in style. If you step back from this and say, "Why? I won't go naked," you've made the same move with respect to fashion that many people have made with respect to literary studies.

The justification for such centering of the fringe nowadays tends to be that literature by dead white males is "universal" only for dead white males—not for Afro-Caribbean writers (or is it readers?). But if most students at places like Vanderbilt aren't Afro-Caribbean, doesn't this mean they shouldn't have to read Afro-Caribbean literature, presumably universal only for Afro-Caribbean readers? Or *is* this universal in a way Homer isn't? Is the claim that Afro-Caribbean literature is as worthy of consideration? More worthy? For whom? And after the top-tier universities are full of people working on the fringes, isn't the next revolution going to be recruiting people who teach Chaucer and Shakespeare? And then won't we look down on all those tired old Afro-Caribbean people, solidly tenured but no longer exciting?

Pig in python

Major new conceptions in the humanities take a couple of decades to work through the system, like a really big pig working its way through a python, being diminished layer by layer until only the bones remain themselves are finally dissolved. First the major new idea is espoused by the Young Turks, who get their batteries charged by the feeling of being kept down and out and having to assert themselves. Then these people succeed (or don't: if enough people lose interest then the idea just fizzles) and begin to set the tone for departments. The graduate students are drawn to these young Turks, because they're younger than the old ones, and full of fire, and seem to have their finger on the pulse of the Next New Thing, whatever that is.

Let's call it X.

Soon conferences are full of papers about X; if you have any pretensions to being interesting you have to have given a paper on X if your colleagues, or those you aspire to be, have done so. Outlyers are considered outlyers, and simply can't compete; there's safety in numbers in academia, as in television ratings: what fails to reach a critical mass simply fails and dribbles off, or is withdrawn. Yet after a couple of decades the Young Turks are Pashas; they've become the graying paper-graders they once so derided. It's likely too their own ardor has cooled as the result of time and increasing acceptance of their notions. And in any case they are besieged in their turn by the newest set of Young Turks with a different ideology to whom the attention of the younger set turns. It's the way of the (academic) world. Only each group of Young Turks fails to see the repetitive nature of what they're engaged in, the fact that all are permutations on the common enterprise of professionalized literary studies, according to which the greatest revolution possible is merely a new set of things to emphasize in the profession.

The most recent really big pig is almost all the way through the python; it's been the influence of Michel Foucault, and has taken about thirty years to work its way through. We've gotten just about all the juice we can out of the notion that works are expressions of power, which many in academia have understood as saying that all power is expressed in works, and hence by words. Related to this is the notion that there is no "master narrative," to quote a concept of Jean-François Lyotard, no one way to tell the story of literary history. Some hold it's okay if we don't teach Shakespeare and Chaucer: they were, it seems, never the center, just the literature of a specific group (white males) that was held out as Literature to countless generations as an expression of (white male) power.[31] Some go further: not only is it no loss we don't teach Shakespeare, it's positively a good thing. After all, substituting *my* literature for *your* literature is the ultimate act of power, so if I can get away with it, I'm going to do it. Only of course we deny that we're doing it as an act of power: that's for the bad guys. We're not about getting power, but about pointing it out when others have it. We're perennially guerillas executing daring raids against the *junta*, even when the colonels have long ago died off or retired and we're the ones in the Presidential Palace: self-conceptions die hard.

Multiple landings

At the beginning of *Philosophy in a New Key*, Suzanne Langer accurately noted that when ideas have been parceled out and worked over enough to fill conferences, working outwards from the central places of their dissemination, this is a sign of exhaustion of the old "key" of things (key in the musical sense), not a sign of its robust health—like a pine tree covered with pine cones or a plant with too many suckers.[32] It's not a good thing. Langer thought that the new key was related to symbols, which turned out to be less seminal movement than she thought it would be. Now we're ready for a new key again. The python has just about digested the last big pig. Maybe we should put the snake on a diet?

Some people sent by their universities to scholarly conferences dread forgoing the sun and streets of an interesting city for sessions of a scholarly conference, where they listen to yet another Assistant or Associate Professor from Wherever College read yet another paper on a currently fashionable thinker, raking over ground that's been raked so often before it shows only the tines of all the previous rakes. If they go to a session, the jockeying for recognition and respect among the (usually) three presenters and the moderator, as well as with the audience (will they support my position? or be combative?) is the most interesting aspect of a session in one of the claustrophobic conference rooms deep in the fluorescent-lit bowels of a cookie-cutter hotel. Not to mention the fact that there are frequently more people presenting in such a session than listening, and those who are in the audience frequently are there out of obligation to the readers. It's a peculiar exercise even for those who make an honest effort to follow what's being presented. (Is there anything more stupefying than listening to someone *read* scholarly prose out loud?) It's like flying in an airplane that makes three landings. At each time you hope you're taken to someplace nice, but what you mostly register is the sensation of being taken into the argument and then being back in the airplane ready for the next descent. Of course there are the True Believers, their eyes glittering at the thought of "hearing so-and-so's paper on the relationship between X and Y," oblivious to the sun outside. I think they're by now in the minority, if they were ever anything else.

Why do they hate us?

When we look at literary studies in the world, what's striking is the degree to which the self-conception of those inside the literary studies part differs from the conception of it by those outside. The situation of literary studies seems comparable to that of a religion that has lost its adherents: at one point people assumed that priestly claims to universality and importance had to be respected. Now no one takes them seriously, and they've retreated to the protective confines of their diminished, but for that reason jealously guarded, church properties.

The perception of those on the outside of literary studies is expressed every year in the spate of articles written in major newspapers about the annual convention of the Modern Language Association. Inevitably the writers are struck by the sheer number of tweedy people taking over a major North American city: most people conceive of professors as existing in units of one, in a classroom. The only time they're otherwise seen in any number in public is at their most picturesque, garbed in the colorful anachronism of academic regalia (all invented around the turn of the last century in America: recent) at graduation ceremonies. People don't usually get a glimpse of so many of them all at once, as if these conferences were the butterfly breeding grounds where all those lone individuals glimpsed in our gardens go to reproduce, trees and ground for square mile after square mile simply covered with the creatures.

The second thing that strikes reporters—which is to say, people who have to explain complex topics in simpler speech that's accessible to outsiders from many walks of life—is the arcane nature of the topics considered in papers, papers that the home universities of all these professors have paid for them to come long distances to deliver. At least arcane to judge by the titles, where academics seem to vie to cram in as many technical worlds and bad jokes as possible. Each of these articles usually contains a selection from the titles that have seemed the most outlandish to the reporter writing about them.

Here's how Scott McLemee summarizes these articles from the perspective of an insider who nonetheless notes the reactions of those outside:[33]

Each December, several thousand literature professors pry themselves away from the comforts of home and flock to the annual convention of the Modern Language Association . . .

Reporters from the local press attend, then publish articles that invariably cite two or three outrageous titles of scholarly papers presented at the meeting. Researchers believe that custom began in 1989, when Eve Kosofsky Sedgwick read her legendary (not to say seminal) paper "Jane Austen and the Masturbating Girl"—a title mentioned in *The New York Times* and cited with horror by neoconservatives ever since.

McLemee notes some of the developments in titles since the 1990s, when the practice was at its most flamboyant:

The use of parentheses and slashes to create unpronounceable puns has fallen off considerably since the mid-1990s, when convention bylaws required every panel to include at least one paper referring to "the (m)other tongue," "hetero/textuality," or "derr(ier)(i/e)da." That tradition continues in a decidedly lackluster vein with this year's session on "Schopenhauer's Corps(e): The Body and the Canon."

He then cites a number of the newer-style titles, including: "Judith Butler Got Me Tenure (but I Owe My Job to k.d. lang): High Theory, Pop Culture, and Some Thoughts About the Role of Literature in Contemporary Queer Studies," by Kim L. Emery of the University of Florida, and "'Dude, Where's My Reliable Symbolic Order?': Gross-Out Comedies and the Rewriting of the Expressible," by Luther Riedel of Mohawk Valley Community College, in New York.

The web site www.insidehighered.com considers the way those inside the bell jar of the MLA convention react to those covering it from without, in an article by David Epstein.[34] Epstein begins: "Coverage of literary scholarship in the mainstream news media leaves some academics asking, 'Why are they saying such terrible things about us?'" This question is the title of a paper Epstein is considering, presented by David R. Shumway, an English professor at Carnegie Mellon University, at the MLA's convention that year, in Washington. Epstein quotes Shumway as saying: "The lack of respect afforded the humanities in the press is something most of us will agree upon." Epstein's summary of Shumway's reaction is this: "Journalists seize on opportunities, like the MLA convention itself, to lampoon what they see as the egg-headed elite and their esoteric, out of touch ramblings." Others at the session apparently agreed, as Epstein reports. "'How many times have we seen the headline "Jane Austen and the masturbating girl?"'" asked Jeffrey J. Williams, an English professor at Carnegie Mellon, to a few groans from the audience."

Despite possible surface differences in titles, the reaction of journalists seems to have changed little in a decade and a half. The article from the *New*

York Times about the 1990 convention was called "Victorian Underwear and Other Seminars"[35]—which gives a sense of the article's unimpressed point of view. A letter to the editor (from an L. S. Klepp—if an invented name, quite a nice one) comments, presumably tongue-in-cheek:

> It comes, of course, as a shock to learn that a large faction of professors and graduate students at the Modern Language Association's annual convention has concluded that there is no such thing as creative genius; it's like hearing that a convocation of eunuchs has declared that there's no such thing as sexual pleasure ("Deciphering Victorian Underwear And Other Seminars" by Anne Matthews, Feb. 10). But I don't think we need be alarmed, just because so many literature professors have finally admitted that they are bored by literature.

And this was in 1991—if they were bored then, think how they feel now. But at the same time, how much more resentful of the way the outside world pokes fun of them so that they vow to stick that much more tightly to their guns. As for all those funny words—well, certainly literary studies nowadays has developed lots of terms that nobody on the outside understands. Those on the inside see this, correctly, as a sign of the professionalization of what they do. If only they'd realize what they've bought at this cost. There's nothing wrong with jargon if it does serve a purpose, any more than there's anything wrong with an arcane but precise tool in the toolbox if that's just what we want. But if our purpose in having it in the toolbox was just to make ourselves feel big with such a well-equipped toolbox, it becomes an end in itself, and at some point too heavy to carry around. Assuming we have to have jargon in literary studies comes from the unquestioned assumption that literary studies works the way science does. And that's just what is so clearly not the case.

Chapter Three

Science Envy

THE ESSENCE OF THE PROFESSIONALIZATION OF literary studies has been its attempt to re-make itself on the model of science. Part of the professionalization of literary studies is the insistence that only specific people can do it. Another part is the assumption that what we do is study it in some systematic way. Both of these are borrowed from the most clearly methodological undertaking available. Scientific methodology works for science. But science has qualities humanities study doesn't. Who says what works for one will work for the other? At the very least we should be justifying our transference of the presuppositions of one to the other, talking about what we've gained and lost, what we've condemned ourselves to by our choices. None of this takes place; instead we merely take for granted that this is the only way to go about our business.

The most fundamental presupposition of science is that the manifold it is investigating, the physical world, merely exists; if there is any explanation beyond "merely" (say, God), this is beyond the scope of science. In order to justify a "scientific" enterprise of literary studies, we have to make a comparable presupposition about texts: they merely are, in the same way that the physical world merely is; anything beyond the fact of the text is irrelevant to the study. That means that the manifold is objective: what's there to be studied isn't itself constructed as a result subjective factors.

Yet literary works aren't objective the way the natural world is, at least not unless we make some very counter-intuitive assumptions—precisely those made by professionalized literary studies. The subjectivity of the authors makes the works come to be, to begin with. That's the first thing we have to assume out of existence. The authors could well have decided not to write, or publish. In addition the random murmur of the world plays a large role in whether or not the text is on the table in front of us days, decades, or centuries after it was written and published: did they have the time and money to write this? Did they have the luck to be published, and then publicized, so that we remember their works years after? Nor are authors the only subjective factors that mesh to determine which works come to be and which don't, which survive and which don't, which catch the public eye and which don't. The choice of what works were publicized or published at all is subjective on the part of editors and publishers, the choice of which among printed works we read is subjective on the part of professors and subject to their necessarily limited knowledge; the focus at all on a certain type of work as opposed to others, say books, is itself is the result of a subjective way of understanding the world. Finally, there's very little about literature that *is* objective. Yet all this has to be assumed away, or simply ignored. We start with what's here, and we study it. Similarly, I could write whole books on the things on the top of my desk (there's a lot). It's here: I can study it. Why should anyone else care?

Why science?

The trappings of science that literary studies have taken over serve only to give the sheen of science, not the essence. The priestly caste in science is priestly because what it does is, potentially, completely public—not hidden at all. You may not understand what's in a specialized science journal, but you have only to go to school and learn the specialized language: then you can judge what's written by comparing it with the world—the results of any experiment have to be reproducible. In professionalized literary studies, you also have to go to school and learn how to talk the talk. But that's become the goal itself: you aren't thereby empowered to run someone else's experiments again and say whether what's said is true or false. After you learn the language of literary studies, you understand what the individual using that language is claiming, but you're no closer to being able to interact with him or her than before—and you can't appeal to an external manifold to say s/he is right or wrong.

To be sure, the notion of "scientific method" is a bit of a misconception even when used with science: there's nothing intrinsically scientific about the process of noting a problem, proposing a solution, and then revising the solution as other evidence comes to the fore. However what's scientific about this is that the process itself takes front and center. We set problems and look for solutions: that's what science does. We don't just note a problem, we go out looking for problems. We don't just by the bye propose a solution; that's what we're supposed to aim at. And we don't just wait for other evidence to somehow drift our way: we look for it, set up situations that test just this solution. (I've considered the relationship of the scientific way of doing things to others in my *Science and the Self*.)

In fact, there's nothing intrinsically scientific about what we do in the laboratory; what makes science science is that we take a normal methodology that we apply in everyday situations—the isolation of variables to determine causes—and put this at the center of things, using this consciously as our methodology. We isolate variables in daily life too, only not so concertedly. If we want to decide whether the problem is the key or the lock to the front door, we try another key made in the same batch. (It's possible both keys are defective, so now we have to test these against something else.) If I want to determine if the problem in my relationship is due to me or my partner, I ask myself, have I had the same problem with other partners? To be sure, quasi-scientific "counselors" sometimes have to force me to pose this situation; most of the time we don't want to be "scientific" with respect to ourselves. Laboratories are about setting up situations that bring this way of thinking to the fore.

Science can never answer all our questions, it just has the framework to show us how to go about trying to find answers. Religious people at odds with science like to point out that science requires a leap of faith too: we needn't have the explanation, only believe we can someday find it. The faith is in the process, not the answer. What makes science different from faith is that the individuals use the presuppositions to assert things that others can judge by the same presuppositions. There's no such thing as private truth in science, access that can't be made public. That, by contrast, is what religion is all about. Religious faith is the answer: it tells us what the bottom line has to be, and lets us get there any way we choose. In science, it's the process that's given, and the bottom line that's never specified.

Fine-toothed comb

The notion that we are always filling in the same framework, only more and more precisely, is one of the bases of the scientific world-view. Sometimes science takes huge steps, jumps ahead to cover a large swath of territory that is only later gone over by generations of researchers with a fine-toothed comb of laboratory fill-ins. We know in general terms how something works; we try for an always more precise set of such terms. This conception has been adopted in the twentieth century by the humanities and social sciences: the notion is that we "make progress" and "do research" on the same manifold to render our understanding more intense, greater in some absolute sense. We ourselves may "specialize" in Hölderlin or Saul Bellow, but we are still involved in the same enterprise as our colleague down the hall who "works" on *Beowulf* or Phyllis Wheatley. This echoes the way two different scientists can be engaged in different enterprises but with a shared assumption that both are working to discover the objective natural world. That's why it's okay for me to do one thing and you another, without asking : If what I do is so valuable, why you shouldn't be doing it too?

No one to my knowledge has ever seriously tried to justify the use of scientific terminology with literary studies: instead it's become part of what I'm calling the methodology, the way we do business. It's merely taken for granted, stirred into the mixture so we can't separate it out. That's what justifies all those references to "X's brilliant insight," "Y's trenchant discovery"—and they're not talking about a new manuscript that's been discovered, but a reading of the old. So too the trappings of objective knowledge, including the jargon of insiders whose result, if not ostensible function, is to separate out a class of knowledgeable insiders all of whom speak the same language, one incomprehensible to those outside, but which is passed off as a technical language necessary to access a non-everyday world of explanatory entities.

To be sure, some of what we do with literature is in fact clearly objective, and this too is mixed in. Older texts need to be understood or standardized, manuscripts sifted through, and so on. But this is not the shift to the scientific that's characterized the late twentieth century. This sort of literary scholarship has been going on for a long time, and undoubtedly will continue to do so. It's not essentially different from comparable scholarship on pottery shards: what are these? How do they fit together? Can we read the inscriptions?

The shift toward the scientific that is at the basis of literary methodology nowadays involves current, already established texts—the work is on nothing so real-world as establishing what they are and how to read them, or deciding variants between texts. This at least acknowledges that works come from the world, and are anchored in the real. Current methodology starts with the texts and treats these as the objective bedrock that can be further elucidated. Our discoveries are the new angles on what was there before, not new shards. We have to have a conference where we meet face to face because our breaking news is that established text X, in a fully comprehensible language, is suddenly seen to be Y (an expression of power by A, the exclusion of B, an example of Bakhtin's theory of dialogic works, a pre-figuring of Walter Benjamin's *Arcades Project bricolage*).[36] If you haven't heard the paper on this, you don't know this, so.... So what? You'll be treating your patients (students) using outmoded techniques? You'll be unable to hold your head up if it turns out you're not referring it to the *Passagenwerk, The Arcades Project* (I use this as an example of one of our intellectual fads that's since gone the way of all fads)? Good heavens.

There are practically if not literally an infinity of combinations of applying approach or text X to text Y—practically infinity in the sense that we'll all die before we've worked through more than a tiny fraction of the possible cross-connections. Perhaps the infinity of literal too: our actions produce new texts that, in their turn, can be combined with each other to produce new permutations, and so on. This makes the enterprise of literary studies completely unlike science, whose presupposition is that we are increasing the Known and diminishing the Unknown. We're not constantly adding to the stuff of the universe, the way we do as we add texts on to texts. (It's surely not coincidental that this work of Benjamin was so outrageously popular in academic circles for as long as it was because it suggested that originality was an outdated concept; one could express oneself by quoting others.)

Too, the reasons we have for applying X to Y themselves aren't objective. Why not A to Y? Or A to B? Those are fine too. But why this right here?

Because we feel like it. Or because everybody else is doing it this year. Or: that's what we happened to do. There's no connection with this application of X to Y and anything outside itself; it's its own end. There's no external situation that renders what's presented at these conferences timely, nothing comparable to, say, the need to cure cancer. They're their own point, and there's no penalty—say, more people dying—in not knowing that this is the way X is being read as Y.

In fact the penalty is in adopting these things, not in failing to adopt them. If we come home full of modish ideas, the danger is that these get transferred too directly to our bewildered students. *Arcades Project*? Maybe the idea of comparing the work on the syllabus to something else makes sense if you already have this other work under your belt (though it's likely to be distracting even then) but it's like telling runners intent on finishing the course in front of them they have to run a side-race twice as long as this one to be eligible to continue. Go read the *Arcades Project,* and then let's talk about how this work, your real assignment, relates to it.

The fundamental problem with this accretive view of knowledge about literature, more being more, is that it fails to see that reading literature or perceiving art is like eating a meal, not stocking a supermarket: we can only eat so much. More isn't more in teaching literature—more allusions, more connections simply make it more difficult to eat, rather than enriching the experience. A few spices: fine. Too many: indigestion, or simple disgust, as we push the plate away.

Knowing more

Part of the reason literary studies has tried so desperately to seem scientific is that we haven't acknowledged that most of life isn't scientific at all. Science is only one thing among the many we do, after all. Talking about "warm reds and cool blues" isn't a scientific way of talking, any more than saying that "she made me feel very small" is scientific. We can't pin either down, which is to say (in unscientific terms) put them in terms that don't move. We can't run experiments to find out, say, if the reason we love our wife is that she's good, or that she has red hair, or (let's say both play a role) what the respective % is of each in our love. We can't run a parallel life in which we're married to a woman who's just as good as our current wife but lacks the red hair, partly because we have only one life, and partly because we wouldn't know how to separate out all the factors that go into an emotion as complex as love. The world of appearances isn't the scientific world, but only because we can't go back to it and find it the same: that's what we do in science, we construct a world that stays put. If what we construct doesn't stay put, we demand an "explanation" for that, and reach a level that does. We separate off the "world of appearances" as we burrow down to the world of science: the two only are as they are through contrast.

Science isn't a model those who deal with the individuals portrayed in the arts and the with individuality of the artworks should even be attracted to. Its goal is something else entirely than understanding particulars; science is about the construction of generals and the complete transcendence of the particular. Science is about finding a location for the unchangeable, placing its focus on a level where change is secondary. We have a matrix that itself doesn't change, though the values within it do. Doing science is getting to the level you can be sure about, which usually means discovering and articulating it, the level of things like the Periodic Table of Elements, of atomic particles, of waves for colors. If these things themselves change more than a negligible amount, we have to explain this change: and that means, find and construct a yet more fundamental layer that stays put, or at least changes in predictable ways.

The problem with science is the same as its strength, namely that focuses on what's always the same, even if the constant is a pattern of change. It purposely sluffs off individuality in order to achieve generality, like a cicada slipping out of its skin. It's always the level of appearances that's variable and, not coincidentally, beautiful, not the level of functionality or explanation. Science goes for the ugly, in this sense, and away from the variable. This need cause us no anxiety; we can accept simply that the two worlds, the world of appearances and the scientific one, are different: neither one replaces the other. The Romantics were still caught in the vise of coming to terms with this: as Goethe puts it in *Faust I* (in the possibly ironic voice of Mephistopheles): "all theory is gray; the tree of life is green." Theory isn't fun, but does that mean it's illegitimate? (Mephistopheles is trying to con a student into abandoning his studies.)

Of course it's true that explanation is intrinsically invariable; that's what explanation is made for, to anchor the transient. We don't have to resist science, the way the Romantics did, or think it's trying to take over: it can't take over, because it can never do justice to appearances, and this by definition. Science does its thing, the everyday world does its. The intersection comes when science helps us explain things in the everyday world that are puzzling to us: what isn't puzzling doesn't need to be explained. The level of explanation only intersects with the world when there's something to be explained.

Professing Literature

What we teach in the literature classroom hasn't always been based on this quasi-scientific methodology, what I call the "knowledge paradigm." It replaced, in fact, an earlier way of looking at literature, what I call the "wisdom paradigm."

Literary studies in nineteenth century America, as we learn from Gerald Graff's *Professing Literature*, was different from literary studies in the twentieth.[37] Graff sketches an involvement with literature that began with a focus on texts in Greek and Latin, largely from a linguistic point of view, was subsequently subject to German influence in the form of an influx of philological studies, and then in the twentieth century began to resemble the "field-coverage" professionalism with which we are familiar today, with its organization into the units of epochs, individual writers, or approaches to literature.

Humanities had had a solid footing up to and through the nineteenth century when it was based on a fixed list of classic texts. But with the acceptance of contemporary literary and even novels as fair game, suddenly it seemed as if the floodgates had opened. This was the crisis to which those who engineered the Pyrrhic victory of professional methodology in literary studies responded. Unable to control content, they learned to control methodology, having looked at science for a lesson on how to do this.

The twentieth century gave a scientific answer to the question, What is the justification for literary studies?, which the twenty-first has so far continued to offer. The answer was: because literature exists, it is part of the world. The nineteenth century, by and large, gave a moralistic answer: because it makes us better people, brings us closer to achieving the invariable moral code. According to this older set of assumptions, the wisdom paradigm, everybody works on the same set of truths or set of texts. According to the knowledge paradigm, the new-fangled twentieth-century one, everybody branches out, sustained by the assertion that they're all part of the whole.

I'm proposing an answer that is a combination of these two. I think literature helps us understand our individuality because it provides an articulation of something in ourselves we hadn't so clearly understood to be the case. Literature helps us to achieve not an invariable moral code, nor an invariable external world, but an extremely variable and changeable thing: ourself.

Most of the problems facing our conceptualization of literary studies in the West today come from the fact that we are only slowly becoming aware of the disadvantages of the knowledge paradigm but don't want to return to the wisdom paradigm, whose disadvantages, being those of a discarded paradigm, are clearer. This leads to most of us relying on an unacknowledged patchwork combination of both, and so to theoretical confusion. We transcend the theoretical confusion only if we return to the practical, the social fact of talking about the work, not offering the talk as an end in itself.

Religions of the book

Literary studies took over the knowledge paradigm from natural science as science displaced religion as an object of general intellectual respect in the mid- and late nineteenth century. That's what I'm emphasizing here, as science was the form that gave literary studies its pattern. Yet earlier conceptions of literature were based on the wisdom paradigm, and the purest form of the wisdom paradigm is religion. The religions the *Holy Qur'an* calls "of the book" (Judaism, Christianity, Islam: the three great monotheisms) seem closest to Victorian literary studies. Of the religions of the book, Islam is the best example of the wisdom paradigm. All the answers to all the problems of the world found in the limited confines of one text (the claim as well for the two religions of the Bible). Where Islam goes beyond Judaism or Christianity is in the belief that these answers are embodied in specific words in a specific language. Gabriel, spokesman for God, spoke Arabic to Mohammed, and not another language. And these words are what God said. For Muslims, the language is in some sense the very incarnation of God, the *Holy Qur'an* the closest Islam has to the Christian corporealization of God in the body of Jesus. Until recently Muslims did not accept the possibility of translations of the *Qur'an*: the classical Arabic is learned and recited by heart, even by those who don't understand its content. Vernacular versions were, and by some purists still are, called "interpretations," the impulse being to require learning Arabic. (This insistence on a specific language stood in contrast to the Christian eagerness to translate the Bible into every known language; we owe many of our dictionaries of non-Western languages to Christian missionaries.)

Even the secular version of the wisdom paradigm, say, studying Greek and Roman poetry instead of vernacular literatures, or limiting curricula to the One Hundred Greatest Books of Western Literature, offers the same advantages as the religious version of the wisdom paradigm. It gives at least the illusion of commonality between individuals. Everyone studies the same texts. Its great disadvantage is equally clear: there is little room for individual definition through the object of study. This may be the reason the wisdom paradigm for the humanities was gradually discarded as literature came to seem a legitimate field of study, and literary studies professionalized as a result.

Nineteenth-century literary studies, being based on the wisdom paradigm, was defined by a relationship with texts that was teleological rather than "scientific" in the twentieth-century fashion. Both the group of texts considered and the nature of the involvement were consciously defined, and the exclusion of those texts not studied was also part of the content of the enterprise. The literary world, the manifold of study, was constant, in addition to being limited in scope—at first to texts in Greek and Latin, later expanding to works in the vernacular, and only gradually to contemporary ones. At the same time, texts were seen as mines of moral lessons, with the lessons known beforehand: the only question left was, Where would these be found?

The wisdom paradigm is overtly reductive. It limits its field to certain texts, or certain kinds of texts, and in the case of many of those it is willing to consider, it "sees" through the text to something underneath which must everywhere be the same, or part of the same construction. The imperative implicit in the wisdom paradigm is: reduce, reduce. The imperative implicit in the knowledge paradigm is: produce, produce. If what you're doing is filling in a view of the objective world, you can't get enough of it.

I also call this the "accretive paradigm" because, in much the same way Marx thought capitalism intrinsically sought new markets, this sort of relation with the world constantly looks for new fields to be knowledgeable about. For the accretive paradigm, more is more. The value of the enterprise as a whole is found in the impulsion forward, though its motion is toward a goal it can never reach, not even asymptotically, namely: complete knowledge about literature. The value of the wisdom paradigm, by contrast, is located in restriction of both the manifold of texts considered and the manner of considering them.

It's already an act of inclusion to allow the study of contemporary novels to serve as the basis for a University degree; it's another act to allow for study of texts outside of a narrowly-defined cultural or geographical radius. An example of this may have been the extension of the manifold of study to include English literature, then (later) American. The presupposition of the knowledge paradigm in literary studies, as in natural science, is the axiom that everything studied is part of the same manifold, and so of equal intrinsic value, whether Romanian epics, Brazilian Indian chants, Leopardi, or Beat poetry.

Postulating the unseen manifold outside of us that we break fragments off of, rather than the reiterated and overseeable manifold taken as the object of the wisdom paradigm, frees us to be attentive to anything we like. It's like postulating God who is interested in each thing we think, say, or do: we don't need anybody else to know these things, as everything we do is part of the bedrock of the mind of God. Yet the proliferation of material that is the result of this forces us to pose the practical question: Who will be attentive to us? It seems so little to have the answer be only, librarians, to whom we are only another binding. We all sense the futility of writing for the shelf, yet who can keep up with everything? Most people no longer try.

The practical result of postulating an objective literary outside world unifying our choice of subjects is that nothing else is needed to unify what we do. And nothing else does. Colleagues with offices next to each other in the English Department have little in common; I need never read the pieces on (say) D. H. Lawrence written by the colleague across the hall, and she need not read those I write on (say) an author Lawrence loathed, or had never heard of. When we pass in the hall, we talk about our children, the weather, or what the Dean has just come up with. What we do have in common professionally, she and I, is only an assumption that what we two do is more alike than either of our enterprises is to (say) the activities of the school's agriculture, or biology faculty, in that both of us are working on the external manifold of "literature." Yet what this is, we probably couldn't say. Thank goodness for the need to provide administrative slots that has led to the distinctions between Departments, Divisions, and Schools within a single institution. These at least give us a sense of identity.

Taking science down a peg

The converse of the insistence that literary studies is *too* like science—which involves a deformation, bending it into a form it can't really assume—is the notion, equally dear to humanities, that science isn't as objective as it says it is. If we humanists can move toward scientists, and at the same time move scientists toward us, the identification will be complete.

Literary professors have been thrilled to hear theoreticians such as Paul Feyerabend claim that science is as much an act of self-definition as (by implication) literature is.[38] Most scientists disagree, maintaining instead that scientists are the servants of the external, objective world. Even if they're wrong, we can still define a spot for an undertaking that is self-effacing before its subject matter in this way: the scientist (or fill the blank with the new word) discovers, s/he neither invents nor expresses.

Literary scholars also loved it when science seemed to admit it lacked the utter stability and closure that had seemed to set it off from more subjective undertakings. This is certainly the reason for the extraordinary attention paid in literary studies to the Heisenberg Uncertainty Principle, based on the realization that bombarding electrons with the stream of electrons of the perceptual device, an electron microscope, blew them away and so rendered impossible the determination of a fixed place for them in the quantum levels around the nucleus.

It's an understandable *Schadenfreude*, but a dangerous one, this saying that the thing you've taken as justification for being objective itself isn't objective after all. I ascribe this to a sort of lingering sense of insufficiency. To put it in Freudian terms, you try to out-do Dad precisely because you admire him so much, and pounce mercilessly on his weaknesses precisely because you're trying to take his place and can never do so as long as he seems invincible. If you didn't admire him you wouldn't be so unforgiving of his shortcomings; they help you cut him down to size, so you can hope to fill his shoes.

Sokal Hoax

The biggest joke of the 1990s in American academic circles was the "Sokal Hoax," where NYU mathematician Alan Sokal authored a "sham" article in the journal *Social Text* purporting to show the intrinsic lack of objectivity in science, with many references to commentators in the humanities and social sciences who questioned the objectivity of science. The editors published the article, only to have Sokal claim in another article, this one for *Lingua Franca*, that it had been "liberally salted with nonsense," and that he had been out to tell the editors just what they wanted to hear in an attempt to see just how far he could go.[39]

Logically speaking, Sokal's motivation in writing the article is irrelevant if what the article says is correct. Certainly it would have been embarrassing and humiliating to have what seemed to be a turn-coat come-over-to-your-side spy reveal himself to be no turn-coat at all, but only there to make fun. Though I think the attempt to create an alternative objectivity in the form of the manifold of literary studies is unwise, it really is true that we can't access motivation of the author, and shouldn't be asked to: here, I'm with the editors of *Social Text*.

Besides, why shouldn't they have thought it was a good-faith submission? It was very like others they'd published, and a lot of people do talk this way. Yes, it was a "gotcha," but should we be expected to be able to avoid "gotcha" situations? If a man comes towards us with a smile and his hand out, we're not well advised to assume that precisely because it looks as if he's being friendly, that's just the reason he isn't. That's what it means to us to have someone be friendly. The adolescent "joke" of approaching someone as if to shake hands and then dropping the hand before making contact is for this reason tiresome. Of course any one application of a social norm can turn out to be fake. But if it's always fake, we simply change the norm. It's not interesting to be made aware that trickery is always possible.

Of much greater interest in the Sokal Hoax is the apparent deep need of literary (here social science) professors to believe that science isn't objective. The postulate of the objectivity of the manifold of literary study is stirred into the trope: it's assumed without being asserted. In science, it's asserted. Hence the need of those who want to bring their own discipline closer to science to bring science down a peg or two: it's more accessible that way. Once reduced in objectivity, science no longer seems so dauntingly different. It's more plausible to say, literary studies is exactly like science.

The thing is, if we demote science too far, there's no value in objectivity, and we're left with our "wisdom" paradigm. From the outside, it seems odd that literary studies should simultaneously be so keen to make themselves more objective in what they do—their world now the same as the world outside—while denying the power of objectivity in science. Yet from within literary studies, it makes perfect sense. It works if we've assumed we're inside the ark: now it can begin to rain. Who cares what happens to the people outside? They deserve their fate. Only what happens if you're not Noah and Co. but a strange sect that poisons itself with Kool-Aid? How do you know, if all you know is what's inside the compound, within the ark? Both Noah and Jim Jones claimed to have heard the voice of God.

Just as a good deal of post-Modern art makes no sense outside of the museum, much contemporary literary scholarship makes no sense outside of the library and the university, which have become to a greater extent than in the nineteenth century ends rather than means. Texts beget texts, and commentary begets commentary. In order to understand the argument of one commentator, you have to have under your belt a whole diet of previous texts by earlier ones. This both necessitates and gives a justification to the professionalization of the enterprise. The more rigorously accretive the view of the knowledge paradigm, the more absolute our adherence to the social structures which must replace the unity that the increasing fragmentation of this knowledge destroys.

Yet this is so only on the surface. Within this rapidly expanding and theoretically unbounded universe that is held to provide the basis of the knowledge paradigm, the wisdom paradigm is still very much with us, though it is largely submerged and unacknowledged. We pay lip service to a knowledge paradigm, but we have largely ceased to believe in it, and our actions continually serve a residual wisdom paradigm which actually ends up being the source of much of our sense of value in literary studies.

Fields and figures

We provide the immediate justification for literary studies not in the manifold purportedly holding together our individual objects of scholarly attention, but instead in what we define as fields or figures, sub-divisions of that manifold that we hold to take on some degree of objective definition, so that we don't have to defend their study in turn. These sub-divisions are the units of professorships and scholarly papers. Though the entire manifold is theoretically unbounded, each field within it defines itself both by inclusion and by exclusion, the hallmark of a wisdom paradigm. We "make progress" in Thomas Mann. Nobody talks about how that means we're failing to learn anything about Molière, or are forgetting what we knew about Schiller. Or worst of all, the fact that we never read Kant at all, and don't know the difference between Monet and Manet. Knowing X means not knowing virtually everything else. Perhaps our brains really are zero-sum games. Sherlock Holmes suggested his head was like an attic: filling it up with one set of things meant there was no room for others.

More fundamentally, more material means we have to spend less time with any part of it if we want to include it all. Our lives haven't gotten any longer, nor our powers of concentration better. There aren't more hours in the day. Certainly our students' willingness to plough through material hasn't increased over the decades. Nor have class periods gotten longer: if we feel we have to start with the tail of the kite, the commentaries attached to the work, we'll never get to the kite before the bell rings.

In addition there's what the East Germans called *die Qual der Wahl*. With the Berlin Wall standing, there was virtually no consumer choice in the East, so you simply made do with the one version of something that was available, when it was: problem solved. After the Wall fell and the West rushed in, shelves were full of a bewildering repetition of apparently identical choices, so that frequently the mentally overloaded Easterners would return home empty-handed, feeling *die Qual der Wahl*, the pain of too-great choice. With so much to choose from, they'd choose nothing. More isn't always more.

So we've learned to limit this rush of new material, all the time pretending we aren't doing it. We're only organizing it, we claim, not curtailing it. In fact we're beating back the tide, albeit without admitting that's what we're up to. It certainly makes sense to beat back the tide; what's unsettling is the duplicity in doing so. Why not just admit that the presupposition that produces this tsunami to begin with is invalid, rather than trying to place roadblocks in the way of a flood we ourselves have created?

The list of fields isn't static, but its acceptance of new members takes place by well-established and limited patterns of association; this is one way we try to slow the rush of information and give ourselves the illusion of making absolute progress. If we take a specific author as our field, we can at least read every word the author wrote and a large proportion of the criticism. The manifold can be seen as a whole, and becomes finite in the way the manifold of all texts is not. We polish off *Ulysses*, if our projected area of competence is "Joyce," and prepare ourselves for *Finnegans Wake*. Thank goodness for death, we sometimes think, at least that of writers, which at least limits the things we have to read. If we're more ambitious, we declare ourselves Modernists, and have enough material for many decades of work. (Even here we limit ourselves to artists, probably writers, and to the works that look like each other, not, say, including the popular literature of the 1920s—unless that becomes precisely our "field," and its study the flavor of the month.) Because we postulate a fixed manifold, we say we "make progress" in our work; we know more about Joyce, or Modernism. The simple filling in of the boundaries provides the value of the undertaking. The more we limit our field of vision, the more it seems we make progress: compared to yesterday's state, today seems like more because we've added A and B. But what if that meant we'd forgotten C and D? Or never learned X and Y? Or if the alphabet isn't finite, but infinite? What's A and B compared to infinity?

This creation of or adherence to solid sub-divisions of the manifold endowed with value allows us to sleep at night, having Accomplished Something (which is to say, having filled in one particular pre-determined box), and to begin again the next morning. We have a map of the terrain and so are able to define progress. Without these sub-divisions, we can never have specific goals, and hence cannot regard any given job as moving closer to completion.

The delineation of any field of this sort is a fact of taxonomy, which means it's conventional. (That taxonomy is conventional is one of the more trenchant points in Foucault's *The Order of Things*.[40]) Joyce is a field, Joyce plus his contemporaries who were writing in the same way is a field (Modernism), Joyce plus his countrymen is a field (Irish literature). For some reason, however, Joyce plus authors who look like him is not a field, nor Joyce plus authors who were born on the same day. It seems arbitrary that we can't "make progress" by finding out about authors who look like Joyce, or that we'd be dismissed as a crackpot if we wrote an essay on writers whose names contained the same number of letters (perhaps we can create a system whereby each letter gets a certain number of points; we could focus on writers whose names add up to the same number).

The fact that fields and figures are what are actually providing the structure of literary studies shows how unlike science it is. Fields and figures are uniquely unsuited to fill the role of *de facto* source of value in literary studies, being extraordinarily mutable. (The *de jure* source of justification for literary studies is still the postulated manifold of the knowledge paradigm.) What was on the approved list of fields and figures this decade or this year may not be so in another year or another decade, or even another year. To a large degree, this is so because things like geography and the vicissitudes of politics, factors unrelated to the information contained in fields, are what delineate them to begin with. Accidents of language play a large role in our divisions of literature: typically we're in a department of French, or of English, or of Chinese. Most people read only their native tongue, and even comparatists rarely go beyond two or three national literatures. They don't typically read philosophy or sociology, much less biology, chemistry, or agriculture.

Literature can't function like the objective world for a science-like sub-discipline, literary studies. The literature available to us to study, and the fact of our studying it, are the results of chance. They're what float up from the depths we never plumb: they're not the depths themselves. The manifold of literature is what it is at any particular moment as the result of a great many factors, ranging from individual power grabs, the fact that the python of the scholarly world is still digesting a very large pig, the result of what's available, the result of what got written and what didn't, what got publicized and what didn't, what got conceived and what didn't, what got started and what didn't, what got finished and what didn't. Writing is a highly specific activity: writers can use their time in other ways, and sometimes do. So if they had, these things wouldn't be here to end up on a reading list at all.

The fact of our attention also creates and destroys the manifold. A reading list is like a lifeboat, things rescued from what otherwise is, for the purposes of this course and these students, oblivion. There's not room for everyone: in a given course, everybody but those in the lifeboat perishes, in the sense that nobody pays attention to them. In order to justify one group in the lifeboat we either have to assert they deserve it more—a claim we hear quite a bit from formerly marginalized groups—or we have to believe that the others don't disappear from the lifeboat, they just tread water alongside for a while: they'll be there when we return. But if they are, it's the result of specific political and economic factors, not a presupposition, like science.

Before the twentieth century realized it could try to turn literary study into something like science, writing a history based on names and dates was as scientific as we can get. That wasn't very scientific; instead it waited to see what actually got made, and then listed it. Of course, even then, there was a strong tendency to think that the works that were being listed were the ones that had to be—that literary historians were somehow also doing eschatology: this lay of the land was fated to be. If so, then there was a purpose to literary history other than merely saying what happened: it gave patterns that had some substance on their own. But it still wasn't science.

Literary studies led the way in trying to turn the study itself into something more like science, probably because literature seems so solid when compared to most artistic products. Too, the paradigm that had previously reigned supreme was that of a small fixed library of "classics." We began to expand that, but if we expanded it to all the products of the contemporary world—rather than waiting for history to cull these for us, for good or bad reasons, to a manageable few—we suddenly realized we can't include them all. But based on what did we exclude? Since our mantra had become inclusion, we now can't stanch the flow of things, and the arbitrary nature of our exclusions—now defined by facts of the profession itself—are clear.

Vector arrows

There's another reason why the presuppositions of a basal underlayer to everything—the presupposition of the objective world that underlies science—can't be applied to a sub-sector of that objective world, namely literature. If it's applied to a part of the whole, such as literature, it's necessarily applied with a vector quality: it's being used to change things. And this is something science, which postulates the largest manifold of all, can never do.

Things like electrons and the periodic table are articulated so as to be they're non-controversial: they're neutral. It's the *use* of science that's normed, not the science itself. We do pure science, as we call it, "as if": to hold things in abeyance for the day when we might need them. Pure science by itself has no purpose, nor is it held to have one: it's useless to be able to explain the inner workings of something that's going right if somehow you could guarantee it would always go right.

We're not helped in knowing what the elements of the periodic table are if there's no payoff to doing so, nothing this knowledge helps us do. After it was discovered that the Earth revolved around the sun, this information was useless for most people, who continue to say that "the sun rises" and "the sun sets." Because we accept that this explains things that otherwise are inexplicable—and moreover, makes possible things that weren't, like space travel—we're willing to acknowledge that this is so all the time.

The useful aspect of Freud's attempt to turn psychology into a science, thus, was not his explanations of what is always the case. It was using this to apply to things that went wrong: hysteria, obsessions, even minor glitches like strange dreams, jokes, or slips of the tongue, where it seemed he could get some purchase on things. By the nature of his explanation system, these simply couldn't be exceptions; they had to actually be the rule. Exceptions can always be treated as exceptions, and need no explanation. Yet in his quest to be "scientific," Freud had to express what he said in the terms of an all-the-time underlayer, make statements not about the exceptions but the rules. All boys want to marry their mother and kill their father, for example; all dreams are wish-fulfillments; all children are polymorphously perverse. But if there's no way to actually apply statements like these, they're as pointless (sure, why not?) as saying that all of us are made of packed-together elves that you can't see, touch, or taste. Or maybe we're made of metaphysical green cheese. Or invisible carrots. Yet if the elf-theory could be use to explain why some people vomit elves, suddenly it would have a justification.

Sometimes science does enter the realm where people care, as a player rather than an overseer/guide. As I've considered in *Science and the Self*, religion always grows out of the world; if it lasts as religion it focuses on "belief" of things that aren't amenable to proof. But it hooks on to the world at specific points. And at these points, it makes statements that science can later challenge. A small example is a statement like this: the Shroud of Turin dates from the twelfth century. A larger example is: the Earth revolves around the sun. Or: the animals that exist were not all created at once, in six days, after humans. If religion is wise, it will simply smile and retreat on these issues: it doesn't need them as part of a belief system that can't be disproven. But here science is as guilty of over-stepping its bounds as religion is, and science is probably the aggressor: religion has to have some admixture of the real world, which only later is discovered to be wrong. It has to attach to the real world, after all.

Science should simply say: Here's the evidence of dinosaur bones that indicate by our measures they lived and died before humans. And here's what we conclude from this. What are you prepared to pay in terms of isolation of your belief system from the mainstream to conclude something different? If religion is willing to pay the price, it will of course continue on its way.

Problems only arise if it balks at the price. Science hasn't proven religion wrong. Everything is possible, it just comes at a certain cost.

Science is therefore not well advised to try and strong-arm people who don't want to accept it. Instead it needs to identify the price these nay-sayers will pay if they don't draw X or Y as practical conclusions. For most people, it's fine to say that the sun rises and sets. So why try to correct them all the time? If really there is no payoff to saying that the Earth evolved over hundreds of millions of years, why argue with the "creationists?" If someone is convinced that AIDS can be cured by eating garlic and raw onions, s/he can't be unconvinced. But when that person dies, others might be. Science really is objective, but this is circular: science is the neutral sub-stratum, not what gets involved in arguments between them.

Science always seeks a "more fundamental layer" that escapes the world of subjective disagreements. This is the nature of science. This more fundamental layer is *hors combat*. The problem with trying to go to a more fundamental layer to explain literature is that the "more fundamental layer" in literary studies is itself always contentious. It's not fundamental enough, by truly scientific standards, and can't be separated from the uses to which it's put. Further, we can't even agree on what the problems are—what uses it's to be put to. In science we non-scientists accept the periodic table (and many other things) because we agree that our goal is to cure cancer or go to the moon and these things are shown to help us. The things we deem "scientific" are by definition removed from intra-human wrangling.

This is intrinsically the problem with the "social sciences": they purport to be able to prove something, and yet always have the potential for arguing with you. They want you to see it their way. It's also the problem with other disciplines than science itself that try to apply scientific methodology. Yet people who want to do something aren't going to be willing to accept control by someone passing as "scientific."

Science's assertion of a manifold itself, therefore, lacks a vector quality. In literary studies and the social sciences, the comparable assertion of a manifold is used with a vector quality: to force people to do something they don't want to do. In literary studies, it's been used to buttress the claims to importance of the priestly class, and to provide a justification for an enterprise that, with the rejection of an overt wisdom paradigm, has ceased to have one. Now, the forms the wisdom paradigm takes—fields and figures, periods and conference topics— are defined only by the enterprise itself, like a faded version of the call to moral arms of the nineteenth century. But they do make it professional, and this by necessity: you have to come inside the profession, follow its rules, to be able to enjoy the benefits of justification it offers. Only if you're "working on" a recognized field or figure—which means, one recognized by the profession— can you tell yourself you're adding to the sum of human knowledge, making progress. Otherwise you're just doing what people do: filling time, making the day pass.

Partial knowledge

To the extent that we acknowledge the manifold of both primary and secondary texts as constantly open to alteration, we must conclude that literary studies neither is nor refers to a scientific layer of explanation. There will always be newly-written literary works; they are being added now, and will continue to be added. This means that we are always damned to the partial knowledge of anyone who is not living at the end of time. Matter is constantly being created in literary studies, though not in the physical world. If physical matter were conceived of in the way of the manifold of literary studies, as mutable, in the process of creation, and potentially infinite, two cubic feet of it wouldn't get us two times closer to encompassing the whole than one cubic foot. In the same way, we can double, treble, or even multiply a hundredfold our literary studies, and still not be any closer to knowing more of the manifold, though we may say (paradoxically) that we know more than before. Like Lewis Carroll's Alice, we're running twice as fast but not getting any further.

There's no reason to assume that we even ought to be trying for a "scientific" version of literary studies. We can carry on just fine without this. The mere fact that we can pay attention to something in the moment doesn't mean it's scientific: nobody says cataloguing all of what a neighbor says and does is scientific, or noting the patterns made by clouds every moment of every day, or taking down (how?) all the words exchanged on a single day in a medium-sized American city. We shouldn't confuse the activity of science with paying attention to things: not everything is science. In fact it's one of the bizarre fallacies of the modern age to think that all things aspire to the condition of science. They don't.

In order to reconcile the fact that the body of literature is constantly changing with the requirements of anything capable of being rendered a science, we have to be as overt as Northrop Frye that he was uninterested in new works on the ground that they were merely reiterations/recyclings of invariable matrices in the same way that a product put on the market is irrelevant to the Periodic Table of Elements.[41] But Frye's particular version of the explanation behind specific works has not caught on as the universal one; indeed it's not clear that any "universal" structure of literature could be so. It's turned out to be a subjective objectivity, which isn't the way science is constructed: science is constructed so as to be accepted by all. That's the only way it can function as an objectivity.

Tyrrany of perception

It is of course true that what is seems to us inevitable: this is the basis for taking the manifold of literary works as the equivalent of the natural world. Understanding this means breaking the tyranny of our perception. We might say, for example, it's a fact like the fact that the Earth spins around the sun that the two greatest Italian opera composers of the late nineteenth century were Verdi and Puccini. We might even have some consensus on what their best works are—not, for example, Puccini's "Fanciulla del West." So the list of what we teach in an Italian Opera course seems self-evident. What else are we going to concentrate on if not works like "Aida" and "La Bohème"? They define the landscape of what we concentrate on; it seems disingenuous at best and uninteresting at worst to say: another landscape would have been possible. The fact is, it didn't come to be.

Consider Thomas Gray's point in "Elegy: Written in a Country Churchyard," that "many a flower is born to blush unseen/ And waste its sweetness on the desert air." Is Gray telling us that other operas were in fact written that were simply swallowed by the tide of indifference? This seems unlikely, since anything that made it to the stage of being a full-fledged opera could be found again, in all likelihood, in some form or another (it's possible that the single score could have vanished, of course). The reality is more subtle, closer to Virginia Woolf's point about Shakespeare's sister, in *A Room of One's Own*: Shakespeare's postulated sister would have been so busy doing the housework she never got to write. Or perhaps, it was never suggested to her that she could. Or perhaps: what she wanted to write, could she have articulated it, was so at variance with what other people were writing that she never was able to articulate it as something that could be written.

If we live in a world where certain things are held to be the norm, we have to be very strange indeed to go against that norm, or a least that hooks on to this norm at an identifiable place, like playing dominoes: we can change to fives, but only by matching threes. What the Romantic artists, and the Modernists after them, were concerned with in their insistence that artists challenge norms rather than adhering to them, was people who actually produced the works that failed to win them glory. We see this concern with acknowledgment in Shelley's "Defense of Poetry," where he announces—somewhat desperately—that "poets are the unacknowledged legislators of the world."[42] We see it too in Gertrude Stein's Modernist assertions that true artists are always ahead of their time, and hence, it seems, by definition unappreciated—until the times catch up to them.[43] So any unappreciated artist is merely waiting for his or her time to come—as Gustave Mahler insisted his would. And amazingly, did.

But the reality is much more complex than the Romantic/Modernist concern with unappreciated masterpieces, or even with flowers "born to blush unseen" (which at least blush). This is like being very very concerned indeed with the second-place winners, and feeling we're being inclusive by focusing on them. What of those who never competed at all? Who couldn't, or had other things to do, or got distracted? Making artworks is no different from the way any articulation changes form before it's ever come to be, and sometimes doesn't come to be at all. In a social situation, we weigh the possible ways of saying something, and then perhaps say nothing at all. What if Flaubert had never written *Madame Bovary*? He could have been too ill, not had the money, not had the experiences necessary to the vision behind it—or simply been too taken up with an affair to concentrate on his writing. By what right do we wave away all these things that the finished product we're paying attention to presupposes— which include having the talent and inclination to write to begin with—and merely postulate them, saying: a world without *Madame Bovary* is unthinkable? That's in fact what we do when we think that what we do with literature is even vaguely scientific, that we're analyzing an objective world that merely is. Of course we can say: if it's here, let's read it. That's what I think of as the alternative to "literary studies." But that's not typically what we do in the classroom nowadays.

We do things that seem appropriate; our thoughts move in the channels given us. Even those who manage to work in other channels—and this can be for a number of reasons, including inability to work in the normal ones, such as the limitations that psychologically abnormal people suffer from—may not even be able to articulate their vision, much less bring it to fruition and expression, get it into printed form, get the printed form appreciated, and entered in history books. There are just too many places where the process can derail for us to think there's anything inevitable about it when it doesn't. Of course we can write a history of all the winners in the Olympics, and that will be a history of all those who won in the Olympics. But it's not a history of the world, and there's no necessity in this list: it could have been much different, and there are many things in the world it leaves out.

When this point is made the artistic Social Darwinists jump on it: we seem to be saying that losers count just as much as winners, in the same way that the Annales school of history insisted that history couldn't merely be written as a list of "great men." But again, my point is even more abstract: it's an easy adjustment to write a history of the others who competed in the Olympics but didn't win; this is what literary scholars try to do who want to save from oblivion an author they feel to be unjustly neglected. But these also-rans actually made it to the Olympics, published works which have survived well enough even to be rescued: they're already the runners-up. What of the runners-up to the runners-up? Those who for whatever reason never competed? For every unjustly neglected author there are a theoretical myriad of people who never became authors at all, but who in a different world might have been—not just flowers that blush unseen, but plants that never become flowers, flowers that never open, flowers that open but have no perfume at all. They're part of the world too: when we look at the works we're looking at, we forget that what sets them apart is that we're looking at them. We could look elsewhere.

It's perfectly true that the list of Olympic winners is the list of Olympic winners. It's just that this doesn't tell us anything more fundamental about the world: there's no necessity behind what actually was, just that this actually was. Part of what actually was, of course, can be that someone simply was faster than all others. But what if s/he had tripped? Gotten ill the night before? An infinity of presuppositions stands behind every thing that was. It may well be true that Puccini and Verdi were the greatest Italian opera composers of the late nineteenth century, but this means, greatest when all other things have been eliminated: their early death, for example. So in order to get the sense that the tips of the icebergs had to be the tips of the iceberg—rather than, merely were— we have to be blind to all the other things we shouldn't be blind to.

There's nothing wrong with defining what we're going to concentrate on. It's just that we shouldn't forget that we're the ones who've decided to concentrate on what we concentrate on: we do forget this when we further assert that what we're concentrating on in the arts is like the objective world. Not at all: this is what comes up when we put certain search criteria into the search engine, nothing more. It's possible to teach a series of works about which we can say things (including that they're like other works in some visible way); this doesn't imply the next step, the one that professionalized literary studies has taken, of seeing necessity or coherence in the list of things that are. Noting that works come into and out of "the canon" all the time doesn't do more than scratch the surface in understanding that everything that is, is surrounded by things that aren't—what Wittgenstein, in the *Tractatus Logico-Philosophicus*, called the "logical possibles."

Unlikely from the outset

Indeed, it should have seemed unlikely from the outset that an assumption about the whole world could be applied to a specific part of the manifold, here literature. The result will clearly be what we currently see: namely, that the specific body of data, treated as if it were the same as the entire objective world, has broken off from the rest of the world as a micro-world and gone spinning into its own orbit. A structure meant to apply to everything can't be applied to a sub-set of everything without denying the connection of sub-set to whole. The attempt to treat a micro-world—here the total of works of literature—with the same objective terms used for the whole world necessarily splits off that micro-world. But this is the Modernist assumption that literary studies has taken over. The rebellion of Modernist theory was against using what it called "extrinsic" approaches to literature: using literature to impart pre-determined moral lessons, or as examples of exemplary biographies.[44] Literature should be left alone to be itself: this was the central Modernist conviction from the Russian Formalists to the Anglo-American New Critics. The advantages of this approach were that it allowed people to actually pay attention to individual works, rather than seeing them as instances of types. But this can be taken too far, and has been. Now we can see the disadvantages of this approach, disadvantages that weren't at all clear at the time.

I should note that my consideration here is itself un-scientific. I speak in generalities, my argument buttressed by anecdotes. The way to counter this sort of argument is to say: It's just not this way. I don't think too many people will be saying this, because it is. Nor does my consideration have much to do with the technical debate opened as long ago as the early 1980s, perhaps with Steven Knapp and Walter Benn Michaels' much-read article "Against Theory."[45] Knapp and Michaels were against applying an overarching theory to literary studies; so am I. The question then became, is it applying an overarching theory to deny the validity of an overarching theory? And so the argument went, an attempt to end bickering becoming itself food for further bickering.

This entire debate is internal to what I'm calling the professionalization of literary studies: it's all something only professors do. The question that's central to my undertaking here is this: what's the relationship of the classroom experience to the world outside—the world students come from, that books were made from, and that literary scholars increasingly leave at the classroom door?

Chapter Four

Mutability

NOT ALL ACCRETIONS OF DATA ARE THE equivalent of engaging in science. Some are just accretions of data. The corollary of this is: just because something can be turned into a coherent body of knowledge doesn't mean there's a purpose to doing so.

Here are some points to consider.

1. The world is awash in data that can potentially be regularized, turned into the object of a discipline, most of which never will be regularized nor even something we'll ever be aware of.

2. Anything can be regularized, turned into an object of study, if you are willing to do it alone or in a small group.

3. Not everything that can be regularized is worth regularizing.

4. There are other ways of dealing with the world than regularizing it.

Look out of the car window as you drive. See those broken lines painted on the middle of road that say you can pass or be passed? (If you don't see broken lines out your car window, wait till the next straightaway to find them.) Each one is different from the next: the pattern of bumps is different in each, the particular shade of white, which may vary within the stripe. Postulate as your field of study the painted broken lines between this telephone pole—there, THAT one!—and the next.

You start off by numbering them. Let's say 1-220. And then you set about categorizing them. There's an initial group of 1-30 that's largely straight, then things get wobbly for 12 stripes, then even out, but slightly off center. And so on. After many years of study, you're an expert: how many stripes of course, but where the ones are that lean ever so subtly to east and which to west, which with the broken ends, which with large stones within them, and so on. You set about teaching on the subtle differences between one strip and the next, specializing (say) in the greater beauties of 177B with respect to anything in the 1-44 group. You set students looking at hitherto-uncharted parts of 59A (let's say they're in pairs, double broken lines). People take courses on and pass tests on "the 20s." There are intense arguments as to whether the last stripe that begins at the further telephone pole belongs to the series or not.

Those in literary studies will object: isn't what we do in fact different than this? Isn't *Don Quixote* in fact more interesting than a road stripe? Probably most of us would say it is. But why? Perhaps because we know the choice of just these stripes is arbitrary—the stripes continue beyond the telephone pole, and this road is only one among so many so there are millions of other unconsidered stripes elsewhere. Besides, they're not very long-lived. The road will be repaved at some point and the stripes renewed. Still, it's possible to be meticulous about these stripes, turn them into an object of study the way literature has been turned into an object of study.

If being equally meticulous about *Don Quixote* isn't equally pointless, someone needs to explain why it isn't. Literary studies nowadays never addresses this question; instead it merely rabbits on, studying *Don Quixote*, or insisting that we should instead be studying works by unduly neglected female writers of the period. Perhaps we can right a wrong in the sense that someone who wrote a book hitherto unread and so who deserves attention now gets some (even if it means someone else who also deserves attention doesn't), but how do we right the wrong that a book that should have been written never was? Or that could have been written in a specific way was shaped into another for whatever reason, authorial decision, market forces, outside influences, or all of these? Or that a book that should have been published never was?

What about those art forms that don't involve publication? If we're somehow master of all written things before we die, we're by definition ignorant of, say, painting: there isn't enough time in one lifetime. And the example is meant to be a joke: we all know we can't even read everything that's been written, even everything on the list of canonic books, when that existed. Can we see all the clouds? Count all the blades of grass? Look at all the road stripes? If we had an infinity of time, perhaps we could do more, but even then we couldn't do all: we can't look at these trees waving and read *Paradise Lost* at the same time, and by the time we get back to the trees they're waving in a different way. Perhaps *Paradise Lost* has changed too: or at least we have, and see different things. While we're writing the definitive work on author X, perhaps our children are growing up without our influence and input: that too is a choice, a whole set of things we haven't experienced and been part of. Life is choices—which means, in any given moment, all things but one fail to be chosen. And then we die: whatever we've come to know about the world dies with us, or takes the form of other works that the next generation may spend time on, or not, must choose from to fill the limited hours of their limited days. What if we've contributed the definitive work on X to a library—and the library burns down? Our book goes unread? What if the book itself wasn't so definitive? The fate of George Eliot's pedantic Chausabon, to spend his life on a meaningless study, haunts us all. His book never appeared; the mere fact that ours does doesn't mean it's any different than his would have been.

Worthwhile

Not all systems of study have to be as narrow as road stripes. But we have to keep our eye on the big picture to say whether or not they're worthwhile. To believe in the value of literary studies, we have to believe that books somehow are intrinsically more valuable, somehow richer, than the rest of the world: this is the element that's gone by the wayside in contemporary literary studies—any explanation of how books *do* relate to the world. Perhaps they do have more point than road stripes. But what would that be? Now we just don't pose the question; literary studies is just what we do. But that's what we'd expect a Doctor of Road Stripes to say too.

I have an answer, the one I'm proposing here: literature gives us the vocabulary and situations for understanding our own lives. To be sure, it doesn't do this in any consistent, coherent way, or in any way that can be predicted. That's why literature has to be read in great quantities, or with someone who can tailor it to what s/he knows to be our own situation. Most people need the teaching situation to get much from literature, need someone more in their world (at least not in, say Elizabethan England) who can be the middle-(wo)man. Literature, to be useful for most people, needs to be retro-fitted to its particular audience. That's what teachers do, and that's why the way literature can have value for most people is in the learning situation.

But that presupposes a teacher who sees his or her purpose only as mediating the literature, not as offering a View of Mt. Fuji that's different enough to be interesting. That's not what we get in literary studies: in literary studies, we get people presenting Information To Be Learned. To what purpose, we never say, except that that's the subject being presented. A Doctor of Road Stripes would say the same. This is Road Stripe 27! Start taking notes now!

Expendable products

Our lives are full of expendable products: words, gestures, shrugs; things we do merely to buy gas, interact with someone at the store, comfort our children, run off the too-big dinner of the night before, or help our neighbors—all of which may be summarized as carrying on the process of living. What if we do not, with our "definitive article on X," put yet another stone in the pathway that one day will lead us to a better tomorrow, but instead merely keep our bosses, the Dean or college President, happy enough to give us more money that we'll off and spend on a vacation in the Caribbean? What if there's no progress in literary and humanistic studies?

There isn't. Any manifold separated off from the world, here literary texts, can't be treated as if it were that world. By separating them we rob them of foundations, and that means they bob about every time we poke at them, like rubber duckies in the bathtub. They'll never stay still, prod at them as we might. We can arrange and re-arrange them in different orders, and write learned papers on duckie #4, the cute small one with the slightly crossed eyes. But that won't be science, because we can never get them to stand still, and don't have a clue how they came to be in the bathtub.

That's fine. It makes clear that what humanities departments inside the ivory tower do is in fact just like life outside the tower. There wouldn't be anything wrong with that, except for the decades during which those in the tower have been told that what they do is fundamentally unlike what those outside do. It isn't true.

Perhaps people in literary studies think the Dean won't pay for them to go to New York or Vancouver for the MLA (at least it's a place to go between Christmas and New Year's) if they admit that they're merely re-arranging the rubber duckies in the tub. Actually there's nothing wrong with playing with the rubber duckies: it helps people understand themselves. That in turn has many justifications, if this alone doesn't seem sufficient.

Many things can be explained in computer analogies: an individual figuring him- or herself out, identifying the center, is like de-fragmenting the computer, freeing space and making things run smoother. In addition, if we've done the work of figuring ourselves out we run cleaner, and more efficiently: we don't all the time have to be coming back to these issues; we can concentrate on other things. Thus becoming centered is actually efficient for people, aside from the fact that it means they become, typically, more at home with themselves, which means more peaceful, less agitated, more accepting of themselves and, typically, of others. But these benefits of reading literature that helps us understand ourselves is all something they'll have to explain to the Dean. They'll have to explain what literature can do for people, and acknowledge up front that reading and teaching literature have nothing to do with science.

Now they continue to insist they're disseminating knowledge, being scientific, and so on. I'm proposing that that justification could come from relating literature to the world, and to students' lives—or rather, insisting that the students themselves have to do so. The professor can't do it all; all s/he can do is fill the time in a way that gives students something to think about. But if we acknowledge that literary studies isn't really about literary study but about making sense of lives, we may get that funding after all—if not to the MLA, then perhaps to go to Florence and sit in a café and sip our cappuccino before wandering over to the Uffizzi or into a church. How much more productive all around that would be.

Lifeboat

All the acknowledgments of mutability we've included in the enclosed world of literary studies have been from the point of view of the enclosed world, looking out. So long as talking of mutability is a minor concession, we can concede it and stick to our pretensions of stability. Some scholars devote themselves to works that failed to get the acclaim due them, for whatever reason. A few exceptions are actually good for the system, like a person swimming along behind the lifeboat whom you haul in: you get to feel you've saved one more. But if a flotilla of people far more numerous than the few in the boat suddenly appears, you have to turn your back on them all. If and when we see that stability is a tiny raft floating on a sea of mutability, we cease to see much purpose in sitting in the raft and acknowledging the fact that it rocks—we should be more concerned with the sea.

Literature, the object of literary study, consists of a collection of the painstakingly-produced flowers of countless bushes that grow wild, sometimes in very odd places indeed. Many hundreds of acres can exist without harboring any bushes; many bushes produce no flowers; many bushes that produce flowers produce only stunted ones. Some produce dozens of smaller ones and a single beautiful blossom. And some flowers are undoubtedly born to blush unseen, or at least unappreciated. On the side of things that literary studies considers, there are only works that do some day get appreciated, see the ones that do ultimately get seen.

Formalized literary study—and the more it's formalized and the greater the degree to which it's a study, the more this is true—begins with the flowers, painstakingly produced and even more painstakingly gathered and brought back, spread out on a table. It can't afford to take the point of view of the bush, that strains and strains to produce a single blossom, or maybe produces dozens of stunted blooms. It can't afford to consider the fact that in order to produce each blossom now arranged cheek-by-jowl with the next, a bush usually produces what it does in isolation from the other bushes, or the fact that the blossoms that are produced are vampires on those that aren't: each one that exists prevents a theoretical infinity from existing. Flaubert's writing *Madame Bovary* may well have meant that other works failed to come to be in the same way that each child occupying the womb prevents others from being conceived.

We don't have to take the attitude that we study these things because they're the best or most worthy. We can acknowledge that they're just what we have, so long as we can justify studying them on the basis of the effect they have on the readers, us or our students. We can say, I don't know how many competing titles died along the way, but I can't do anything about it. This is what we have. No point in thinking of the children who might have been conceived; this is the one who was. I love *this* child.

But this isn't what we say in literary studies, because this requires us to be concerned about our relationship with the work (or child), and our students' relationship with the work. And that contravenes our conception of ourselves as adding to the fund of human knowledge about literature. In fact, we needn't be upset that we've only "covered a fraction of the material" if our students have had a useful experience three 50-minute periods a week for a semester, which is all we promised them. They'll never read everything, we can't teach everything. Besides, "everything" isn't all that was ever planned, written, or even published, but a tiny percentage of that vast amount, most of which both will never, and can never, be catalogued. Yet instead of taking this attitude, we persist in giving "objective" justification for classroom hours: this is the most important literature of its time, we have to cover it, they have to know it.

Stock market of taste

The closest literary studies has come to an acknowledgment of the radically arbitrary nature of what comes to be is the scholarly consideration of the mutability of literary reputations among the upper layer of people who ever acquired them to begin with. It's been remarked that, say, the Nobel Prize winner John Galsworthy is largely unread today, and that Emily Dickinson was unknown in her own time. The first realization was behind the Modernist attempt to transcend questions of taste, such as T.S. Eliot's "impersonal" theory of poetry, or Frye's monumental but at the same time futile attempt to openly separate the study of literature from literature.[46] These in turn led to our current predicament, in which we turn prayer wheels of scholarship.

We can accept that writers we currently consider major, such as Emily Dickinson, were unknown in their day. Others have had reputations created posthumously, such as Kafka. Still other reputations rose as the result of critical intervention: Edgar (Allan) Poe, "created" by Baudelaire; Melville as an American classic was "created" by F.O. Mathiessen.[47] We can accept this because it seems that the discovery only goes in one way: we can correct the mistakes of our dunce-like forebears; indeed it's part of the Romantic trope that artists are only appreciated after their deaths. But, we tend to believe, once the mistakes of our predecessors have been corrected, they're corrected. We're not going to decide that the world is flat again.

Yet most artists who die unknown stay unknown, and many people who were lionized in their day, or even "discovered" after it, don't wear well with time, and become a footnote to historians or, more likely, disappear from the official version of things altogether. How our head spins, walking through provincial galleries full of the once-famous artists of the nineteenth century. The rooms are dark, the air dusty—the visitors few. And yet these all won the Prix de Rome! Was it for this, we might wonder with Wilfred Owen, that the corn grew tall? Let's hope they had fun in their lives, at least, and left a few people at their deaths who genuinely missed them. And then there are the basements of these same museums, still of yet more obscure paintings, and the numerous levels down from that: the dark dining rooms with a painting of flowers, a bowl of fruit, or a placid cow meadow by Auntie Tess, the garage sales, the "antique stores." And below that, the people who never applied paint to canvas at all.

Out there

Most scholars, in order to avoid a welling sense of pointlessness, tell themselves they've contributed to the store of human knowledge by publishing an article or a book: at least it's "out there"; it's catalogued, somebody can get it someday, should they be interested. It exists; somebody will notice it. But this too seems a dangerously unrealistic point of view, even if we limit our point of view to rich, politically stable Western countries. For one thing, the burgeoning of self-published or print on demand books in recent years have altered the landscape of "getting information out there." There's so much information, much of it of the personal sort, we can't possibly accept it all as a "contribution to human knowledge." This implies there's someone out there knowing it. Yet it's not clear that the hundreds of thousands of books unread past family members are part of "out there" at all.

Read any military book site devoted to self-published books to see a sobering number of "my life in the military" titles, or read the catalogue of any of the major print-on-demand (POD) companies like Xlibris or iUniverse to be convinced that the world is awash in books whose existence calls into question the notion of "publication." For a time in the first flush of POD publishing, people who had books printed by these businesses were told that their books were listed on the major internet booksellers and "available" in bookstores. Years later, it's clear that most of the internet sources won't list such books, and most bookstores won't even order them; at best they'll complete a special order, pre-paid in advance. They aren't reviewed. No one can even find things in the morass, much less plough through them. There's no longer a "there there" in "out there": the sheer volume and unclassified nature of information makes it impossible to hold to the classical scientific paradigm of an ordered objective world waiting to be discovered and catalogued. Every time we catalogue some of this world of information, ten more units equal to what we've catalogued have sprung up. Reading a book is like cutting off the head of the Hydra.

If this is too much publication, on other fronts there is (in a sense) too little. University presses nowadays have to show a profit, so they simply don't publish many books that at one point would have been published, and given some publicity (which doesn't mean they would be read, or checked out of libraries). Commercial book publishing is even more draconian about publishing only things that fall into well-ploughed furrows: all else, for its purposes, is never allowed to exist—more to the point, probably never thinks about wanting to exist. Thus the new technology has become the Scylla of modern publication: you can publish (or "publish") anything you want. But it's almost certain it'll be to utter silence. The Charybdis is commercial publication, which involves a virtually guaranteed public, as publishers won't give a contract to something they don't think will sell. So probably you'll get some response, at least more than with a POD publisher. But if you publish to some response, it'll be because you've agreed to produce something for which there's already a public. The demand, such as there is, is driving the production; writers become entertainers. All such works do, as Horkheimer and Adorno pointed out decades ago, is respond to current taste.[48]

Green-lighted

The decision to allow a commercial book to come to life in much the same way a Hollywood movie project is "green-lighted." And few people outside Hollywood know that exponentially more projects die at a stage before wide release of a finished picture than make it to a multiplex. Perhaps the earliest level of pre-existence of a movie it even makes sense to say is related to "a movie" is that of a "project" that goes no further. A planned movie can be cast and not shot. A movie (perhaps it makes sense to call it "a movie" at this point?) can be shot and not released. A movie can be released and not publicized. A movie can be released but not to movie theaters, direct to DVD.

Commercial books are comparable to Hollywood movies. What exists determines what will exist in the future: book publishers, like Hollywood, are looking for books "like best-seller X." Originality is not a positive commodity; spin-offs that are guaranteed to make money are. Books are killed by never being born because they're too far from an extant prototype. Usually this means, the authors don't even think of writing them. So they never even make it to the point where they die: they weren't candidates for life to begin with. Thus, a cloud of abortions and still-births surrounds each book or film that actually figures in the history books: here, as all over, history is written about, if not necessarily by, the winners, those who not only think of training to enter the race but do train, do enter, and do win.

Review of Metaphysics

The same cloud of never-weres, failed to implants, and abortions swarms around every article that actually makes it to the starting line of publication as around every book, every movie, and every painting. You can write what you want in an open society. But why would you think of writing it, if nobody wants it? If what you want to write doesn't even qualify as a fill-in-the-blank? Let's say you write it anyway. How to get it off your desk and into someone else's hands? How do you know they'll read it? If they do, how do you know they'll understand it?

Let's say your piece is fiction. You can't send it just anywhere; the *Review of Metaphysics* doesn't publish fiction. There do exist journals that publish fiction, but if there's not one that publishes the kind of fiction you write, you have little chance with them. Having a journal exist means, a group of people have to be sitting (most typically) in a university somewhere doing the work to publish things like what you write. What if there isn't such an outlet? What if they've given up doing so? Or never started? Start one, sure. How to get people to pay attention to yours in a world where there are so many? It's like starting a new restaurant in Manhattan. You may strike it rich, but it's not likely. None of this is about objectivity; it's all happenstance: who talks to whom, who's willing to take on what work and for how long, who has the money. Without these things lined up, the work of literature (or whatever it is) fails to be.

Let's say your submission finds the right journal. Then it has to appeal to an editor, or to two outside readers. Let's say it does, somehow catching the eye of an editor who receives hundreds if not thousands of submissions. It appears in print! You think you're a made (wo)man. You've won the race.

In fact, all you've done is start. Or perhaps not even that. To have your article even noticed by the world at large, it has to appear in the small handful of journals with any common reach in the profession. Otherwise you just have to hope that the journal is at least indexed (not all are) and stays in print for a while. And if it's in a foreign journal inaccessible to American scholars, then, for the American world, it might as well not exist. It has the status of a handbill or an advertisement, printed and in that sense real, handed out on the street, or a newspaper printed in (say) Baku or Sophia. What if you go to Baku to find archives and find them inaccessible, thrown away, burnt or flooded out, or eaten by insects? Is the printed word by itself a contribution to human knowledge? More than the Sunday advertising supplement? Does anybody keep those things, anywhere—the newspaper, the ad agency? It seems doubtful.

It's not enough to play the lottery in order to "contribute to human knowledge," you have to win the lottery. And how many people do? And for how long? And as the result of what concatenation of forces? How does this jibe with the notion that just by playing the game, you're contributing to human knowledge? If you also have to win the lottery, then "human knowledge" has nothing to do with it.

Borges

It's possible to accept smaller-level changes to a manifold of study and still think the existence of the manifold can still give a rationale to the enterprise. But once they surpass a certain number and a certain threshold, there's no manifold left. So most of the time we hold that what seem to be changes to the manifold are only subjective shifts of attention: sure, we're no longer so mad keen about Wallace Stevens and Borges. But, we insist, we could be: they're there, slumbering on the library shelves for the day when we want to go back to them, if we ever do. Yet even this presupposes a stable world of library shelves, something that only makes sense in the politically not too volatile West. It's a real-world presupposition at best, not a metaphysical one, at least not with any weight. When I lived in Rwanda before the civil war, the only books in the country had been brought in by expatriates or donated by various embassies.

There was no overview anywhere; the only bookstore in the country was Church-run, and contained only a few books in French. The largest cache of books was in the library of the National University. Its system, such as that was, was imposed by an American librarian probably out of desperation: books were catalogued in the order in which they entered the collection, the oldest being 1. Otherwise there was no systematization on the shelves, no equivalent of the Dewey Decimal System. And then came the civil war of the 1990s, which destroyed most of the books and scattered many of the rest, leaving a tattered remnant of a patchwork.

Where in this world is there room for the illusion of stability, permanence, and order that lets us think we're metaphorically taking books off the shelf when we teach them (in the case of Rwanda, it was literal: I handed out the books to my students, as there was no bookstore and they had no money to buy them with) and putting them back when we're done, each in its pre-assigned spot?

Oh, we say. That's Rwanda. Things are different in the West: we lead stable lives here. So we do, compared with the Third World. The point is, the stability of our literary world isn't metaphysical: it's practical, political. That's different than the stability of the objective world of science, which is postulated.

Footnote

We can see the mutability built into literature and its study by considering the convoluted process of eliminating the mutable to find a level of the immutable. In literary studies, we achieve the illusion of immutability—allow ourselves to turn away from the iceberg of mutability to focus only on the tip of the immutable—through the footnote. The footnote, with its placement of assertions in a common world of time and space, gives us the illusion that what we do is solidly based. However when we consider the footnote more closely, we realize that the solidity we achieve is bought at the cost of simply ignoring a vast blankness which is not so solid. We float on the tiny islands of objectivity we call footnotes, or citations, but what these in turn float on is a vast sea that's not so objective.

The *MLA Style Manual* explains to the aspiring writer that "plagiarism is the use of another person's ideas or expressions in your writing without acknowledging the source." To plagiarize, it continues, "is to give the impression that you have written or thought something that you have in fact borrowed from someone else." Plagiarism can be avoided by acknowledging borrowings through footnotes or, as the current MLA style prefers, citations in the text. The simple footnote or citation saves us from what the *Manual* calls the "moral offense" of plagiarism. In using citations, we live up to our "professional responsibility to acknowledge 'academic debts'."[49]

Subsequent chapters of the *Manual* list an extraordinary range of things we can cite and acknowledge in our writing—indeed if we take the book's opening admonitions to heart, the extraordinary range of things we *must* acknowledge. We might even get the impression that there is nothing not amenable to documentation. We are obliged to acknowledge our debts not only to books and articles, but also to television shows, recordings, information services, performances, works of art, private letters, unpublished manuscripts, speeches, private conversations, fliers handed out on the street if we can somehow nail them down by location, and Internet pages that disappear moments after we access them (here we include the date of access).

This list suggests that the world of literary studies is in fact an objective one like that presupposed by science, where absolutely particular identification of incidents is possible. If we're asked to ascribe a thought, an idea, or a phrase to one person, clearly the assumption is that there is a point in doing so. This means that a person fixes words through utterance and makes them his or her own, so that these words carry that person's name attached to them, like the plaques that go up on the faces of houses where famous people have lived. The second presupposition of the situation, what I am calling the objective presupposition, is that the world is both fixed and accessible enough that we, or more probably our reader, can return to the place we've pointed at with the footnote and find the thing we've indicated.

Newton's Laws

In science, the individual is subsumed almost completely to the thing discovered, at which point the necessity to document the source of what's discovered dissipates. Though we still speak of Newton's laws and the Michelson-Morley experiments, the facts these individuals discovered are quoted and synthesized without citation; lesser scientists with lesser discoveries simply go by the bye like long-dead plants that help create the loam on the forest floor. The world-view of the footnote holds that the subjective never completely disappears in literary studies; the individuality of the discoverer takes precedence over the discovery and the language of discovery is largely replaced by one of "argument" and "assertion."

The personal element of the footnote, the "who said it?" aspect, is a development and transplanting of the Romantic, and then Modernist, emphasis on the overweening importance of the artist. The artist is now denied the crown, which has (at least according to those in literary studies) moved on to the professor. Perhaps the next step will be for librarians to demand the same importance of their subjective contribution and deny it to scholars?

The first assumption of the footnote is like the comparable assumption of science: if it's itself mutable, it's not science. Similarly, if it's mutable, it's not footnotable. Change by itself doesn't flummox us in either case; when the ground we're on crumbles we don't panic, we just move one step back to solid ground. Because web pages appear and disappear so rapidly, we can't document

with merely an address. We have to include the day we accessed it: the fact that
we accessed it on this day in the past isn't mutable, though the page may be.
Similarly, a private conversation is long gone, but the fact that it happened at
such and such a time and at such and such a place isn't. No one but us may be
able to confirm it, but at least we've made the gesture of putting it in objective
terms.

Children's songs

Most of the bulk of the rest of the world escapes even this sort of
footnoting. We don't try and footnote the songs children make up, sing once,
and then forget, though we can footnote someone's printed reference to these, or
a film of one of them. Neither do we cite the chance pattern of trees blowing the
wind or the motions of clouds. It takes a John Cage to put some of these on a
public stage in controlled circumstances. Such performances we can begin to
footnote: then we can refer to a piece with this name (that someone else may
remember; besides, there's the printed program), performed at this theater (that
we can find again), in this city (we can go there if we're not there already), on
this day (that can be located on a calendar). If Cage makes a film of these
performances, we are on even more secure ground for the purposes of
footnoting; if the chance patterns are printed in script form in a book, we can
footnote that.

Yet Cage's point is that these uncontrolled patterns are far more numerous
than the few reproducible patterns we call art. The assumption of fixedness,
while valid so long as we keep going until we find a layer where it "works,"
actually only applies to a tiny segment of data in the world. The same is true of
the other assumption of the footnote, that of accessibility. Most of our footnotes
in America refer to books published by the same handful of publishing houses in
the cultural capitals of wealthy, politically stable, largely Anglophone countries.
A book published last year in London by Faber and Faber is a paradigmatic case
of the accessibility presupposed of the footnote. It is probably still in print, we
can order it with some hope that it will arrive, and our currencies are
convertible. Indeed, the local library may already have it. Something published
in Lisbon is now once again accessible, as it probably wasn't during the Salazar
years. But what of something cranked out on a hand press in Maputo? Of course,
we can treat it for purposes of reference as if it were a Random House book. It's
far more likely we'd have to refer to it, the way we'd describe a hand-scribbled
Post-it note on our refrigerator, not try and document it.

What falls within the purview of the footnote is what's accessible to us to
be footnoted, which is not the same as all the world. Just as books and articles
aren't paradigmatic of the world of the other arts, that part of the world which
enjoys stability and is sufficiently accessible that there is a point in citing
individual works isn't paradigmatic of the whole. Accessibility has always

meant, accessibility to the airplanes of the industrialized West; the necessity to footnoted expanded with the reach of our means of transportation. In America we conceive of all printed works as accessible because they've entered a central data system: books to the Library of Congress, articles to bibliographies, dissertations to a central storehouse in Michigan. "Researching a topic" consists of checking these standard sources. No one will fault us for not getting the single-copy handbill from Baku. And if we have too many references to sources in the library in Addis Ababa in our Ph.D. dissertation, our advisor is likely to question it.

Even more difficult to footnote, though not yet at the unfootnotable level of the Post-it note, would be something like a handbill produced somewhere in central America that we heard about via the grapevine. There's of course a way to footnote this, either as a conversation in which we heard about it or by placing the handbill in some context that seems to us part of the objective world—perhaps the name of the printing company and an address in a real city, if we can find any of that information. We keep going until we find a layer of reasonable accessibility; the point once again is that this hides the fact of all the rest that is merely passed over as unsuitable.

There are usable footnotes and sham ones: this is verging on a sham one. It doesn't take very long to get to the level of sham footnotes; mostly we learn to stay within the realm that allows real ones. But how little of the world is amenable to "real" footnoting, and how much trouble we usually have to go to to find a footnotable level! If a conversation can be "sham"-footnoted, what do we do with, say, an exhalation of breath? A water bottle sitting on my desk?

I let my glance travel upwards from my fingers on the keyboard. How many of the objects on and around my desk are "footnotable," in the sense that they can be pinned to a precise time-space continuum, referred to something outside themselves rather than being described? How far would the description have to go before it would hit the bedrock of an objective world? The calendar comes from a precise publishing house in Switzerland; that's easy. The computer is from a precise company, with serial numbers. That's equally easy. How about the "spirit buttons" I have stuck into the cloth covering the ugly metal of my cubicle, large wearable pin-ons to advertise football games of the U.S. Naval Academy? I don't know we can find out who made them, or whose design they're from. How would I refer to them except as individuals, as 'the spirit buttons on my desk"? Probably our best chance at hooking them to an objective world is the connection through the Naval Academy, a locatable single institution. How about the cloth on which they're pinned? Could this be put in the time-space continuum through the manufacturer of the desk? Could it be traced to its factory? What of the computer-generated announcement from the English Department taped to another surface? Is the "publisher" the particular machine that printed it out? The English Department here at the Naval

Academy? Our best hook to objectivity on all these is probably the Naval Academy itself, equivalent to saying that what we know about a book is that it came from "England." What of the little hand-painted leaf card from India that's propped up on a shelf? Probably the best we could do would be to say: "From India." The source of the plastic water bottle? I'd probably have to give up on that and hook it once again to the Naval Academy whose label it carries. Finding something to footnote is like focusing a camera: you just zoom it in and out until you hit something in focus: something it's near, sometimes it's far, and sometimes you never get focus at all.

There is an enormous area between the Faber and Faber or Random House book, on one hand, and, on the other, the single piece of paper of uncertain provenance and date that we've merely heard about. And written things themselves are only the tip of another iceberg.

Take a political pamphlet published by a tiny now-defunct printer in Samarkand in the late nineteenth century. This may exist in more copies than the handbill, though we would probably still cite from a single copy, and some library in the world may own it. But the chances are that we won't be able to get it on inter-library loan here in the US: such libraries as might have it (a provincial collection in Uzbekistan?) aren't even listed on the data bases, which is to say, the Western data bases. Perhaps the copy that still exists has long ago fallen victim to moisture, rot, civil war, or fire. This book was published but, we might say, it may as well not have been: it's gone from being a general in the world to a particular, something as particular as the pattern of clouds. It's not accessible to others.

We don't footnote a work believed lost; instead we refer to it. We don't footnote a one-of-a-kind work; instead we say "the Leonardo in the National Gallery, Washington." This is fine in a way that "what my three-year-old said last night" isn't fine: the first is public and accessible; the second isn't. Footnotes always gravitate to the level of the immutable and accessible.

Joyce's Stephen Daedalus speaks, in *Stephen Hero*, of publishing his work in a "manuscript edition of one copy."[50] This is meant to be wryly humorous. This presupposes a footnotable world and reaches out to include what did not seem footnotable, much as if we referred to a particular cloud pattern over my house at such and such a time. It can be done, but it's done either to make a point (Stieglitz's "Equivalences," pictures of clouds, make this point) or to give the illusion that the whole world is within the purview of these presupposition. If we come at this from the other direction, not reaching out from the island of immutability, it seems merely part of the mutable world, that world of the patterns of all clouds, the positions of flower stems, the precise shadows thrown by grass in lawns, jokes, social palaver, and body language that provide the greatest bulk of the world, all of it unfootnoted and, except as a sort of joke, unfootnotable.

In some sense, therefore, the presupposition behind the footnote is justifiable: we can, if asked to do so, find a level that allows us to refer to anything, even body language in a single conversation that nobody else heard. The point is that doing this is a specific choice. We can't do this with everything, as there isn't time and even if we find an immutable layer, this leaves unconsidered all the things that are particular to this situation, just as speaking of the Periodic Table of Elements leaves unconsidered the way any person, whose body is made of elements, looks and sounds. Speaking of light waves ignores the way a blouse shimmers, and an analysis of evaporation on the skin doesn't explain the way a tree's shade can feel deliciously cool on a hot day. This isn't because science is soulless—as Wordsworth and other Romantics seemed to suggest (as Wordsworth put it: "We murder to dissect").[51] It's because that's the nature of science.

With literature, here's the equivalent of the patterns of clouds: the ideas a writer had and gave up without writing down (if s/he wrote them down once we can refer to the object of a diary, or to a printed version if it appears), ideas that never were because so wide of the mark as to have been rejected without consideration, early versions of a completed work (the computer now eats alterations, unless we save each state of a MS as a separate file or print them out—think of all the pages to plough through!—worse than reading a lengthy Gertrude Stein work, which in fact usually do include rejected versions of things as part of the flow), works planned in the head, works written and printed but never entered into the relatively small world of works we have to take account of, works printed outside the political centers of power of the West.

Looking at vs. seeing

The greatest source of mutability and unscientific accident in the study of literature is, however, none of the above: not the fact that books come to be or don't be by accident, are printed or not as a result of accident, become famous enough to be short-listed by accident, physically survive as the result of political accident. All these deal with the existence of the printed object.

The most intensive source of mutability, and the reason why "literary studies" is a sort of oxymoron, is that there's a difference between understanding words and understanding the point, what in literature is the equivalent of the difference between looking at something and seeing it. We can test people on whether they've understood what's on the page: Madame Bovary did this and that. But what's more difficult is whether they've understood why it should matter to them. At their best, essay tests allow that, or a really good student paper. So all isn't lost in the halls of academe. But that's not the "literary studies" I'm talking about. That's what I'd like to see more of: the "this is my connection to the work" essay. "I see myself in Madame Bovary because—" You don't need to use big words to preside over such a classroom. Nor do you need to go on about intertextuality, or say there's no world outside the text, or call it a text at all, except insofar as it clearly isn't a table, or a trashcan.

Each of us is simultaneously many things—including things we won't have thought of. I'm a human being, a father, an American, a man, a middle-aged suburbanite, an athlete, an insider, an outsider, and so many other things I can't list even a fraction, and this by definition. *Madame Bovary* is in the same way many things: the story of a woman, of a French person, of a too-pretty-for-her-own-good peasant, a person, a young person, a wife, a women without a job, an unwilling mother, and so on. It's not something strange and exotic about literature that we can be aware of some of these sometimes, others of these at other times, and some of them never. That's the way we live our lives: we think of ourselves as the child of our parents, until one day we don't. We see things differently.

Considering many of the concentric rings that all center around the character Emma Bovary is what a good professor can do: many people are unused to considering the fact that they themselves are many concentric circles, so they fail to apply this knowledge to others, or to fictional characters. The young, especially, are unused to shifting between one such circle and another, playing many roles: they're still trying to solidify one. This is why a sympathetic professor can be so liberating to students: s/he suggests other rings than the one the reader gravitates to. If enough circles are put on the table, one of them is likely to fit each person, for a total of close to all. Professors help students find rings that fit them.

Sometimes this is expressed by saying that "the mark of a classic is that you always find something new to say about it." That isn't true; what is true is that if it's complex, you can shift from ring to ring. What literature gives many people is precisely this sensation of shifting: in the world of our everyday lives, we have so much invested in the shifts we're unlikely to be aware of them as shifts. Plus they change so much of our lives, we're unlikely to see them in a disinterested fashion.

The most frustrating fact of all for those who are interesting in professionalizing the teaching of literature is that people can be made to pass tests on any aspect of a book without it ever actually touching them. It remains something looked at, rather than something seen—only it seems to have been seen, as they can talk about it. But just as we can talk about death without realizing in any way but intellectual (as we say) that it applies to us, so we can read a book without in any way making a connection to ourselves. We simply don't find a ring that fits us: we can say what happened, but we can't say why it matters to us.

The Catholic Church rejected what it came to call the Donatist Heresy, the insistence that the lives of priests be pure in order for the sacraments they presided over to be valid. How can you run an army if you worry about what the footsoldiers think, rather than do? You can't, and the Church rightly insisted that whatever the priest's private life, the sacraments he administered were still valid. But that's only the point of view of someone trying to run an organization. My point is that we don't have to be organizational with respect to literature. In a way, I'm trying to re-introduce the Donatist "Heresy" into literary studies. We can say that the material has been transmitted if the students can pass a test on it. But this really doesn't amount to much. I can certainly understand that we can't give or grade tests on what the student has really, truly, deep down understood: we'll never get at that; we'll only get at what's on the test. (There are tests that allow more of this to come to the surface, tests that allow the students more leeway and aren't under the illusion that they're testing "material.")

However this requires accepting that even the student doesn't always know what s/he has gotten, or not. And in many cases the payoff of the literature isn't now, but twenty years from now, when suddenly they "get" it, or understand what they didn't understand. And there's no objective viewpoint that says, this really is here in the text and you did or didn't get it. We can't say that *Madame Bovary* must be understood as being about women, or French women, or people, or young people, or people of a certain sort: all these are possible, and may or may not be applicable to the reader's life, either now, or later.

Some years ago I got an e-mail from a former student. "I really disliked you," he wrote. "I didn't see the point of what we were reading, why we were reading X, Y, and Z" (he reeled off the exact texts fifteen years later). "Then three years into the Marine Corps I got it." For me the amazing thing was, he could say exactly how each text he'd read as a college freshman in my class, when he'd initially been a surly uncooperative student, related to his life. And then he went into combat in Iraq; now he wants to be a writer. I would have guessed he'd retained nothing. Instead he filed what I said, and pulled it off the shelf when he needed it, at which point he could eat it. Presumably he didn't dislike me any more, either. Even that can change.

Not everybody who "gets it" writes to the professor. Most who don't "get it" never do. Most never "get it." There's no "it" to get, in most cases: I'm not saying he "got" the wrong things the first time, and the right ones later on. My only concern is that he use these works for his life, which I'm not ultimately privy to. He's the one who decides if he can use them to conceptualize what he's lived, and if he can use them, how much and in what way.

Lamentation

The function of literature in specific and the arts in general is that they give us conceptual frameworks for what's happening to us. You can teach the content of the literature, but you can't teach the connection with what's happening in the perceiver's life, because nobody—usually, not necessarily even the perceiver—knows what that is. Martha Graham liked to tell the story that a woman came up to her after a performance of her own one-woman dance *Lamentation*, performed in a stretchy sheath with the performer sitting on a bench, rocking back and forth and clasping her hands without ever leaving the bench. The woman wanted to thank Graham for the dance: she told Graham her son had died and she'd never been able to cry. But after seeing *Lamentation*, she could, and it was the beginning of acceptance.

Before going into the theater, that is, this woman presumably wouldn't have been able to say there was anything that needed doing, such as weeping. Seeing a dance that for her seemed a stylized representation of mourning, however, triggered something in her, and the floodgates opened. Would seeing this dance have triggered similar floodgates in other people who had lost children? Not necessarily. Nor would we be able to say, except for the title, that this is a dance about mourning: it could just as easily be of a soul in torment, compelled to do something she didn't want to do. In any case it hit a nerve with this viewer: this is what art can do for us, and this is precisely what cannot be taught.

The really frustrating thing about art—frustrating at least for those who want to professionalize it—is this: you never know how people are going to react, or whether they're going to react, or when. You can't ever say they haven't "gotten" anything from the works (see my former student, above). If we insist on maximizing the predictable facets of interaction with the arts, or literature in particular, we'll end up with the pointless "literary study" we've created for ourselves nowadays, all syllabi and grades and hiring decisions and self-important "I have breaking news about *Madame Bovary*" professors.

The alternative is simply to unlax, as Bugs Bunny puts it. You understand that the teaching situation is theoretically primary: you have contact with a group of (typically younger) people to talk about a book. That's your playing field; that's the game too. All else feeds into that. The game is the classroom, which means, the human interaction on the subject of the book is its own point. You give the students a forum for reading, you throw out ideas, you remain sympathetic to the fact that not everyone is at a point in his or her life where s/he will be receptive, you acknowledge the fact that what you see in the work is what's appropriate for your life (though if you're a little older you probably have a larger repertory than most of the students), you encourage them to think, you're clear about what the grade is based on, you grade, you wish everyone well. That's about the best we can do. And that's probably enough.

More is not more in this world: more predictability is sham predictability. It's negative rather than positive to have more conviction that you're changing the course of their lives (you just don't know), more conviction that you're beating back the darkness of ignorance about this work (in fact you're merely taking a different view of it, which means all the others go begging), more sense of your own importance in following up a particular viewpoint.

Sure, follow up the viewpoint. But the world is full of things you do out of your own curiosity. We don't expect people to applaud them; why should they applaud a "brilliant insight" into literary work X? You got to have it; that ought to be enough.

The unhappiness endemic in literary studies nowadays, the malaise that makes so many people glum, is the sense that more was promised. Fame, perhaps, if not fortune. But if we just give up that sense of what's realistic, or makes sense, we won't be disappointed when we don't get it. The result will be a much greater sense of contentment all around.

Filters

So it's not the literary world itself that's objective. Instead we've postulated objectivity and keep going in our references until we find something that functions that way. If we're in geographical territory where objectivity is hard to find (most of the Third World, for our purposes), we withdraw quickly. We stay within the boundaries of what we've created. What we have to reference isn't merely what is; it's what is seen through a particular filter. One such filter, as I've noted, is who's on a sort of short list of people to whom we have to genuflect. This list can be created accidentally, by facts of language or geography, or consciously, by a ruling political class—or by intellectuals eager for control. Once the filter is on, we can go back to our insistence that we footnote: we've looked beyond the vast amount of data that is mutable to find the level that isn't.

Language, again, is one strong determinant of the filter. Anyone who's taken part in the intellectual life of the Continent (mainland Europe) knows that many highly developed intellectual linguistic societies exist other than the Anglophone one, with completely different benchmark authors. Much intellectual discussion in the German-speaking world, for example, proceeds from a knowledge of Hegel, who is still a topic for specialists in the United States.

Politics is another filter. Before the Wall fell, all of Eastern Europe used Marx and Lenin as their points of reference. Americans, by contrast, have never had to refer anything to Marx and Lenin, even if there was a similarity to be noted. Political control isn't of this sort in America. But in intellectual circles in America in the 1980s and 1990s everything had to be referred to and filtered through Derrida; in American academia, people read the same quotes over and over just as those in the East read the same quotes from Marx over and over.

In any given sub-world, thus, whether defined linguistically, by politics, or by intellectual fashion, there is a short list of "individual" sources; the others blur off into the common fund of nameless ideas. If someone is not on the limited current list of our society's benchmark authors, we may borrow this person's ideas without acknowledgement. The precise contents of this short list of people who must be acknowledged is determined in intellectual sub-worlds, such as the world of American literary studies, by the actions of individuals sufficiently powerful to have intellectual epigones spread their ideas. If Althusser is hot this year, then things Althusserian are translated and published, and form the basis of MLA papers. If the thinker of the moment is Adorno, then the character of things that enter our data system will alter because more will be written about him; our references have to become more precise to show we're "up to date." These are examples of the wisdom paradigm at work: it's only by narrowing our focus that we can get a field sufficiently restricted that we can say state B is progress with respect to state A: two books published on our author, for example, rather than one—though we're not likely to be able to say how many people read either. We can track sales, but not readings. And in readings, how do we track what percentage people understood?

Spectrum of art forms

We've abandoned the lists of classics that used to produce a small fixed manifold. Still, we've tried to hold onto the illusion that the manifold of what we study is fixed and finite. If this is already an illusion on life-support in the case of literature, it's simply dead in the case of the other arts. For this reason, those most dedicated to literary study as a profession are typically those who most blatantly turn their backs on the other arts. Seeing even how much less most of the other arts lend themselves to being made into a study might cause those focusing on the small immutable quotient in literary studies to falter or even abandon their calling.

Many other art forms lack the initial canon that gave Modernism something to expand on, and rebel against—but which at the same time gave people the sense that in their world, things were fixed. Musical performance ceases when the players put down their instruments and scores are handwritten documents that may or may not be preserved. Paintings all exist in "manuscript editions of one copy" and so fall victim to wars and misplacement. And dance, until quite recently, had no score at all to disappear, being kept alive, if at all, only in the so-mutable memories of dancers and ballet masters.

The fact that literary studies is largely run by people all but ignorant of the other arts—and why should they not be? there's no pressure on them to be literate in anything but their own "field"—is comparable to the fact that people who study, say, Portuguese literature, don't also study Chinese, or most any of those who study Anglophone literature anything but Anglophone literature. There's nothing objective about the separation of bits of an external manifold into language-based pieces, nor the separation off of written arts from non-written ones. That's just one way to do things. If suddenly we realize that the line that had seemed so absolute is merely a line in the sand, what it's delineating suddenly loses its apparent coherence. Literary studies is in fact held in only by lines in the sand: what language we speak, what country we live in, what art form we focus on, what department hires us, what books and thinkers are "hot" this year.

Of the art forms, literature has seemed most congenial to codification in the form of a professionalized "study." Its products seem to stay still (as opposed to the products of, say, acting), it's in words that look like the way it's studied (as opposed to the way words about paintings seem to enter a different realm), and we can hold them in our hands in the way we can't with, say, music. So the professionalization of literary studies has gone the furthest among all the art forms. Other arts have tried to develop their studies too, but typically this has been by using literary studies as a model. We might say that the other arts lag behind literature in this respect—except that the direction literature has been taken hasn't been salutary, so it's just as justifiable to say that the other arts have ended up out front.

Dance

Dance, for example, has only recently even become remotely amenable to treatment like literature. Until the twentieth century, dance was only annotated by notes and descriptions. As a result the "same ballet" changed from version to version with only dancers' memories providing what small degree of similarity they had. Even so, it was considered perfectly fine to cut and paste, or start again: dance in this sense lacked any immutable text. The first version of *Swan Lake* in 1877 apparently wasn't much like the version that forms the basis for most of our versions, from 1895. (The earlier one was a flop, to the same music, but with different choreographers than the Petipa-Ivanov version that is the basis of most productions today.) Even today it's considered kosher to vary almost every element of the "same" ballet, including choreographer and basic story elements. If we read that a ballet troupe is putting on *Nutcracker*, for example, and want to know if it's something for the kiddies, we should ask how "traditional" this version is. Is it even set to the familiar Tchaikovsky music? Is it set at Christmas? (A version by the American choreographer John Neumeier is set to Tchaikovsky, but at a birthday party: there is no tree, no snowflakes, no Christmas gifts.) Assuming it's basically the familiar story with a little girl who gets a present (the titular nutcracker), we should ask: are the "children" real children, or adults? What's the framework of the second act? Is it the Kingdom of the Sweets? A dream landscape? A ballet studio?

The variations are so many that the shred of immutability we can muster—a name, a composer—seems very small indeed. Partly this is so because individual choreographic steps weren't, until the twentieth century, held to be of much value: what counted was the whole spectacle. Dance lacked a text; variations were all.[52] In literary studies, it was held to be of interest to insist that readings of texts varied widely[53]. The intellectual interest in pointing this out was because it seemed new information, given the presupposition that the text stayed fixed. In dance, this was never a point worth making more than in passing, since, until the twentieth century, variations were part of the definition of the work: we didn't have to further insist on them.

With the advent of Modernism, exemplified in dance by Martha Graham and George Balanchine, came an increasing focus on the precise movements, as Modernism in literature focused on words and Modernism in painting on the painted surface. With the conception of ballet as a sequence of precise steps came an increased emphasis on notation, which gives us a firmer basis for documentation, something common we can use to refer to "*Nutcracker*"—or perhaps at least "the Joffrey Ballet's *Nutcracker*." Notation in dance takes several forms, ranging from the stick figures of Laban notation to the most common form nowadays, videos and movies. Yet Laban notation is a notation by an individual of an individual performance, and a movie is always a movie of a particular performance and production. What we end up footnoting is the precise version rendered in Laban notation, or the precise movie.

Once again, we can keep moving back to the solid land until we have something fixed enough to be used as a benchmark of immutability. But this by definition abandons and leaves unconsidered all the things that are not in this sense immutable. They don't cease to exist, though they cease to be considered. It's like shining a flashlight/torch into the dark: all we have is the little area picked out by the light. The darkness is dark; it's simply not considered.

Souls

What reigns in literary studies is a kind of tyranny of the actual, something like what causes religious fundamentalists to insist that every person who exists was meant to be, and has a soul. People who aren't, don't have souls. We see this doctrine working out in the so-dogged insistence on not having any blurry edges that would show this fine delineation to be contrived or arbitrary: two cells together in a zygote is a person, presumably with a soul, and abortion is murder, just the same act as if a 21-year-old is killed the day s/he graduates from college. Yet to a mother who's tried repeatedly to get pregnant, had several failures-to-implant, and is finally delivered of one viable in vitro fertilization (while multiple other fetuses remain frozen or are thrown away), it's a little far-fetched to say that this one person who does come out is the one being who was destined to be a person. The circularity of the position is clear: whoever is born is declared to have a soul, to be the real person—not the theoretically possible people who weren't made when all those other sperms swam slower (only one makes it). If a zygote is a person, isn't a sperm or an unfertilized egg something?

Many of us have the sense of a crap-shoot with children: bits and pieces from so many people are put back in the spinner and spun around, then only a little is dumped out. Who hasn't looked at his children and wondered, What if s/he had been X, or Y, or Z instead of A, or B, or C? But that's no great tragedy, as we ourselves were a cup of the great communal soup. What's so fabulous about having a son who looks like us? We ourselves may look more like Great Uncle Gus—or nobody in our family. And what's so important about a nose? We can have a nose just like Dad's and be his exact opposite in temperament.

Talk about sex-change operations ("I was a woman in a man's body") seems so odd to most of us because our gender is such a fundamental part of our personality. But most of us are willing to play with "what if" scenarios with qualities that seem less fundamental, on the order of "what if I'd been taller/shorter?" "What if my parents had been someone else?" "What if I'd been born to money?" Of course in a strict interpretation, any alteration, no matter how slight, means you aren't you. And being born to other parents isn't slight; first of all the chances are overwhelmingly against a child of two other people having any similarity at all: you, as you, can't have been born to two people different than your actual parents. Even having been born a blonde rather than a brunette can have altered your life, or with a nose that didn't have to be straightened. Indeed, not everything can be altered. Some things we can alter, like hair color; some not. And some qualities admit of limited possibilities for alteration. Tall/short is probably somewhere in the middle. We can wear higher heels or platform shoes, if too short. Tall girls sometimes slouch, but it's not recommended. There's even a way to saw out bone or lengthen it with surgery and excruciating braces, but in any case this is cumbersome and never adds more than about an inch. Hardly worth it, one would think.

Can I be "me" if I lived in Connecticut? We might initially respond: Sure. Heck, I can *go* to Connecticut right now if I hop in my car and don't have to be there before dinnertime. Surely I'd be me whether I'm in Maryland or Connecticut? No, comes the response: that's not what we mean. I mean, if I *lived* there? That might mean, another job, which might mean, another personality. Am I still the same person? We're postulating a quick visit, right now. I won't be appreciably different from an hour ago. But what if I stay in Connecticut? Couldn't that change me?

If I would be different in Connecticut, isn't everything further away even more certain to imply fundamental change? For example: would I be different in Istanbul? Well, it depends on what the question means. I can visit Istanbul, and seem to be the same person. But what if the question means, if I were there not as a tourist? Do we mean, would I be a different person if I were am American diplomat of my age and education living in Istanbul temporarily? There on a Fulbright? I could apply for Fulbrights right now. These things don't seem to imply any great change. But who says "living in Istanbul" means that it's living there with the smallest possible damage to the rest of my qualities? What if the wish I had magically granted was merely to "live in Istanbul" and I forgot to say, as a well-paid Western diplomat? (The Cumean Sybil asked for, and got, eternal life, but forgot to say that she wanted eternal youth.) What if I found myself suddenly a Turkish shoe-shine boy? What if I postulated myself as a Western diplomat, but forgot to say, as a man? Or as a tall man. Or as a tall white man. Or as a good-looking tall white man. Or as all of the above and not crippled. I couldn't think of enough qualifiers to escape being a person with all the things I'd asked for but without something else that turned out to be fundamental. In this case, my life would be different; I would be different. To ensure that postulated alterations don't change "me" we'd have to postulate them as not changing me, whatever that would mean.

Locke and the Empiricists made the attempt to decide what qualities of objects, if any, were necessary to defining the objects. We might ask: is the peach no longer *that* peach if you take a bite out of it? We'd probably say: it's *a* peach, but not *that* perfect waiting-to-be-bitten peach. So is this quality an essential one or not? In a way it's the same peach; in a way it's not. The question loses urgency when we realize that things are constantly having qualities added and subtracted from them. We say that things remain "unchanged" when their qualities remain unchanged with respect to other things that change more rapidly, or with respect to what we expect. If a person "hasn't changed a bit" this doesn't literally mean s/he hasn't changed a bit, all it means is that s/he has changed more slowly in the areas we're concentrating on (presumably things like face and hair) than other people we know, or than we know people to change. All change we notice is with respect to change we don't. We expect children to change more than adults from year to year, so we aren't startled when this happens. We expect them to change size radically over time, and expect their teeth to loosen and fall out—whereas both would be grounds for alarm in an adult, and so on. But we don't expect them to lose their arms: that would be a change we'd notice. Still, we can imagine if it were the natural way of things for children to lose and grow arms the way they lose and grow teeth: if it was normal, we wouldn't be startled when it happened. We simply fail to be surprised by the change we're expecting: they're part of the constant person. Unexpected change need not be unexpected, and wouldn't be if we were used to it. But is there any real difference between expected and unexpected change other than the fact that we expect the expected change? Change is change.

Thinking that there is some ontological weight to the books we're actually studying aside from the fact that we're actually studying them, or perhaps to the small number of books people we know are presenting conference papers on, is the equivalent of getting self-righteous about the people who made it fully formed into the world, reading some sort of necessity in anything but a postulated way into what is. That's the way it is, but there's no further weight beyond that fact, no need to conclude that the world is unimaginable with even the smallest change. We can imagine any change, and that means the things we take for granted (for example "me") will change too: if I were blonde I might not be the same person. If I lived in Istanbul I might not be the same person. In order to ensure that I am the "same" person, I have to determine what constitutes the "same" person (is the bitten peach the same peach as the unbitten one?). There's no way to know the answer to this; we just have to give one.

Pangloss

We're welcome to say, whatever is, is good—in the manner of Voltaire's Pangloss in *Candide*. Whatever literature we study is what we're meant to study, so in that sense it has the weight of ontic inevitability behind it. God knew all the options, and chose this as the best. So we don't even have to speculate about what isn't: by definition it's worse, or at any rate lost the race for existence—presumably because it deserved to. But that frees us from actually articulating, or even worrying about, what the other options were. We just wait patiently to see what comes out of the machine's slot, and that's the best, the only, God's will (the locutions can vary: all they mean is, we're not going to worry about it). The disadvantage of this point of view, as Voltaire notes, is that we have to accept the things we don't like as God's will/the best too. Why do bad things happen? Why do they happen to good people? Why do things happen that don't seem to have anything to do with people at all—like earthquakes?

Perhaps we can justify what we teach on the grounds that they're what we're ourselves interested in. Or that they're what the institution demands. Or that they're what we were taught. But I think we should stop short of Pangloss's addition that "that's the very best in this best of all possible worlds." If anything we do in literary studies was meant to be, how can we relate to a world outside, or deal with questioning? Pangloss can't deal with questioning; everything that is, is right. And if the opposite happens, then that too, because it happened, is right.

Dragons

Reading and commenting on literature is an activity like keeping our bodies in shape; it's not piling up knowledge. It's not scientific. We don't "make progress" in studying literature, any more than we "make progress" in solving the fundamental problems of life: ageing, loss, death. Every person, every generation, has to go through it all again: it's called life. All of us think we are going to avoid the mistakes of our forebears, and ultimately have to admit that we have not done so. Each of us begins convinced that s/he will slay the dragon, and exits without having done so. Or perhaps (never say never) we do slay a dragon or two; for every person who slays a dragon, there are many more who try and don't. The dragon-slayer can in theory be us, or someone we know—just as it's theoretically possible we'll be the one to win the millions in the lottery.

But probably it won't be. Perhaps there aren't enough dragons to go around, to begin with. We can't all kill one, any more than we can all win the lottery.

What's true of literary studies is true in large part of the other humanities too, certainly the studies of other art forms than written—art history, music history—and of philosophy. It's also true to a degree of the social sciences, those odd birds whose name makes clear their attempt to mix science with the human factor, a combination that places them firmly on the structural fault line: they forever tilt back and forth becoming more scientific (and less human) on one hand, and more human (and less scientific) on the other. This doesn't mean they're intrinsically illegitimate, as some have claimed—either they're social or they're scientific; they can't be both—just that they're always pulling back and forth and threatening to break up. In fact, they can be both, and are.

Chapter Five

"Repellent to Ordinary Americans"

IF YOU DON'T MAKE THE CLAIM THAT the object of study of your own particular discipline functions like the objective world—the claim that allows literary studies to cast itself in a scientific vein—you can share the same world with others. That means you can talk to other people outside the walls, and even discuss what you do with them. You don't have to paint yourself into a corner, as literary studies has done. If you *are* the world, by contrast, any criticism is simply anathema, and nothing can be changed about what you do. Problems are no longer individualized problems that can themselves be considered in the objective world—and so which others can address. They're problems that go too deep for anyone to address: we've proven that we're right because our presuppositions cut to the very base of things. This is the nature of the "linguistic turn" in humanistic studies too, considered in the next chapter: it makes claims that assert control not over a bucket of water taken from the well, or many buckets, but over the whole well. This gives us a feeling of power, but it also means others will avoid that well. And then we wonder why we're all alone with our well.

An article in the *Chronicle of Higher Education Review* helps show us that in literary studies we've managed to re-cast all questions others could help us with into questions we alone can consider. That's not its intention, however. Ellen Schrecker, a scholar whose work focuses on the McCarthy era, is using the article to warn against what she sees as right-wing "encroachments on academic freedom." Students at some campuses, Schrecker reported, are being encouraged to protest if professors offer liberal or left-wing views in the classroom, or fail to give what conservative students think is sufficient air time to their own views.

The most interesting passage for me in Schrecker's article, which appeared while I was teaching a course at the Naval Academy under the rubric of "Multi-Cultural Literature," was the author's reference to "the late Palestinian literary critic Edward Said, whose work, it is claimed [by conservatives] so dominates the field that its practitioners not only promote an anti-American worldview but also subscribe to the trendy postmodern discourse on race, class, and gender that makes contemporary scholarship so repellent to ordinary Americans."[54] This is implied quoting: it doesn't seem likely that Schrecker is signing off on the notion that the philosophical basis of humanities nowadays is in fact "repellent to ordinary Americans." But I think she should, because I think it is repellent to ordinary Americans, at least to judge from reactions coming from my students. They're politically conservative, to be sure, and more driven than many students. But they're geographically diverse, and almost all middle-class kids from the usual collection of small towns and suburbs. And they're ordinary at least in the sense that few of them want to become academics. If academics could understand why ordinary Americans do find their way of proceeding so repellent, literary studies might be able to re-join the common world rather than insisting that it is its own world. Academics know those outside tend to find them strange or repellent, but react by licking their wounds, or rubbing ash in them to make sure they remain fresh.

The day after I read it myself, I brought Schrecker's article, called "Worse Than McCarthy," to class, and read out loud to my students the passage that caught my attention. Did they think the author was right that courses based on Said were "repellent to ordinary Americans"?

They did. And then we talked about why this might be so.

"A bloody racist"

By that point in the course my students knew about Said because we'd read large chunks of his now-standard book *Orientalism*. The first week was *Heart of Darkness*, followed by Chinua Achebe's celebrated essay/lecture in which the novelist accused Conrad of being a "bloody racist." This had set the stage for Said. What was striking was the difference between Achebe's critique and Said's, though the two overlap to some degree.

A critique like Achebe's, at least in some of its claims, allows a response, and so can actually change people's actions. It's situated in the objective world, one assumed to be held in common with those outside the wall. A critique like Said's, by contrast, is what's come to characterize professionalized literary studies. It allows no response, so it gets to feel it's invariably right. That's the good news. The bad news is that nobody's going to change as a result of hearing it either. It makes claims that are supposed to be valid whatever particular things they do. Whatever people do or don't do is already explained it and filed away. This kind of thinking has painted itself in a corner, become "repellent to ordinary Americans." Or at least irritating, and finally irrelevant.

Achebe's point was that though the narrator of *Heart of Darkness*, Marlowe, might hold beliefs that were enlightened for the time—he clearly disapproves of the Belgian treatment of natives in the Congo of King Leopold's time—his creator Conrad wasn't ultimately so enlightened. Achebe compares the amount of text devoted to characters of color with the amount devoted to white people, and finds that the people of color are left with the lesser amount. Conrad, that is, makes a book primarily about the white people; he fails to give equal air time to the natives. They served only as the "backdrop for the dissolution of one petty European mind."[55]

This is an empirical claim, one that others can react to by saying it's true or not true. It's clearly true. Then the question becomes, so what? One way that text can be devoted to characters is through offering their words, what they say. Here too Achebe is disapproving. The white people get to speak standard English; the non-white people don't. This too is specific, and seems in fact to be true. In any case we can confirm or deny. Most of the non-Europeans say nothing at all, at least nothing that's reported by the narrator; presumably he couldn't understand their language. When they do speak a version of English, it's pidgin, certainly not educated English speech. When asked what he intends to do with a fellow Congolese, one of the cannibals driving Marlowe's boat replies succinctly: "Catch 'im. Eat 'im." And T.S. Eliot made the book's most famous dictum his epigraph for "The Hollow Men": "Mistah Kurtz, he dead."

It's true that the Congolese of *Heart of Darkness* do not talk like Chinua Achebe, delivering the Chancellor's Lecture at the University of Massachusetts. Partly this is so because Conrad was writing about a time earlier in the colonization process than Achebe experienced, which came outfitted with European-style universities; partly it is so because the Belgians, even later, weren't fond of setting up institutions like universities and the British, under whose domination Achebe was educated, apparently did. How do we react to that fact? By cursing the colonialism that gave Achebe the tools to attack it?

"The Question of Orientalism"

Achebe's more deep-seated accusation—namely, that Conrad was a racist at some sort of deep-structural level—brings him close to Said's most striking claims, though Said too begins with an empirical observation. The midshipmen and I considered this in Said's *Orientalism*. Said's work is a *j'accuse* at many levels. It does, to be sure, contain the relatively concrete accusation that writers from the Middle East—in the nineteenth century referred to as the "Orient"— exhibited overt disdain for the people they were writing about. This is provable by looking at snide turns of phrase in texts; it's roughly comparable to Achebe noting that the characters speak pidgin.

However the charge that has given this book its longevity and its power is the more far-reaching claim that all writings by Westerners about the non-Western world are guilty of what Said calls "textual orientalism." This is a more difficult-to-articulate stance of the offending text itself, rather than any particular authorial opinion or content. The potential reach of such an accusation is staggering. Ultimately, Said seems to disapprove of any member of one group writing about members of other groups at all, whatever the particular content of their writing: the other people is reduced to the status of something caught in the text, like a butterfly wriggling on a pin. If I'm writing about you, rather than the reverse, I get to say what I want, and in any case it's my point of view. That, for Said, seems to be bad. But, I ask the students, wouldn't that have a chilling effect on any kind of attempt to understand the world outside? Isn't that like saying that everybody should stay in his or her own intellectual corner and never attempt to get out?

The venerable (and unrepentent) "Orientalist" Bernard Lewis, in a critique of Said's work which I considered with the students the following week ("The Question of Orientalism"), asks the same question.[56] Lewis begins with what seems a fairly ingrown criticism, by questioning Said's scholarship. Lewis points out that Said has the chronology wrong by several centuries in his dating of the development of Orientalist studies Said, Lewis notes, seems to think it only started up in the nineteenth century. Further, Lewis is puzzled by the fact that Said focuses so narrowly on English and French writings. Why, Lewis asks, does Said brush aside the equally important German and Russian?

It becomes clear that this is not in fact merely a narrow scholarly disagreement when Lewis proposes a pattern in what he takes to be Said's factual errors, of which, for Lewis, the worst are these: moving "Orientalism" forward to the time of colonialism, and focusing on English and French intervention. Lewis suggests that Said must have adopted this strange view of Orientalism by looking at English writing about India, where, he agrees, this view of colonial writing is valid. However Said is using British intervention in India as a pattern for understanding Western interest in the Middle East, where (according to Lewis) it's egregiously false.

Said, Lewis suggests, is furious most of all at the *fact* of colonialism, and in order to critique that, attempts to include in his fury all Western study of the Islamic world—which, as Lewis points out, began not during the period when the West had the whip hand over the Orient, but when the Orient was the dominant civilization. Thus Lewis believes Said is wrong precisely where Said is most interesting. Instead of making a concrete accusation, which could be confirmed or denied, Said has made the sin structural rather than factual. It lies so deep as to be inescapable. But if it's inescapable, all you get for pointing it out is that you're guaranteed to be right, and nothing will ever change. The more fundamentally you locate a truth, the less it's something that can ever be escaped.

The intellectual interest of Said's work for academics, people who deal primarily with texts, is his claim that texts have the power that is usually ascribed to things like guns and jailors. Texts control. Most "ordinary Americans"—or, for that matter, ordinary anythings—would probably find this ridiculous. It's a counter-intuitive reversal of what common sense tells us is so. Guns, jailors, and judges control, most ordinary people would say; texts merely mirror or express this. Sure, they can abet it too: but without the real-world versions, texts are pretty weak. However this focus on the power of texts is tremendously flattering to academics, who can imagine themselves at the center of things. If texts are primary, rather than secondary, then people who deal with texts have their fingers on the real pulse of things. Its appeal is thus to people who have no intention of ever changing anything outside of the world of texts. In the late twentieth century, this means, academics. You can show you're right in that world, but you buy this correctness at the cost of being irrelevant outside of it.

Is Schrecker right?

And that's where we were when I came to class brandishing the *Chronicle Review.*

For days I'd been responding to the ongoing protests of a young man fretful at the constant pummeling he'd been taking from our texts. This young man asked the question: "How can you be racist if you don't know you are?" He thought the assertion ridiculous. Similarly, most men grow hot under the collar at the insistence of feminists that, to echo Andrea Dworkin, all men are potential rapists.[57] I take care of my family and pay my taxes, they'll say. How am I a potential rapist? I'm a nice guy.

My students need a little education on this matter, of course. All of us have effects on the world we're unaware of. It's perfectly plausible to say, it's possible that your actions have effects you're not aware of. You needn't individually exploit the Third World, but if you buy products made in sweatshops, you indirectly support its exploitation. Comparably, you can support individual women, but if you take as your due benefits reserved only for men, you perpetuate the suppression of women.

But these are still empirical claims, akin to those that point out the effects on the environment of having a huge house full of many gizmos: the person inside may be unaware of the effects of his or her life-style, but that doesn't mean the environment isn't being affected. This is something that can be proven with evidence, or disproven. Things get Saidian when the claim becomes even more fundamental than that—so fundamental it turns into an unreachable metaphysical assertion that no one can ever take away from you with anything so concrete as disproof. Dworkin's argument is Saidian in this sense. It goes far beyond the provable into the unprovable. It seems to say that though an individual man personally never has raped nor ever wanted to rape, his size and power means he's reserving the right to do so should he have a yen. To this, of course, there's no possible response. A man might well say: why are you even talking to me if I can't do anything about it? Said's thought works the same way for colonialism: any approach to the non-Western is a structurally guilty one. There's no meaningful distinction between good and bad involvement. Said isn't trying to get people to change their actions, just tell them what they're really doing when they think they're doing something else. He gets to feel justified whatever happens.

Making verities so certain they become structural givens (and thus, matters of faith, rather than empirical disproof) is a specific enterprise, a way of doing things. Said inherited it from the great anti-Enlightenment thinkers of the Victorian era, most notably Marx and Freud, who suggested that our individual view of ourselves was irrelevant. We may be convinced that we're doing A and B, but in fact we're doing X and Y. To learn the truth we have to appeal to the priestly class that alone can explain it all to us. Academics love the way Marx and Freud think, even now a long time after the content of their thought has been discredited. These writers invented the thought pattern that's at the basis of literary studies, and of any self-enclosed hermetically sealed sub-world that seeks to assert theoretical hegemony over the rest of the world.

 The pattern of thought in both these thinkers, and thousands of other lesser lights, is this. The individual is not the measure of all things: I, the commentator, am the measure of all things. You always have to wait for me, the academic or theoretician, to explain it to you. For example, you're *really* doing A and B because you're a member of a certain class and accept its presuppositions. Or: you're *really* doing C and D because of now-inaccessible events in your childhood. What you personally think about this doesn't matter. In Said's case, the claim is that if you're a member of the more powerful society, you're really "Orientalist" even when you don't think you are: you can't help but be so, because you're considering someone who's not you. Even if you say you *like* the someone who's not you, it doesn't matter. Your sin is structural, not one of content.

Such structures are so airtight that they've even taken account of those who think they're wrong. The louder the screams of protest of those being explained, the better those insisting on their point apparently like it. Like the howls of agony of those being roasted to death inside that the hollow bronze bull of Daedalus transformed to sweet music, protests prove the very point they're protesting against, at least to those who hear them aright. All howls of denial (I'm not sexist, I'm not repressive, I'm not a colonialist) are translated into this to the ear that knows how to hear them aright: I'm protesting so strongly because I know you're right; I'm showing how deeply I've repressed what I deny I'm repressing by denying I've repressed it. The devil fights hardest when he's in greatest danger of being exorcised.

The creation by the academic community of its own bell jar has largely been based on its embrace of structures like those of Said, making claims at so basic a level that there is no possible response. The point isn't to change facts or incite actions, but to prove that one is right under all circumstances. The victory is one of words, and has no practical effect save to increase one's sense of self-righteousness. Do you agree with Freud? It's because he's right. Do you disagree? It's because you're repressing. Do you disagree with Marx? You are merely showing your class allegiance, and so proving him right. Do you think it's possible to write in a way about an Other that brackets out your own position? Guess again.

Marginalized "R" Us

American academic shrillness in the last half-century has been devoted to defending the interests of the marginalized. Marginalized is cool, non-marginalized isn't. Too, it seems to infuriate academics that the non-marginalized don't simply acknowledge their utter un-coolness and fold their tents, silently slipping away in the night.

For those exultantly manning (as we once would have said) the barricades against the straight white male majority, the unwillingness of the majority to simply walk away from its power position when that is demanded by others as its right seems proof of the necessity to keep on at the barricades. But if we could contemplate the possibility that the majority has other motives than merely self-interest (which of course is also the motive of those at the barricades) we might begin to see the reason why "ordinary Americans" find what's coming from Academia so "repellent."

It's because what they hear seems wrong to them. Not that it's threatening, not that it's unwelcome. But wrong. I'm filling in for my student sputterer here: over and over he'd begin at "ridiculous"; I'd show him that it wasn't "ridiculous," at which point he'd edge towards "that's not the way it is." What he could never say was why not.

The marginalized, aided by academics, have been telling the non-marginalized for decades that removing structural impediments to their particular marginalized group (people of color, women, gays, non-Westerners) will solve their problems. At least this is the form in which it reaches the non-marginalized. If the point is simply that it will allow them to compete on a level playing field, this point has not come through: the insistence has been so great, the shrillness so shrill, that the mainstream has concluded, not unsurprisingly, that if it matters this much to the marginalized, there must be some intrinsic advantage in it. Not: that it makes their situation less negative, but that it actually solves problems. This is what's false.

The fact that someone seems to those outside to have won the lottery in this sense—is, let's say, a tall and reasonably good looking straight white male—does not mean he can merely reap the rewards of this position rather than working to attain his goals. He's allowed to try, but there's no guarantee he'll win. In fact, the likelihood is great that he won't; there are only a few winners, and many strivers. For most of the non-marginalized, being non-marginalized merely means they can compete, not that they will win. Equating being non-marginalized with winning is a mistake only someone on the outside looking in could make. If the have-nots could suddenly be sitting where the haves are, they seem to imagine, they could suddenly be without problems, without goals. The non-marginalized, those competing among themselves, know this isn't the case. And so they object: things aren't this way. Inevitably, the marginalized think the non-marginalized are protesting only because they want to hold on to the benefits of their position.

Storming the palaces

The academic versions of Freud and Marx, and now Said, have turned revolution into sullen name-calling: the object is no longer to storm the palaces and take from the wealthy few, but to heckle from the outside. The non-marginalized are bad people. We've proved they are. We can't take over in fact, but we can establish moral superiority. Inside the academic walls, the bastards can't take over. But what sense does this make? What the marginalized want is to be like those they are bad-mouthing. Instead, all they get is an intellectual structure that shows how absolutely they will never be anything but marginalized.

The whole intellectual structure of asserting things to be structurally true (which means, true already and forever, which renders immaterial any actual action, any attempt to achieve them in fact) relies on a nineteenth-century intellectual paradigm, which is outdated. The vocabulary used by the marginalized to assert their intellectual if not factual superiority reeks of Marxian analysis developed in a pre-democratic age of European titles and privileges. In that older world, the privileged were a tiny minority, and did not in fact have to exert themselves to be something. It was the majority that was marginalized. This vocabulary cannot be transferred without problems to a world in which the non-marginalized are in fact the majority. The marginalized want to be these people, not take things away. The non-marginalized of today are not structurally compatible with the aristocracy of the nineteenth century, from whom the marginalized have borrowed vocabulary to describe them. What we have is not a tiny minority keeping down the majority, but a majority to which the minorities aspire to belong. What good does it do for the minority to badmouth the majority, show how racist/sexist/fill-in-the-blank-ist it is? That's what it wants to be.

In order for the marginalized to effect real change, they must turn away from the "trendy postmodern discourse" following Said, with its breathtaking assertions that suggest those in the power position do everything they can to perpetuate it, even when they don't think they're trying to. If this is true, there is no hope, though saying it may feed the academic need to hear things the way they wish they were. Far better would be for the marginalized to make clear they are merely asking that structural impediments be removed. And this means presupposing that impediments, once identified, *can* be removed. Said's invective runs so deep he suggests that what he's talking about can never be rectified; it's a structural fact. This is ultimately the theory of the weak, not the strong—not even of those who seriously hope to become strong one day.

Chapter Six

The Linguistic Turn

THE FORM THE SUICIDE OF THE INTELLECTUALS in the twentieth century took was "the linguistic turn" in philosophy and humanistic studies. This notion too was part of Modernism's re-alignment of the intellectual and artistic world: Modernism emphasizes the medium of the work, here words, over content, however we understand this content. In its post-Modern phase, Modernism went so far as to claim that all content is medium, or that content as something discrete doesn't exist at all.

Language studied as a discipline has to situate itself at a level where variations are not so numerous and so inexplicable that the system is overwhelmed. But that is not how language actually works. Words are only part of a much larger configuration that is so vast we can never sketch it in any given moment, a configuration in which the actual is almost always the victor by default: we don't even know what its competition was, usually. There's no sense in seeing it as a system of signs which get their meaning from each other: they're too small a part of the big picture, and they're in turn related to an infinity of other things, most of which are never considered, much less articulated.

We define reality by defining a part of a spectrum we can never see until we've defined it. Nobody but us can say before the fact what we were aiming at; only we can say after the fact if we've achieved it. This is how literature works too: we don't know what the options were, only what in fact was produced.

Signifier/signified

The two most influential linguistic theoreticians of the twentieth century were Ferdinand de Saussure and the Ludwig Wittgenstein who wrote the *Philosophical Investigations*, sometimes called Wittgenstein 2, and thought of by many academics as the "good" Wittgenstein. Wittgenstein began his career with a work that has become almost talismatic in its fame, though now it is almost universally considered a huge error: the *Tractatus Logico-Philosophicus*. This, it's held, was written by Wittgenstein 1, the Wittgenstein before he realized his errors. Intellectual life in America in the last part of the twentieth century is based on a rejection of the *Tractatus*, such as intellectuals believe

Wittgenstein himself effected in his later work, the made-from-fragments *Investigations*. The *Investigations*, together with Saussure's *Course in General Linguistics*, hovers over much of American intellectual life in humanities and social science departments. They've produced the involution and airlessness of much contemporary academic thought, spinning around its own center and largely cut off from the rest of the world. In following their lead, we've gotten ourselves in a very bad position.

Like Freud or Marx, Saussure produced ideas that had to be stripped of a good deal of their original specificity to be usable by scholars in other disciplines. Most fundamental to Saussure's conception of language as a system of signs was the realization that language could be studied from without, be its own subject. This is a perspective that allows us to "get a handle" on things: transferred to literature, it conceives of the manifold of study as something that has some real existence. It makes sense to stand outside this manifold and make utterances about it.

The next most appropriated of Saussure's notions was that language was a "structured system of arbitrary signs." *General Principles in the Course in General Linguistics* begins with a concept that has been much mulled-over: "The main object of study . . . will . . . be the class of systems based upon the arbitrary nature of the sign." (Saussure is here conceding that some signs seem to be "natural": "mime for instance.") "For any means of expression accepted in a society rests in principle upon a collective habit, or on convention. . . . Signs of politeness . . . although often endowed with a certain natural expressiveness (prostrating oneself nine times on the ground is the way to greet an emperor in China) are none the less fixed by rule. It is this rule which renders them obligatory, not their intrinsic value. We may therefore say that signs which are entirely arbitrary convey better than others the ideal semiological process. That is why . . . human languages [are] the most characteristic of all" (68).[58] "Arbitrary," Saussure cautions us, "must not be taken to imply that a signal depends on the free choice of the speaker." Individuals, he explains later, aren't in a position to make up their own signification.

Important relations therefore go sideways, not outside the system; the notion of a system at all implies some high degree of permanence in its members and a high degree of fixity. Not that Saussure denies that language changed. The pair of "synchronic" and "diachronic" offered two ways of looking at language: the first, how things are right now, and the second, how they change over time. Nor can we as individuals effect changes in language single-handedly. What we speak is *"parole,"* our individual products. These can be meaningful or nonsensical, correct language or incorrect. What people in general speak is *"langue,"* which changes slowly and over time, being composed of many individual *"paroles."*

Saussure's view of language was vaguely Darwinian—even, as we might say, social-Darwinian. He acknowledges the fact of change, but all he looked at were the changes that survived. If they're there to be analyzed, it's because they won over other changes: individual alterations, blips of *parole*, fell by the wayside, or were corrected; all the other changes that could have happened and didn't are never considered. Applied to literature, this social-Darwinist attitude—part of what I'm calling the methodology of professional literary studies—means that the mere fact of someone paying attention to a work of literature suffices for it to join the ranks of literature that *should* be paid attention to. Literature is what's studied by the professionals: we create the nature of what we study. Hence the vitally important nature of getting sure "your" book gets its place on the syllabi. If syllabi and classes and reading lists are the world, then the content of those things determine the world. What we don't do is add the caveat: that world is only the world of syllabi and classes and reading lists, professionalized literary study. There's a much bigger world outside. It's true that anything we do in a classroom takes place in a classroom, but that doesn't mean it has to be about the classroom. This is the conclusion that intellectuals drew from Saussure and Wittgenstein 2. Literature professors were aching for someone to show them how to "professionalize" their discipline: these thinkers provided the vocabulary that made it possible to assert this plausibly to the outside world.

No sticky threads

Saussure taught us that in language, units get their meaning not from a relationship with an entity outside themselves, but only by relationship with each other. "Bat" means the thing you hit a ball with, or a flying rodent: it doesn't mean "but," which is virtually identical but means something different: because "but" exists in its own right, choosing one rather than the other is a choice that means something. Not everything is an alterative: if we said or wrote "baat" we'd probably realize it was a mis-writing or mispronunication of "bat," in a way we might not, or not as soon, with "but." A smile is an alternative to a frown, but no expression at all may merely mean the person is listening.

Nor does "bat" somehow reach out to an objective world and attach a sticky thread to it, as if it were a spider. Some signs, Saussure holds, do seem to do this, since they're mimetic—comparable to the ideograms that so fascinated Ezra Pound in Chinese writing.[59] But these are the exception that, for Saussure, prove the rule. The assertion that "bat" somehow does reach out to the world— that words somehow pictured the world, at least nouns like "bat"—is what's held to be the error of Wittgenstein's *Tractatus*—at whose center, it's usually held, is what's called the "picture theory of meaning.". But it's not an error, though the theory itself doesn't make much sense (whoever really thought a word could "picture" the world?). It's an assertion in a larger context, a way of thinking that's challenged, so that the whole work is like a play in which characters interact with each other. It's as much an error to say that the bottom line of the *Tractatus* is the "picture theory of meaning" as it is to say that Shakespeare, through the character of Lady Macbeth, is telling us that regicide is the way to go.

The interest of the *Tractatus* from my perspective, by contrast, is that Wittgenstein tries again and again for the kind of clarity and certainty such a "picture theory of meaning" implies, but each time acknowledges that it's unattainable. He includes this picture theory, with the illusion of absolute self-evident clarity it seems to offer, as one element in his larger work, and then repeatedly acknowledges the limits of this certainty, noting the end of clarity. By the end of the work, he is speaking helplessly of "what cannot be said" and "the mysterious"—and then the work itself ends, its ending famously a renunciation of speech. "What can't be said—we have to be silent regarding it" (7). The *Tractatus* taken as a whole isn't an assertion of the picture theory of meaning as a take-home point. Instead it's a drama of the conflicting principles of clarity and its lack, control and chaos, the acknowledgment that this sort of certainty is only one part of a larger mosaic: not unattainable, only limited. The concept of absolute but limited certainty is one of the central notions of the *Tractatus*. (I've laid out this view in greater detail in Structure and Chaos *in Modernist Works*.)

The insistence that words mean what they mean because they have a fixed, self-evident connection to the world outside (the "picturing" of the *Tractatus*) is what Wittgenstein 2, as one of the patron saints of contemporary academia, is supposed to have abjured. According to this way of telling things, the *Philosophical Investigations* jettisoned all this nonsense about words having fixed meanings by connection with a world outside: words have meaning (only) in use. Because the *Investigations* so conveniently followed the *Tractatus*, many readers have concluded that "meaning in use" is a rejection not only of the picture theory of meaning espoused in the *Tractatus*, but of the notion of connection of words to an outside world at all. But that doesn't follow. At least the picture theory was attempting to express that words somehow link to the world, even if we can't ultimately say how. The *Investigations* was understood as abandoning not only this particular articulation of the link, but the notion of any link at all, because that's the reading most congenial to academics bent on creating a sealed world of words.

But saying that words get their meaning from use doesn't mean that there's no alternative to words, or to using words. Sometimes we don't use words at all: the number of situations in which any words at all are involved is quite limited, an island of verbosity on the sea of other things: facial gestures, body reactions, as well as the utter lack of reaction as a reaction. The world of human interaction is far larger than words, or their use. So long as you're within the small world of words, it's easy to miss the fact that this is only part of a larger whole, and so to fail to understand that we have to relate any words, and their use, to a larger world in which they are quite minimal indeed. The relation may not be that of "picturing," but words are by definition part of a larger world. That's already their relation to the world: they play a role in a larger whole. Now we have to say what that role is. This fact, that words aren't the world, is what readers of the *Investigations* eager to justify a self-enclosed study of words missed.

Nor is it even true that we have to answer the question, How do words mean? before we can go on with life. Those who want to consider words will say, even saying you don't want to consider words is in words. So you have to consider words. But this doesn't follow at all. Any of the "most fundamental" questions that people have considered have seemed to them at the time to be "stop press!" kinds of questions. What is the nature of the afterlife? Surely this is more pressing than any other. What is the nature of our soul? This in its way is just as fundamental as the question, How do words mean? We are at every moment on our way to the afterlife, so we have to solve this problem before all others. What is the nature of objects? Do they exist independently of us? Surely in a world of objects, our bodies among them, this question has to come first. And so it's seemed to each new group of questioners. The consideration of words is something that can be foregrounded, or simply set aside, like all other questions: we're not left with nothing, we still have our lives to live.[60] We can simply use words, and worry later (if at all) about how they mean. I'm always a tall white male, but sometimes that becomes the issue. Presumably here, in print, it isn't, so I simply move on to other things.

Posing the question of how words mean has already set the basis for discussion. It focuses on words, separates them from things they aren't, at least for the purposes of analysis, and then asks what their relationship is to the rest of the world. Whatever the answer is, we've still isolated words and focused on them. In fact, the question of how words mean—is it by referring to a world outside them? Or by forming alternatives to each other in a self-enclosed system?—is itself an academic question that assumes a) it's possible to discuss language in this manner without doing it violence and b) it's worthwhile to do so.

Never were

Language—something that is, in the sense that born people are someone— is part of a larger complex of things that never were, both verbal and non-verbal, a range of responses going from silence or even physical absence, to glossolalia (or chatter-like "verbal diarrhea") on the other. Making a self-contained verbal system to be considered in words from this one small part of the world is as self-serving as having people who actually made it to birth congratulating themselves on being the only ones with souls. All it means is, they're the only ones who are; of course they're the ones doing the congratulating. What else do we expect them to say? If you make a "linguistic turn" in philosophy, what else do you expect philosophy to say about the world except that words are somehow either primary or all there is? Neither is true. The insistence on "meaning in use" is revealed as trivial when we understand that unused language is also meaningful, as is the lack of any language at all.

The theoretical mistake of twentieth-century philosophy after the "linguistic turn" effected by an allegiance to Saussure and Wittgenstein 2 was confusing what is with inevitability. What is, is merely what is: we can acknowledge the tyranny of the actual without giving in to it. Of course we're generally going to focus on the people who are rather than the people (almost-people?) who aren't. Of course the book you read is more real than the book you don't read. And what you actually do at any given point is what you do, whereas what you don't do isn't what you do. But language philosophy of the "linguistic turn" assigns to what is done an extra value in addition to the fact that it filled the bill: it takes over, nothing else was ever an option, things had to be this way.

Deadlift

Sometimes an alternative to language is silence, not merely other language or articulation. Whole dramas can play out inside our heads. What the other person sees is nothing; there's no evidence that it ever happened. But that doesn't mean it didn't. "Meaning in use" seems beside the point given the fact that use of language itself is only one option. Sure, we can insist that only used language has "meaning." But if this is a limited set of cases in the world, why should we care so deeply? Whatever you say: decide how words get meaning if you like, but meanwhile I'm going to continue to use the whole spectrum of possibilities, not just words. And when I want to use words, I'm going to use words: I don't have to wait for you to tell me how they "mean."

Let's consider an example: I am standing next to another man at the deadlift station. Between any two given stations is a rack of weights for the deadlift bar. I usually take two weights out of one side and two out of the other; usually I am alone here at this hour in the weight room, or any other users are on the other side. Now I am ready to put back my weights. But when I look over at the rack between us I see there aren't enough empty spaces both for the weights I've taken, and for those he's taken, to go back. Or has he taken not from the one on his left (my right) but on his right? I look over to see if all his weights will fit there. I don't want to fill up all the spaces that—who knows?—perhaps I've been using against some unknown-to-me protocol. If those are his spaces to fill, I don't want to contravene the system.

What do I say? Do I say, "Hey, are you going to put your weights back there?"? He probably wouldn't know why I'm asking. Unless he's using the other rack, in which case he might just be puzzled, and say: "Nah, I'm using the rack on the other side." What if he says, "Yeah," but says so in such a puzzled tone it's clear he has no idea why I'm asking? Then I'll have to say: "Is that my rack?" He might not understand why I'm asking, and we'd both stand there while I lay out the issues and my thinking on them—too much talk while we're supposed to be working out. The talk itself would fail to work in the situation: words aren't always appropriate.

Better would be to articulate the problem rather than asking a question to solve it: "I'm trying to figure out where I should put these weights back." That's friendly, brings him on to my side with the problem he can help solve rather than being confrontational. But it does require some time away from lifting, and it breaks the cool-air calm of the place. Only one articulation will actually be used; all the others, ranging from statements to questions to fragments, are going to be rejected. The world is full of things we never say; it's a misdirection of attention to assume that what we do in fact say, assuming we say anything, is what had to be. It's only one choice among many, some of which we may be aware of. No philosophy of language that starts only with what in fact is said, or that fails to acknowledge that what isn't said is far more complex and numerous than what is, can do justice to the reality of the world. Asking how the words actually used relate to the world is focusing on the tip of an iceberg.

And what about my tone of voice? My body language? Neither of these is in words, so a "linguistic turn" in philosophy will similarly fail to take account of these: we can of course articulate any particular case, but those words too are couched in tones of voice and with body language. Here, I consider, I need to have an even, non-confrontational tone of voice. Not a sharp "Is that rack the one for your weights?" with an edge. That's almost certain to get his back up, or have him reply in a weary "Hey buddy, why are you being such a jerk?" tone of voice. I need a tone of voice that says, "Hey, no problem here, trying to do the right thing, don't want to take your space." And the body language can't be that of the puffed-up gorilla chest, rather the "at ease" of arms pushed out by lats.

But this is all far too complex for the problem. Another option is simply, have no communication at all. And in the end, that's what happens. I notice that he's doubled up the thinner weights in one of the divisions of the rack, like a toast rack, and I do the same on my side. I end up not having to interact verbally with him at all: talk takes time, isn't what guys working out do with each other, and just makes things complicated. So the path I chose was ultimately that of no interaction of any sort. Words were considered, and rejected. Any philosophy that considers only the linguistic wouldn't even take account of this engagement.

Of course words can consider any one situation after the fact, as here, and even point out (as I am doing) that they fall silent. That, after all, is what Wittgenstein was doing more dramatically in the *Tractatus*: showing the point at which language fails. But Wittgenstein presented this as a great tragic renunciation, the end of his work. In fact the failure of language, in this sense, is quite a quotidian event: language is always only one option among many, and not speaking is always an option, one that's frequently exercised. All of these options including but not limited to language are the cards I hold in my hand, or perhaps each card the placeholder for another fan of cards on its own, and each of these for yet another fan, and so on. Or at least those are some of the cards I can enumerate after the fact: how many did I actually have at that moment? I'll never be able to say. I can only be conscious of a few cards at once, but that doesn't mean the others couldn't have been played—usually we don't know we have a card until we play it.

Any focus on language as a synecdoche for life will be inadequate: language is merely one card in a hand that will by definition never be defined. We can articulate, which is to say, put into words, the non-language options of any one particular situation. But while we're doing that we're choosing, in this case, to focus on the tip of a new iceberg, the words used in this situation. This too was chosen as an option among many. We can never articulate all the rejected alternatives in all situations, because we're too busy doing the things we haven't rejected.

Most analytical frameworks in words fail to capture the living moment: what can you say about a football play, for example, that even goes near what it feels like to be in the moment of play? We know this when the moment itself doesn't involve words, such as athletics. But for some reason if it does involve words, we've tended to defer to them: they are all that counts. That's not so; they're only part of the whole. Silence is an option too, not just speech. And even silence has many gradations.

Doing it wrong

So words are only one small part of a cloud of factors, most of which we never articulate; these include as well still-born words. This is especially true, perhaps, of situations between men, where I'd say a larger proportion of the information is below the water line than above it. Consider again the weight room. Someone over on the other side is clearly doing the exercise wrong. Are there ever any circumstances under which another man can use words to set him straight? It's wisdom to realize that the answer is, "Never say never but probably never—but if there is an exception you just have to be aware of it when it happens." In the weight room men are supposed to ignore each other almost as much as they're supposed to do so when lined up at urinals. But of course if you know him and have a sort of mentor relationship to him, you may speak. If he accepts that the relationship is that you tell him what to do and he does it, you merely say, "Hey [insert name here], let me show you how to be more efficient at that." Even so you probably don't want to impinge his masculinity: you want him to ask you for help, not resent you. It's difficult to think of a case where you could get away with saying, "You're doing that wrong"—you'd have to be his brother to make this one work, and his older brother at that. With a stranger the only case where this would be appropriate would be if he was actually in danger of hurting himself and you were intervening to save him.

It's similarly difficult to figure out not just when to say something in praise, but what. The impulse to praise another man in the gym is itself something controlled by circumstances. If we sense him as competition, there is typically no impulse to praise at all. He may be throwing around 50 pound dumbbells for his curls as if they were toys, but if he has bulging biceps we're not typically going to put ourselves in the subordinate position of even acknowledging we've noticed them, especially not if he's showing off (ripped shirt, Spandex). He knows he looks good; we don't have to tell him.

What we say to him, if anything, will additionally be determined by his manner: if it's cocky "get out of my way," we certainly will not be praising him, merely pretending he isn't there.

Let's say, however, he catches our eye with a friendly grin. "Hey man," he might say, "can you give me a spot on this one?" He's talking to us like an equal, so we respond in kind. "Sure," we say. He'll typically now say what he wants: "Can you just give me a pop-up on the first one, on three?" "Sure," we say. "How many you going for?" Let's say he says, "six." So we verbalize a couple of "push it up"s and maybe a "one more" at the end, or an "it's all you."

We've seen him sweating rather than not sweating, so we've bonded with him. He's been flat on his back and weaker, not towering over us and stronger. So now we can probably say, "Good job, dude." If he's egregiously muscular, we may at this point find ourselves able to say "You're huge, man." Not just "you're huge"—you want to use a term showing equality, to take the admiring edge off it. You want to give him a horizontal compliment, not a vertical one.

He'll shrug it off. "Hey man, thanks," he'll say. Maybe he'll add a sort of self-diminishing phrase here to indicate that we're in the process together, the thing that allows men to bond over what they share rather than form a hierarchy over what separates them. Whether or not he says anything in return about us will depend on how big we are. If we too are big, he can't ignore the friendship overture of someone as big as him complimenting him first. So he'll say, "You're pretty huge yourself." We say "thanks": we've bonded. If we're noticeably smaller than he is, he won't lie by saying we're not. In fact, if we're a lot smaller, we might have to acknowledge the reality by saying, "Hey man, wish I was huge too, but that's just not my body type." There's a fine line between excusing ourselves for something we can't change and correctly describing the situation. Two men can be equals even if one is muscular and the other not if the smaller one says, in the right tone and at the right time, the right thing: perhaps, "hey, I'm an endurance guy, look at my body type." If it seems he's comfortable with this, then everything is fine. If he says it in a regretful tone of voice then it's not fine; the bigger guy can't do anything about it and is somehow being asked to solve his problem. If he says it first off, that's bad too.

Limited

The "linguistic turn" of contemporary Anglo-American philosophy is therefore small and quite dry. It's not just words that we need to consider, it's many other factors too, and even silence—so many other factors that we can't list them. We can of course take any particular incident and say what factors are at play: we can analyze the tone of voice from a recording, the body language from a film, and the words on the page. But these too are words, which for their new situation are neglecting all the other things that aren't.

And who's to say we've got even the major factors? By definition we don't have them all. This situation at the deadlift station was anomalous in that I actively considered actions I subsequently rejected, such as speaking. Most of the time we act without laying out the options on the table in front of us like cards before taking one. So my description of my options in any situation won't necessarily be correct: I'll only be able to access the options I seriously considered, which is to say look at situations where there was no clear front runner. Most of the time we "do the right thing," which is to say some horse simply streaks across the finish line. We'll never know what the others were because we didn't have to pay attention to that race.

Rejecting an option means it had more of a chance than options that aren't even articulated enough to be rejected. And there are a million slight variations on what we can articulate, things that simply didn't happen. As Hegel famously observed, the owl of Minerva only flies at night: you have to wait for things to be resolved before you can start analyzing them. The problem is if you think that what you can analyze is all there is, or was in some sense inevitable: that leads to self-involvement, precisely the state of contemporary literary studies.

Words are only a tiny fraction of all the responses possible, and the words that are said tiny fraction of words. When we've exhausted what can be said about words we still haven't touched the vast reality of a situation, especially given that silence is always an option—say, replaced by what we call a "withering glance," or a pleasant neutral exterior. Yet in a world where we're told that everything follows the "linguistic turn" in philosophy, we believe that focusing on words is more than what in fact it is, focusing exclusively on a small cache of options. We can speak about the "withering glance"—after all, I'm doing that here. Of course we can always use more words: they never dry up. But in each moment of words, what are we leaving behind, failing to say, pushing into darkness, and ignoring? A gulf opens around each micro-second if we realize that what is holds no special ontic weight. And have we exhausted even this moment we're analyzing, now increasingly in the past, by limiting ourselves to "withering glance"? Of course not. What of the other factors present—the weather outside, the temperature of the air, the way I felt, and so on? Each moment implies the whole world around it, if we choose to embed it properly. We can spend our whole life on a single moment, and still not exhaust it.

The advantage of a work of literature is that we're open about the fact that we're taking time articulating these things in the work of literature: we are turning things not in words into words, but we're not even close to claiming that life is made up more primordially of words than of other things—which is the implication of language philosophy. When we use words to analyze the non-verbal elements suggested by a work of literature, we are merely using words, not claiming that they're theoretically primary: the analysis is secondary to the work, which may evoke more non-verbal factors than verbal, even if we use words to discuss them all.

Spectrum

Even choosing the direction I'm going in verbally, say at the deadlift station, doesn't mean the precise words used have any sense of inevitability. We aim, as if by instinct, at a general place within a spectrum we don't even define. The precise articulation of the general ball-park position within the spectrum isn't relevant. And the act of aiming at a place in the spectrum can never be brought to the surface except in particular cases. This means that by definition the words that are used are infinitesimal compared to the words that aren't used. We fail to use a myriad of words in the chunk that we're aiming at, as well, of course as all the other words in the other chunks.

We're always aiming in a general direction, and always hit a precise one: anything else in the same general neighborhood would have worked just as well. If I meet someone I know, I can say, "Nice day" or "How are you?" or "What's up?" or "Working hard?" How many things am I unlikely to say? We can never articulate them all, and in this time we'll grow old and be unable to articulate how we articulate any of the things we articulate in this time. I don't say "Screw you" because that's not the part of the spectrum I'm aiming at. I don't say "Aren't you my mother?" because I know he's not. I don't say "Blue is my favorite color." I don't say "the population of Madagascar is X according to the last census." I don't look away, because I know the person and that would mean something here (other times it might not). How do I know all these things? I just do. It's like asking an athlete how he knows what to do in any given moment: he just does. All we can usually say is what we do do, not what we don't do. Of course, we can analyze what's done come Monday morning. But who says we're analyzing everything? We only stop when we run down. And that's time that could have been used for other things.

Nor can language itself ever articulate this fact of aiming at a place on the spectrum, except in any particular case. It can't run around behind its own back—this is the realization that haunted Wittgenstein most consistently his entire life. Language itself isn't on the other side of the glass watching language come to be. It's only in the room with what actually comes to be. Language works like a newspaper: the column inches have to be filled, but how we fill them is up to us. We can talk about how the space was filled up, but talk doesn't explain how it gets to be filled up. And talking about filling up the space fills it up: there's no room for anything else. Occasionally it can talk about some of the alternatives that bit the dust, or didn't run, or were never written. That's what I'm doing here. But this is the tip of an incalculable iceberg, one that by definition we can never measure. Let's say we try to articulate what any given column inch was an alternative to (another assignment, more on a movie star, another way of writing the same general story). Still, what about the icebergs that each subsequent moment produces? We could write volumes on a single iceberg; by the standards of what's usually written on icebergs, that would be a lot. But it wouldn't do justice to the iceberg. And it would leave all the others— and each micro-second, each column inch, has its own iceberg—unconsidered.

Library

Here's an example of the ballpark, the general area of the spectrum I'm aiming at, where the articulations on either side of what in fact I say could have worked just as well. I go into the library at the Naval Academy. It's after semester end, and the library is all but deserted. Behind the desk are two men I've joked with over the years: they know my name, never require me to show a card. My options for interacting begin with a) a polite smile and move to the slightly more engaged b) "Gentlemen?" through c) "How's it going?" and ultimately to d), where I choose to pitch my interaction. "Do they pay you two for standing around when there's no business?" I ask, adding theatrical "google-eyes" to make clear it's a joke.

If I've done it right, the people I'm talking to "get" the part of the spectrum I've aimed that. And within that part of the spectrum, any response they give me is fine. It can be "Hey, yeah, your tax dollars at work"; it can be "Man, we work so hard with all these students we're entitled to a break"; it can be "What about you guys over in academic buildings?"; it can be "Hey, this is the good part." None is better than the other.

In fact, what I get in return is this, initially somewhat puzzling: "Hey, I'm just taking time off from writing my memoirs." It's not quite clear how this fits into what I said, but it's clearly from the same "joshing" part of the spectrum I accept it. It would be rude to say, "What does a librarian have to say that would be of interest to the world?"; it would kill the moment to launch into a serious discussion of how hard it is to get a memoir published nowadays or what stay-at-homes have to say that's of value. That would be to misunderstand the tone of voice.

In fact, they responded in the same part of the spectrum that I responded in; they understood where to look for their responses. What they say is irrelevant;

all I was looking for was a correct identification of the part of the spectrum. If we had parts of the spectrum numbered (an impossibility because the spectrum changes with each and every interaction, second to second), they could just as well have said, "That's a sector 32a response." Anything in that sector is fine, we needn't waste time picking one in particular. Similarly, I sometimes feel disinclined to open thank-you notes from an elderly aunt to whom I occasionally send flowers. The fact of its being a thank you letter is what counts, and this I can see from outside the envelope. My wife has to open them and read them, all very by-the-book.

For that matter, much of what we do (which includes what we say, and don't) is an arbitrary particular within a precise, usually unarticulated, field of possibles. One morning I came to work dressed in blue jeans and a t-shirt. Since classes were over, I knew I wouldn't see students, and most of the other faculty members who were around were in shorts. That day, however, there were many other faculty members about, and puzzlingly enough, dressed in our normal teaching attire: suits and ties. Suddenly I remembered that there was an awards ceremony in the department library. It was not, I reflected, a hugely public affair, but it was one that required better than t-shirt and jeans. I didn't have to go at all, but since I'd been seen, it would be taken as an affront if I sequestered myself in my office and didn't go at all. If I hadn't showed up at all, by contrast, this would not be the message sent. I was trapped; I'd have to go. But that meant, not in a t-shirt.

No problem, I thought. I had a suit in my office, with a tie and shirt, stashed there for such occasions as these when I forget one. But I'd never had to use it. Having to use it made me realize what I'd forgotten: shoes and socks. I was wearing tennis shoes. White tennis shoes: impossible with a dark suit, both because tennis shoes and because white.

First I made the rounds for shoes: in a department with military personnel, there will be dress shoes. I finally found a pair down the hall. Too small, but I could walk in them. I had thought the white socks wouldn't show when I tried them on, but they did. That meant I had to go foraging again. Where there are black Corfram shoes, there are black socks. I found a pair of these from another officer. I had achieved something conformable with the necessary generic, if not the precise one I would have picked.

Could I have gone in my t-shirt and jeans? No, better not to have gone at all. Completely the wrong part of the spectrum. That made me wonder: is there ever an occasion where a t-shirt and jeans would have been possible at a function like this? It's difficult to come up with one, but it's not impossible that under certain circumstances—say, I was the guest of honor for a surprise event—it could even be considered charming. My relative undress would be proof of just how unsuspecting I'd been.

If I were the master of ceremonies, of course, no such laxness would have been even thinkable: it would have been a poke in the eye at the formality of the occasion. The officers are in their dress uniforms; unless my house had burned down with all my clothes I could not have showed up in this.

The reason I had to be properly, if not nattily, dressed, was not that I was important, but precisely because I was so unimportant. Indeed, I was merely wallpaper. There needed to be a respectable number of civilian faculty members present to fill the chairs, and also to balance the number of military faculty who were more numerous, as they had to be around anyhow. All I had to do was come, look pleasant, not interrupt, say nothing, clap when the others clapped, and leave at the end. I could see the events coming to an end when the master of ceremonies began saying things like, "Well, ladies and gentlemen, that concludes today's events." There could be only a few more sentences after that: he would thank us for coming, he might invite us to coffee and cookies in the hallway, he might say something to the awardees. In fact he did all these things. But I couldn't jump the gun: I could have saved three sentences, but the nature of the situation meant I had to wait. I could be the first person standing up, but it couldn't be by much. And in fact, I forced myself to wait until I wasn't even the first. Then I was free; all I had to do was fix a pleasant smile on my face and exit.

I had aimed at, and achieved, a generic, through piecing together specifics, no one of which was what I would ordinarily have chosen. Most of the time we're unable to distinguish the specific from the generic, never ask how far from where we were we could have been, because we have an acceptable specific ready, and don't have to construct it.

Pool

Odd situations, or uncomfortable ones, can make us aware of the generic spectrum, and of choosing our actions and words, in a way we aren't usually aware of doing. For example: one day at the pool, I sat in my Speedo pulling on a pair of shorts. Across on the other side of the pool I saw a female student of mine—or at least she'd been a student until a few days ago when I turned in her grade. I had seen her perhaps a handful of times here, me in my Speedo, her in her midshipman swimming suit. Each time we had acted appropriately: as if we'd implicitly agreed not to mention the fact that neither of us had many clothes on. She called me "Professor Fleming," and made appropriate conversation. My demeanor to her was no different mostly naked than it had been in the classroom. It was, after all, the swimming pool: a suit in the classroom, a Speedo in the swimming pool.

She'd done quite well on the final I'd corrected the week before, and I wanted to tell her so. Besides, she'd written me a note at the end of the exam about how she'd entered the course with great trepidation but had ended up really enjoying it. I motioned for her to come over—the motion was appropriate because I was the superior. My lack of clothing wasn't suggestive, because this was a pool. But I was in the process of putting on my clothes. I continued doing so to show that she was irrelevant to this process; it had nothing to do with her. Here the part of the spectrum I was aiming at was that none of this meant anything. I did things in exactly the same order and with the same timing as if I'd been alone.

We talked. The conversation too was exactly what it would have been if she had been in her uniform and I in my suit. I told her she had been a good student. She told me she'd really studied hard for the exam. I said it showed. We talked about her leg surgery. I didn't stare at her leg, only indicated it visually in a very general way. I didn't ask her how she felt about having the ACL of a corpse, which is how, she explained, she'd gotten full mobility back. We talked about her service selection: she'd wanted pilot and had gotten surface warfare because it turned out she had an allergy.

On leaving, I shook her hand and wished her well. The whole encounter was completely proper, though from start to finish it involved a lot of skin. For this reason, I was acutely aware of what not to say in a way I infrequently am. I considered everything before I said it, made the choice for silence in many cases, made sure before uttering it that it was completely unrelated to our situation of semi-nudity, and was very aware of not even appearing to be visually, physically, or tone-of-voice suggestive. Some things would have been grossly inappropriate, starting with the obvious—either of us making any comment about the other's body. But any undue hand pressure on either part, any straying of the eyes: all would have hit the walls of this encounter, which was like steering between obstacles.

Usually we're not so aware of the boundaries, the things we're avoiding. But even when we're aware of the boundaries, the fact that they fill our concentration doesn't mean that they actually all are there is. Who knows what else I was avoiding? Much language is like this: we choose the thing we choose, which means many other things aren't chosen. But there was nothing inevitable about the thing we chose: it was generically the right thing, one of many, but not specifically. We only have to get one thing within the generic that we're aiming at: we don't even have to know what the others are. One's enough.

We may be particularly conscious of this in foreign languages: if we realize we're shaky on subjunctive we change the sentence in midstream to an infinite so as to avoid it. We've still spoken correctly by avoiding a possible mistake. And who counts what's avoided? All that counts in communication is coming up with something that works, not everything that could have.

Speech Acts

The huge popularity both for twentieth-century philosophy and study of literature of John Searle's *Speech Acts*, which focuses on the very few cases where interactions have been stripped of everything but words and where they are almost perfectly programmed, suggests to me that we want to believe that our interactions with each other are predictable and frozen in words.[61] In fact they are neither predictable nor frozen. To be sure, it's true that most interactions are things we do correctly predict. But that's what it means to correctly predict them: they turn out to be what we think they are. It's what we're expecting, but we're expecting it to be this because of the nature of what we've experienced. Nothing compels this to be yet another X, however; that's a call of our perception, of what pile we've put it in, not something that determines its nature.

"Performatives," words that (in Searle's terminology) seem to be themselves actors, are exceptions that prove the rule. They're situations we've set up so as to be at the absolute end of their particular spectrum: words in situations where the options for response are limited to two: saying them or not saying them. In a wedding, saying "I do" gets you married, or at least makes the presiding authority pronounce you married. But words only appear to do things under these circumstances because all the other options have consciously been eliminated. Normally we have some wiggle room, even in the most routine of questions: "How are you doing?" We are, to be sure, expected to say "Fine thanks, and you?" But it is possible to say something else and have it "fit" equally well. "Not bad for a Monday," "Pretty good considering who's President," "Really super, it must be the weather" or simply "Can't complain." All but the most relentlessly binary of situations have at least some sense of the generic. And even the "I do" situation the choices, though set up to be binary, never are. What if you start singing "I do, I do, I do" at the top of your lungs like a mad(wo)man while you are running away? The runaway bride scene from the Claudette Colbert/Clark Gable movie "It Happened One Night" comes to mind—very photogenic, a long veil billowing in the wind. Would you be married or not? Surely we not only have to say "I do" but fail to be running away while we say it? But who could have said this before it happened? We may have set up this situation as an airtight binary—say it or don't say it—but the fact is, someone, somewhere, will find a way to make it other than binary, blur its apparently sharp edges.

Analysis only analyzes what happened; it can't get us from where we are to what we do. For that there are simply too many factors at too many levels of evidence or consciousness—however we choose to articulate it. We're constantly shaping our actions, always in the middle of many structures, holding many threads that come sooner or later to an end, depending on whether they're long or short. Here we are ourselves the Three Fates: we determine their length, we spin them, and we cut them off. We are continually falling off a cliff, picking ourselves up, and moving forward again. We're constantly muddling through with language, sometimes by the skin of our teeth, sometimes handily. That is, when we do muddle through. It's more typical to muddle through than not, but that's only so because of the nature of "typical": we expect what we expect based on what what's happened in the past. Muddling through means achieving the expected. But even the expected has to be made to happen; it doesn't happen by itself. And it only happens if the other person lets it.

Separation anxiety

Making meaning (in use? Picture theory?) the center of your attention already separates language from its surroundings. You've therefore already missed the point of the world, which is that words are part of a much larger picture, grow from it and are subsumed by it. But because you've chosen this one limited aspect of the world, language, to be your center point, you have to answer the following question: How does it relate back to what you've separated it from? But if you never separate it, you don't have the problem. In a similar way, Romanticism began by separating the individual from his larger social context. Then the question becomes, how can he be re-attached? Through nostalgia? Longing? Sympathy? Art? The means varied, but all presupposed the initial split. The pre-modern world doesn't seem to have made the split: man was a social animal, that's all there was to it. So it didn't have the problems of re-inserting him in a context. Thus limiting our choices to these two, those held to be exemplified by Wittgenstein 1 and Wittgenstein 2—namely that language reaches out to the world or language doesn't reach out to the world—already presupposes the answers to some basic questions, and implies other problems.

It's curious that the second alterative has gained so many adherents. It seems so odd in the world. (My point is that we shouldn't settle for either one.) Who doesn't use words to do things, and not in any way like the strangely frozen museum artifacts of Searle? Language is entwined with the world, and not because it either mirrors it or is more primordially used than not used: it's a part of a larger whole; its relationship with the world is not so limited either as picturing or "use." (Sometimes we fail to use language; that's a use if everything has to be a use—but at this point we see the theory as hollow.) My just-turned-two son says, "I want water," and he gets water. If the almost four-year-old forgets to say "please," we ask: "What's the magic word?" And it is magic: it gets him what he wants. We don't have to look in the rarified corner of Searle's speech act theory to find performatives: language is intrinsically performative. How could we have been so infatuated so long with the almost trivial fact that signs are arbitrary? That's like saying that money is only paper and metal—or whatever it is: cowries, sticks. It's also money, which means it can be turned into a million and one other things. By the same token, insisting that language is used is trivial: what else? But this doesn't mean that it's only language that's used: language is one among many options, and any specific language one among many more, few of which are ever visible or articulated, whether physically or mentally.

Es stimmt

In German we say that something is the case by saying "es stimmt"—it's the same locution as to "tune" a piano, *ein Klavier stimmen*. It's on pitch. This is in fact our sensation when we search for a word or a phrase, or go back and correct something that seems false to us. We are bringing words into unison with an unseen postulate. And that process is what we mean by "meaning." Of course both the unseen postulate and "meaning" are mystical, which means we can never haul them *in toto* into the light: that's I think Wittgenstein's point in the *Philosophical Investigations.* Why have so many people been eager to understand him as saying that there's nothing we're aiming at, nor any process of aiming? Of course there is. But it certainly makes things simpler if everything that exists is right here on the table, ready to be analyzed and categorized. There's nothing else beyond what' seen. It's no longer frustrating like trying to bob for apples or get the rubber duckies in the bath to stay put.

People interacting with each other are like boats where somebody has a hand on the tiller. No outsider can look at the patterns of the boat's wake and conclude that this was the only possible pattern it could have taken. I could have said a dozen things that would have kept the boat moving in almost the same direction—which is to say, where the variations would have been uninteresting (we needn't have talked about exactly the things we talked about). And yet at each moment, I could have pushed the boat in another direction, or the other person, who wasn't part of my program, could have done so and I would have had to react. If the boat had gone in another direction, that would have opened up a dozen more things for that moment, and a dozen for the moment beyond that, and more beyond that. After the fact the pattern it takes seems fixed, but in fact it wasn't while it was unfolding.

That most boats keep a straight course most of the time rather than flitting all over is merely something we realize, not something that has to be. Or rather, what is, is. We learn how many are in "most boats" or "most of the time." We come to learn what the bounds of predictability will be: there's nothing written in the stars that says that certain things must change and others mayn't. A child can appear before us suddenly missing a tooth, and we say merely, "I see you lost your tooth." We have to learn that that's not unusual. A Martian wouldn't know what to expect as usual. Sometimes even we don't know what to expect. Why is John happy one moment and sad the next? If we know him to be bipolar (manic-depressive, as we once said) we're not surprised—but outsiders might be. Outsiders might find the demeanor of my autistic daughter strange. I do not.

Sometimes we're aware of our hand on the tiller, but usually not. And by definition most other people aren't, most of the time. To the extent they are, it's because they know the world, have experiences that tell them someone's story isn't holding together, someone else is upset, someone has other motives than he says: they've paid attention to surfaces. This whole book, in a sense, is a plea for surfaces: instead of a pseudo-scientific "literary study" with the pretense to objectivity and to striding forward into the unknown, I propose merely paying attention to what's there. Patterns will form, or not: they help us process what we see. Being alive to surfaces is its own end. We can still read and discuss literature without "studying literature."

Timing

Words are a small part of this interaction: the words that don't get said overwhelm those that do, and the elements that are not in words at all, ranging from widening of the eyes to body gestures to clearings of the throat, are by far the lion's share of the methods by which we give and get information about each other. One element attached to words but independent of them is timing: not what is said but when it's said. Couples learn, sometimes the hard way, that timing is all in their communications with each other. You shouldn't hit the other with bad news the second s/he comes in the house—unless, as we say, it "can't wait." In the stereotypical 1950s household, the wife has made the husband's favorite dinner and pours him an extra-large scotch when he comes in the door (this on top of his three-martini lunch); only afterward, when she massages his shoulders and he sinks, half-slumbering, into his easy chair, does she dare to say, "Honey, if you'd like to do something nice for me, there *is* something you could do..."

Nowadays we find the complex lead-in to the *pater familias* demeaning, but of course we have not done away with the fact that timing is part of every utterance. Couples' counseling emphasizes the fact that complaints are to be kept finite, not be allowed to snowball as part of a tirade of vituperation whose form is typically "and another thing..." It's not against the rules ever to say these things to the partner, just not now. Plus the complaint should if possible be expressed as subjective: When you do X it makes me feel Y. Not: You are so X when you do Y.

We're most likely to be aware of timing as a separable aspect if we have already polished up what it is we're supposed to say: if the 1950s wife knows what she's asking for a specific thing—perhaps, to continue the stereotype, a piece of jewelry, or to go on a vacation: she'll know what the words are she wants to say, and the question of when is all that remains to be answered. Is this the right time? Is this? Is this? There's no rule book that will tell her what degree of quiescence the husband has to have attained. And there's no rule book that says how long he'll be amenable to considering her demand. This is the aspect of "striking while the iron is hot" that we're all aware of: how hot is hot? No book can tell us. In the case of complaining to our partner, however, we not only answer the question of when but also of what. We change the form of what we want to say because we know what we'd like to say would be counter-productive. We change "You are so X" to "when you do A, I feel B." We can actually change what we say, not just say it at a different time.

All writers know that there are times when we must "pull the punch" or wait until later in the article: how much preparation do we need? Do we get to the point right away? Do we lead up to it? Can we say it twice? Even once the information is delivered, the decisions aren't over: do we need to do it again? Can we? Should we? In such cases, timing merely becomes one issue among many. Not only the when of the thing delivered but the thing itself must be fit to circumstances. And sometimes the decision is made to not allow anything at all to be delivered: it's the equivalent of the might-have-been baby failing to attach to the uterus. People that aren't have to be considered sometimes too.

Other factors
In any given set of circumstances, it seems possible to apply an external set of measuring sticks. One might be "timing." Another might be "tone of voice." Another might be "degree of aggression." In some cases we might be aware of calibrating what we do and say at particular places on these external scales: perhaps we are very aware of timing. But it's not possible to have all of these external scales equally foregrounded: we can't be thinking as much about timing and content and degree of aggression and body language as if we know what we are going to say (perhaps because we've rehearsed it) and are only concentrating on "when." We have to let these things sink below the surface if we are to remain normal-seeming. We have to be aware of changes as well: perhaps the whole project will have to be scrapped, or one project turns into another. Who hasn't had an interaction with, say, a partner you're splitting up with (or think you are) and have it turn into something quite different, perhaps sweaty sex on the floor, perhaps a shouting match? The roller-coaster of make-up sex is something only the two people involved in it can chart, the moment where fury and yelling is suddenly replaced by another feeling: one partner looks at the other, confirms that the other is thinking what they're thinking, and then things change course.

It's possible our housewife could be so fixated on what she had to say that she'd be unable to change course if instead of relaxing and becoming the proverbial putty in her hands in his easy chair, her husband chose this moment to begin talking in a drowsy voice, confessing something to her: he's lost all their money on a horse race. Probably he'd only confess a weakness if he were sitting in a chair with her hands massaging his shoulders: it would be very odd indeed if he chose that moment, when he was in her power and under her hands, to say something like, "I'm having an affair with my secretary." More typical would be things where he was saying he'd been a naughty boy and wanted to be soothed: soothing would not, all things being equal, be her reaction to such a pronouncement as this.

Yet it might be. The circumstances might be such that he would be making the right decision to say this here: she's always wanted him to have an affair (for whatever reason)—say, because she has, she's been pressuring him to do so to even the score and lessen her own guilt, finally he has given in, knowing she'll approve. Or: he's done it before, she's made clear she sees it as a mere character flaw rather than a major blow against their marriage; he's confessing yet another to her.

No one before the fact or sitting on the sidelines could use the tools of extant analysis—these aspects, say, starting with "timing"—to say what he will say, or should. Nor is anything stopping someone from saying the wrong thing, or something that is less than ideal: the rulers, that is, can neither predict nor influence what happens save to the extent that the people in the interaction choose to have them do so. Interactions are so multi-faceted that no set of measuring sticks can ever do justice to them: we don't know which of the measuring sticks we are even required to be conscious of, nor how to use them (people with no "radar" can't be given one by learning, in an academic fashion, about these measuring sticks). You can't develop good timing by learning that one measuring stick for an interaction is "timing," for example: perhaps this isn't even one we need to consider, or is subsumed to a measuring stick for "content."

Any attempt to set up a rigid meta-terminology of factors that we can use to consider our actions, or that can be used to consider what we do and say, will of necessity be limited and too mechanistic to capture the reality of how we choose among options, many of which we're unaware of until we need them. I don't usually think, "I really have to get the timing right on this one," nor did I usually ask myself "Where on a scale of tones of voice will I pitch what I say?" I aim at a target I haven't articulated—and this each and every moment of every day.

Blind date

The words that are uttered are tips of icebergs. We jump from tip to tip. But even so, we can fail to have any of the iceberg emerge: it's work to get some of the iceberg out of the water.

Let's imagine a blind date. The man sees the woman coming down the street. Since he's not quite sure it's her, he assumes a position of interested waiting, somewhere between the full-faced grin he'd reserve for somebody he knows and the blank "you're not on my radar screen" look of just someone waiting out his time. She comes closer, and he turns towards her, making contact possible but not inviting it. He looks to see if she breaks stride, or is looking at him. She is slowing and moving towards him. He puts a friendly smile on his face and, when she is at the right distance (what's the right distance?) says, "Are you Karen? I'm John."

"Yes," she says, and smiles, a real smile. He lets his friendly smile deepen several degrees (but how many? What's a degree?).

A blind date is largely about identify the correct ball-park to pitch utterances in. At this point one or both parties is supposed to express something that shows consciousness that the other has put some effort into coming. He could say to her, "I hope you didn't have any trouble finding it" if it was a place unknown to her, or perhaps "I hope you didn't have problems parking" if she had indicated she was having to drive in. If she just walked, he has to find something else: "I appreciate you getting off work early." But it can't be too craven (how do we measure this?), as if to indicate that he's not worth her doing that.

She, for her part, could say something like "I hope I haven't kept you waiting"—she can say this even if she's right on time. In fact, this probably works better if she's right on time. If she's a minute or two late, he doesn't want to indicate he wasn't punctual himself, so he says, "No, of course not, you have perfect timing." He doesn't say: "It's only a minute late, why would you even say such a thing?" If she's, say, ten minutes late and he's only just got there, he could get points by making a mock confession: "You know, I had trouble getting here myself and was worried I'd keep you waiting." He doesn't have to say that he himself has only been here for a minute, or even a few seconds. Why give away an advantage? He can leave the length of time he's been there vague, make it sound as if he was worried for five minutes. In any case they're both acknowledging the importance of punctuality.

How to greet? A handshake, and she should stick out her hand first. A kiss would be inappropriate, even a brotherly one. Her offering the hand gives her the sense of control—women on blind dates always feel a little vulnerable, even if in broad daylight in a public place. The handshake should not be a manly "professional" one on her part, but instead a kind of back-of-hand-up that in an earlier age would have had the man clicking his heels and bending over it for the simulacrum of a kiss. However it shouldn't be too dead-fish-like (how do we measure this?). Yielding, therefore, but not too yielding. How would we explain this to a Martian?

Where are they going? Venue counts. It shouldn't be in a sports bar: the territory is far too male, and women on blind dates don't like feeling like tag-alongs. Unless, of course, the source of the commonality is the sport. Even then, the noise level in a sports bar makes it difficult to talk: perhaps heaven for the man, but not what most women have in mind at all.

Let's say the man is aware of this, and has gone with the default of a restaurant. It's right here, so they go on. The man is expected to have made the reservation, so he's the one to interact with the hostess. Besides, it shows an ability to steer things in the world, assume responsibility. However, he takes care to be very neutral with her: restaurant hostesses are invariably attractive young women with whom he would probably normally kid around or flirt a little bit. This is a very bad move in a blind date when he must give the woman the impression that he is paying 100% attention to her.

They are led to the table. John stands back and asks, "Is this okay?" Probably he should give her some options to let her get out of this table more easily if she really doesn't like it. He should therefore add: "Would you rather be closer to the window?" Usually restaurants try to save the tables by the window for four people, and put the two together somewhat inland. However if they're not busy, and let's say this is right after work—early, for most restaurants—they may be willing to do it, either because he breaks the rule above and does in fact give the hostess a huge smile as he asks, "Any chance we could get one of the tables over by the window?"—probably he should ask this before he even gives it to his date as an option—or because the hostess sees that the man and the woman are strangers, intuits the circumstances, and putting herself in the woman's place, wants to make her evening as pleasant as possible. (It's more likely she'd do it as a favor to the man than to the woman.)

"Maybe over there by the window?" says Karen, not committing herself to saying she'd be unhappy if she stayed here.

This could be either before or after it's determined if that's an option. The hostess saying, "Well, we generally hold those for parties of four and our crush is about to start" could put an end to it. If she merely says "we generally hold those for parties of four," she's being inconsiderate: lumping Karen and John in the group of "generally." To be factual without being inoffensive, she'd have to say something that indicates she has no control over the situation: "I'm sorry, but those are reserved." She doesn't have to say reserved by whom, or for whom, or under what circumstances.

At this point Karen is supposed to give in: the man has tried to give her options, been checked, and that's the end of it. "This is fine," she'll say. More discussion indicates that she's unnaturally interested in the placement and not primarily in spending time with him.

They sit and smile while they unfold their napkins. Now John should introduce a subject; doing so shows initiative and oomph. If Karen gets there first with the subject, however, it needs to be a mere place-holder, probably something about the restaurant. She says, "This is really nice here up on the balcony." She'll have to add something so it doesn't sound inane. Perhaps: "Sort of like those wine-cellar restaurants you occasionally see in Paris." Perhaps: "You can see the people walking below." This second one may be the wrong decision too, especially if they've tried and failed to get a window overlooking the "below." If so, it's a mis-step that shouldn't be made worse by John's becoming apologetic: "I'm so sorry we weren't able to get a table by the edge." That will require her to say, "No no, not at all, I mean this is fine, you can still see the people, and anyway it's fine." This will be awkward.

The thing about Paris might be awkward if it seems as if she's trying to impress him with having been to Paris (she should assume everybody has been to Paris), or if she's trying a bit too hard to make it clear precisely that she knows everybody has been to Paris. So this might not be the best one either. So she should perhaps stick to: "It's nice up here on the balcony. Quiet so we can hear ourselves think!" Or perhaps: "A different perspective!"

Let's say it's her choice of restaurant. In that case John have to make some comment. But here the waters are choppy too. He can't seem too interested in the venue (she's the main point), but should be approving. Something bland like "I'm glad we got here before the rush" might fill the bill, addressing the situation rather than the place and suggesting that quiet is good because it allows me to hear what she has to say.

Soon, however, a "real" topic will have to be introduced, though the point of all the things said so far is precisely to see if the other person picks the same part of the spectrum. It can be too far out, making the other protest too much: for example if he says "I hope it wasn't too much bother coming out with me," he's kissed the evening goodbye. The presupposition has to be that the benefit will be hers, so if he indicates that the potential payoff for her is close to zero, or that it was a great condescension on her part to come out with him, he's selling himself too short. What he needs to be aiming at is: I'm *worth* making any sacrifice for, but I'd never *demand* it.

If she says, "I hope you can put up with my chatter" she's pitched her horseshoe much too far and makes him go and retrieve it. He can save this mistake by saying, "If you can put up with mine?"—which tries to turn it into a joke. This is about the only thing that could save such a response, because if it's serious—along the lines of her asking, "what is a gorgeous hunk like you doing with a waif like me?"—that's the end of the evening, and they might as well push the chairs back and get up now.

At this point there are many topics that can be introduced, all of which would work equally well. The most logical is to continue the "meeting" theme and ask, "Did you have a good day at work?" Of course he wouldn't ask it in these words, which sound too much like the rote question of a husband to a wife. Probably he'd try for something a bit more personable and without a situational meaning of this sort. Perhaps: "I hope you had a productive day?" He should if possible give a reason for asking such a relatively inane question. He could add: "I mean, with this gorgeous weather you might not have felt much like working." Or: "with this lousy weather you might not have felt much like working." Or: "It is Friday, after all." Or: "It is Monday, after all."

Here she could start with fact, and tailor its edges until it fits the hole left for it. "Pretty productive, thanks," she might say, but it can't be in the "and that's all there is" tone of voice usually used for a response like this. It has to be followed with something that links to what was asked before, or replaces it. Such as: "I got outside at lunch for a bit, so that helped." But then she needs to put some cards on the table. Once it's been decided she's going with the "beautiful day" theme she needs to say something like: "I frequently take my lunch out into McPherson Square to eat. That is, when I'm not snowed under by clients."

The "nice day" theme is probably played out at this point, so he should ask something about the clients. Perhaps: "I gather business is good these days?" if he knows what she does based on previous conversations, say on the phone. Or he could ask for more information: that's always legitimate if you admit ignorance with a smile. So he says: "You know, I'm not sure I quite understood from X [the person who set up the date] exactly what it is you do at Christie's. You're not the auctioneer, are you?"

"Yes," she might say, "that's just what I am." She should avoid saying "as a matter of fact, that's just what I am," because that suggests the next thing is going to be a feminist screed about how women can be auctioneers too, or perhaps, how could he have assumed she wouldn't be the auctioneer?—either one working an agenda he's not likely to have and that would put an end to the evening right there.

She might say, to minimize the damage, "I've only just become one, so I'm quite proud of myself. They don't have many women auctioneers. I'm only the second in the history of the firm." This says to him, "Your surprise is warranted," and provides the information without rapping his knuckles.

"Oh good," he might respond. "So I can get all the secrets of the trade from you. I've often wondered." Then he could try and carry on a bit: "I've never even been to an art auction. Is it like scenes in 1960s movies with Audrey Hepburn, everybody incredibly well-dressed? Or that scene in *North by Northwest*?" He's showing off his culture, but it's middle-brow culture, and it's about what she does, so that doesn't count as being a pain.

"Just like that," she might say, and smile. "Everybody just that well dressed, with pill-box hats and all!" She's really soaring here. "No," she might go on immediately. "No, not like that at all." And then she'll have to elaborate. He'll be already thinking of a hook-on, without knowing whether he'll still be able to use it once she has taken the conversation where she takes it: every addition is like adding another sentence to the story we're making up together. It's not clear he can use the sentence he had in mind once she's done adding hers.

What he has in mind is something that refers to the odd patter of non-high-art auctioneers, that reiterative patter of syllables that seems so difficult to learn and sounds like sing-song stuttering that resolves, abruptly, into "Sold to the man in the blue hat!"

Perhaps she does end it at a place where he can ask, kiddingly, "You don't have to do that funny auctioneer's patter, do you? I mean," he might add, "I know that's not high class like Christie's."

To get away with this comment ("high class like Christie's") he'd better be sitting there with a Rolex watch, that of course he doesn't refer to, and a nice Italian suit. Otherwise calling this "high class" sounds bitter, as if she has to answer for being something he's not.

But it may be that he can't use this comment. Maybe she's gone on to say something like, "Well, actually, I'm still just the assistant auctioneer—they've never let me do one on my own." Here it would seem as if he's not taking on board the comment about her personally if he sticks with a question about the patter, that she clearly in any case doesn't do. He'd be much better advised to hook something on to this last comment directly: "How long does this assistant business—is it a kind of apprenticeship?—last?" Or: "What does that mean exactly?"

By now the waitress should have come. Karen is in the middle of a sentence: John needs to keep his gaze on her until she finishes, at which point she, seeing the waitress, pauses and smiles blandly. She need not look at the waitress, but John does, and waits until Karen pauses until he does. He looks at the waitress with a smile a tad warmer than the bland "I recognize you as a fellow human being" smile but nowhere near the full luminescence he reserves for Karen, and goes into "we were expecting you, thanks for coming" territory. She will say something like, "Have you had a chance to look at the menu?" or "are you ready to order?" It would be Buñuelesque if, instead of taking something from this ball-park, the waitress instead said, "Do you know what the rice crop in China was last year?" If she did, he'd have to assume she wasn't crazy, but that it was a sophisticated gesture, and initially play along. "No," he'd say. "Do you?" Then he'd wait for the subject somehow to be led around to the menu.

What if she tried to discourage him from ordering something on the menu? Perhaps by saying, "I can't recommend you ordering the veal; you have no idea about what appalling conditions calves are raised under, and how cruel. They're tied etc." How would he react? The least aggressive response would be to say, "Are you a PETA activist?" She might say, "Yes." Then he might try for dry humor and ask, "Are you also a waitress?" If she said "Yes" he'd say "Fine, I'd like to order. I'll have the veal."

If she persisted, and was not disarmed by humor, dry or otherwise, a whole other range of options presents itself. He'd have to look at Karen to see how she was reacting—either smile at her conspiratorially or raise his eyebrows. Mostly his agenda is to get along with Karen, so he'd look for some sign that she wants him to turn this strange waitress off. If, on the other hand, Karen is supporting her, sitting rapt at her chutzpah, John should realize this was a no-win situation, and back off, acknowledging the evening a waste. Of course he might, instead of trying to deal with it as the male interface with a hostile world, simply throw it into Karen's lap. "What do you think of that?" he might ask her directly. Or he might limit himself to a "gee, what now?" face at her.

Derailing

Every moment of every interaction holds the potential for being the moment at which things take an odd course, just as every moment of a car journey can be the moment of an accident. We know what's likely, what we want to happen, but things can derail or change course at any moment. We consciously keep them on course.

The whole of this interaction, which in reality might have lasted five minutes from meeting up outside the restaurant to sitting at the table, presupposes that both people are anticipating reactions and keeping track of responses. So many things are such evident evening-killers, that if I were the man, I wouldn't even put them on the table before rejecting them. For example, saying "That dress makes you fat." Or "I can't believe you wore cowboy boots with that." Or "I think you ought to skip dessert."

The closest I might come to any of these is the second, and it might in fact be pitched as the opposite of what I think: "I think cowboy boots look really neat with that." Or "did you get those great boots in Nashville?" It's not really a compliment so much as something to elicit a response that I can use as further conversational fodder. If she gets cute and says, "Yeah, I know they look goofy but I was trying to get creative. Too creative?" To this I'd have to say, "Not at all," but in any case I've gotten the information I really wanted, namely, does she realize how inappropriate if funky the boots are with this dress? She does, and she's trying to be wild and crazy. Because she admits it, and I'm the reason she wanted to be wild and crazy, I can only take both of these things as positive.

Just as, according to the saying, it's an ill wind that fails to blow someone some good, it's an inept person who can't turn every weakness into a strength— if not for one's self, then for another. If I'm John and tongue-tied, I say, "I'm so sorry, I seem to be tongue-tied tonight, and I know it's a cliché, but you're the reason." I don't think I could get away with it without the admission inside the admission (I know it's a cliché). If I trip on the way to the table, I'd have to say, "My mother always did say I was a klutz, but usually I can stand upright," and widen my eyes on the "can" without flapping my hands or looking unmasculine: the idea is to be boyish without also being incompetent.

The mistake of any analysis, linguistic or not, is to believe we have access to the world that produced the line-up of dominoes that actually end up being laid on the table. We don't. We can move backwards from any particular pattern to explain why it works, or does not. But we cannot stop things in their tracks and use analysis to get us to the next domino.

We have the impression we can, because sometimes we hesitate before placing the next one, making the next comment: is this too evidently a leading question, or should I chance it? But we don't do this all the time, and even so in this moment we've failed to consider a million other factors that, had circumstances been different, might have been the object of our consideration. Because we foreground one criterion of analysis in one moment and another in another does not mean both were present at both moments.

Generally, what the male wants to project on a blind date is: not scary but very competent, not pushy but sure of himself, very interested in the woman but with a healthy self-esteem, able to handle the world without belittling it or being afraid of it. At any moment the things we say or do (including widening eyes, holding gaze, letting eyes linger a tad longer than absolutely necessary on the pair of stocking-clad legs the date is stretching out before him, clearly for him to notice—who tells him how much constitutes admiration and when to cut it off so it doesn't move into the inappropriate?) are chosen with this overarching goal. But not necessarily with this goal in mind: just things that, added to the dominoes on the table, continue the row in a plausible fashion.

The protocol on a blind date for the man is: pay attention, keep bringing the conversation back to her without making it seem you're avoiding answering her questions about you or hiding things, give her ways to shine without being evident. A perfectly attuned woman will be someone who responds in a way that shows she correctly identifies the move. Let's say I'm the man. I'm feeling naughty and throw a compliment that's too fulsome just to see if she'll identify it as such. If she grins conspiratorially and says, "Gee, I must be doing really well to get a compliment like that!" all I can say, admiringly, is "you are!" It acknowledges that the compliment was off-base, and compliments her for labeling it correctly.

But every rule has an exception. A rule might be: Don't stare too long at her breasts, don't go into how beautiful she is. But, ten minutes into the evening, if the conversation hits a lull, I could very well say, looking directly at her: "You have really fantastic legs." I know I'm not supposed to play this card, yet I'm doing it. That's the kind of thing that might just work.

All this presupposes that the man want to get along with the woman, which in turn probably presupposes he finds her attractive. But since it's a blind date, the man could find the woman not like her online picture(s) and very unattractive—or perhaps like it, and still not for him. She can say all the right things and still have the evening be a disaster. Words are part of a larger whole, which means we'll never articulate the whole. The world is, indeed, as Wittgenstein pointed out, mysterious: we can never say what allows us to say what it is we say. So we should stop trying.

Chapter Seven

The Great Chess Game of Life

IN REAL LIFE, WE DON'T SEE THINGS FROM without and with the pretense of controlling them, as in the academic situation, but from within. We don't separate out words from other options of action, and the things we're involved in determine our reactions. Most of the time, we live our lives as if we were one of the chess pieces that imagine themselves, in their own movement patterns, masters of their fate: the job of the other pieces is to be true to what's expected. And that means, divergences from what's expected produces friction. If the knight failed to move two up and one over, the other pieces would be puzzled, perhaps extremely so. If the pawn suddenly moved more than a square at a time, these other pieces would undoubtedly be outraged. Occasionally, however, we become the person moving the pieces, aware of our own reactions and the fact that they are determined by what we expect to happen: were the rules we have so laboriously learned simply different, our reactions wouldn't be at all the same. The period (which may be perhaps quite a long one indeed) before we explain the variation from what we're expecting is the moment of disconnect, where we sense only the grinding of the gears. During this time, we are conscious only of the sense that the knight isn't moving correctly. Most of our emotions of outrage, puzzlement, and hurt are produced by the sense under such circumstances that the world is out of joint. When we feel satisfaction, by contrast, it is because others see the same situation we see: the pieces are moving "correctly," which is to say, as we've learned they should move. Conflict is the result of different understandings of the lay of the land, expressed by different formulae of interaction; a sense of belonging is a result of seeing things the same way as others.

To be annoyed or not to be?

At one point recently, my wife and I had a colleague and his fiancée over for dinner. I realized with a start a week or so before that I had semi-invited him at a department get-together recently when he told me he was getting married and that his fiancée had moved down from New York. If left un-followed-up, this became one of those numerous "oh, we have to get together some time" vaguenesses that serves as a way of saying goodbye in an amiable fashion. But since the ostensible occasion was a wedding, leaving it at that was more impolite than it should have been, saying that even something as special as this could be treated in so cavalier a fashion.

Luckily, though two months had passed, these were toward the end of the semester, and I had been away. So I could plausibly plead end of semester crush. I did so, and after consultation with my wife, sent some specific dates to choose from. None worked, I suggested he give me dates, one of these worked, they came.

I was preparing the dinner alone, with two little boys milling around. The guests were almost an hour late, though I had outlined the "little boys" factor and emphasized that we would eat catch-as-catch-can while dealing with them. They claimed that this was part of the attraction, and in effect signed off on it. I was initially furious—to keep two little boys at bay, already late for their dinner, while first one phone call and then another came, was no mean feat. They were late to begin with, and then took a wrong turning. The first call for directions assured me they were within two minutes of the house by my directions; it turned out they had turned in a completely wrong direction and the blinking light the colleague was describing, which both of us thought the blinking light at our corner, was miles away.

Finally I went ahead and fed the boys. Meanwhile my wife too was late, and I was furious—but at what or whom? It seemed unlikely the guests understood the strain of having to make children wait for their dinner while preparing adult food. Or perhaps they assumed I'd intended all along to feed the boys first? Or that my wife would be there to do that? What they don't know and can't reasonably assume can't be held against them. Still, after all that discussion about children, to be an hour late seemed really bad. Not all of this lateness was unavoidable either; the man thought he knew where he was going and had left my directions at home, so that he ended up combining in his head elements of two ways to come I'd given him (probably a bad idea on my part). And he thought he was going south when he was going north—surely something I could assume he wouldn't think given that his main connector had been going west. To go south you turn left, to go north you turn right. It's that easy.

My wife arrived first, apologetic at being late herself. I agreed that it had left me in a hell of a mess, but the guests were even later, and apparently lost for unjustifiable reasons. "Remind me never ever to invite anybody for dinner ever again," I said, largely to have got rid of some of my resentment.

At this point the little boys were slipping their moorings and milling around Mommy, but at least they had some dinner inside them, and I could continue setting things out for the guests. And soon the doorbell was ringing.

How to react? Surely not with, "I can't believe how late you are." The presupposition is that the guests would be hastening to apologize profusely.

They apologized, but not profusely. This re-awakened my first sense that they had no idea what it meant for them to be an hour late with a host preparing dinner alone with two small children.

And I? I was gracious, which is to say nicer than the situation warrented: after all I had to get through the evening. I said something like, "Meg just got home so your timing was perfect." That isn't what I was thinking.

After a few minutes of appetizers I allowed myself to say, "I'm going to have to ask you to take seats already so the food isn't completely dried out." It was the closest I could allow myself to referring to the lateness.

Dinner went fine; the little boys, running around rather than, as planned, sitting in their seats eating with us, weren't too intrusive. In fact we made it through dessert, at which point my wife offered to put them to bed—something that wouldn't have been necessary so soon after eating if everyone had been on time. And the evening didn't go on too long; the fiancée was a bit flu-y—in fact the husband-to-be had left a message earlier in the day to say she wasn't feeling well but they were assuming she'd rally, just wanted to let us know in case things took a turn for the worse, did I want to call it off to keep her away from the kids? I said it sounded as if she was over the worst, and in any case the kids wouldn't plaster themselves on her if she didn't invite them to do so, but of course they should make the decision based solely on how she felt (the ball-park message I wanted to convey was: this is about your comfort, not mine). I really didn't think there was any danger for the boys, and I'd gone to the store especially to get things to eat—besides, it looked as if alternative dates were few and far between. Better just to do it.

They left therefore at an appropriate time. I still felt that their reaction to the lateness had not been theatrical/apologetic enough, which suggested that they didn't understand the difference between being an hour late for dinner with adults (bad enough already) and being an hour late for dinner for a man juggling two small children. So I allowed myself a joke, or perhaps "joke" about which direction to turn on exiting the driveway: "since there's some suggestion that you're direction-challenged!" (such a statement is only possible if delivered as an exaggerated joke—if you say it straight it becomes nasty, not to mention petty). The colleague reacted appropriately, and good-byes were warm.

The next day I got an e-mail of thanks, saying what a wonderful time it had been, how nice it was to spend time with my wife, and how charming the children were—with hopes that they hadn't gotten them too wound up. (They had, and I had also made a theatrical statement of blaming them for doing so: since having children react positively to guests, which leads to the children being wound up, is a good thing, I could do this without being too negative.) To this message, I expressed my lingering annoyance (is this what it was?) by not responding—this was one of those gray-area moments where a response would have been possible but was far from necessary.

A few days later I saw him in the hall. "I just wanted to say again what a lovely time we had," he began. And though I was on my way out the door, I was appreciative enough of his saying something in addition to the e-mail that we chatted a bit.

So all in all, he and I did see the same set of realities: the one divergence was this issue of lateness with children, which I decided to ascribe to ignorance. In the larger scheme of things, however, this was made up for by all the correct perceptions. However there is no point having social interaction with people who don't have enough correct perceptions to make up for the occasional incorrect ones that might creep in. I stopped inviting students years ago, even before a wife and new family made it impractical. They never seemed to understand that I'd spent all day working on, say, the spaghetti sauce and that they couldn't treat my table like King Hall, the Naval Academy dining hall where they come in, sit, ingest, and leave. Only rarely would I get even one person out of the group writing a note after the fact to say "thank you," and when at table they would continue their USNA gossip to which I wasn't privy, as if I wasn't there.

I'm a chess piece within this game, so I can tell how much is not enough, as well as how much is too much. But how could I justify to someone who wasn't a piece within this game that though once verbal "thank you" after the fact from my guest was thoughtful and appropriate, a second one the next day would be too much unless explained away? Perhaps he could get away with another compliment if he emphasized how odd it was: "You won't believe this, but we're still talking about the salmon." Or "I know you won't be insulted to hear yet again how utterly charming your children are." But it's not clear that anything more can be wrung out of this except a smile and affability in the hall. How to explain to a Martian that this is about as far as it goes, that more would be dipping down into negatives?

Joke's over

Sometimes we do meet people who don't seem to realize when the joke's over, as we say—when you can't keep harping on the same topic.

People with any degree of autism, such as my daughter, are unable to say what is too much—are in a sense the equivalent of Martians, to whom everything must be explained, and who do not understand that once is mandatory, twice is thoughtful, but three times is strange. And even this isn't always the case: there are always exceptions. Even now, in her teen-aged years, she will sulk for hours about some small imaginary slight from me or my mother, though usually my mother will have driven two hours one way to be with her. Grandma didn't do X or Y, she'll wail, and nothing can bring her out of her funk. She just doesn't "get" that this small insufficiency is minimal and cannot be allowed to determine her view of the whole the day. Family activities usually involve me spending at least half the time allotted for their completion trying to talk her out of her mood, with the result that the activity itself is invariably ruined. Because of her autism, she can't put herself in another's place, so she doesn't know what the parameters of interaction are. Hence she can't appreciate divergences from it, or play the elaborate game of under-offering to make a point, or over-offering to be gracious. She's surrounded by the events and can't order them. A friend of mine who barely knows her goes out of her way to send her a present: she barely registers it, and doesn't realize that the friend needn't have bothered at all.

When she was younger she mis-used words and body-language gestures. For a day or two she'd come into the room and make the quick intake of breath we use when something is amiss, or when we burn ourselves slightly on the stove. After the second time I realized she simply was using it because she'd heard it, not because she'd understood it. So I told her, "Sweetheart, we only make that sound when there's something really wrong." She stopped using it. She'd do the same with words too, and with phrases—they were frequently just off center of where they should be. Even now with interactions there's something blurry about them: she's too sugary with her younger half-brother, too martial with the older one, or reacts to a minor incident as if it were a major one. Seeing her interact with the world is like looking at a badly-printed newspaper photograph, with the colors not quite lined up.

There's no rule book that says, thanking your host verbally in addition to the e-mail is thoughtful, but beyond that it becomes tiresome. Except when it isn't. And then we have to flag the exception to the rule: usually that lets us get away with it. Rather than merely setting autistic people aside as defective or exceptions to the rules (the fact is, there are no rules, except the ones we articulate after the fact, when we note that someone has made a mistake), we could learn from them about the vast areas where most of us don't steer our boats, guided almost unerringly by instinct. The least socially aware "normal" person is much better at keeping on the chart than most autistic people. To keep them on track, we are reduced to showing them what to do: we can rarely explain why this is so.

The world that the autistic reveal to us is the world we're only rarely conscious of. Those who live with the autistic aren't outraged at seeing others off the track, making movements that seem inappropriate to their chess piece: the probability of getting off track is so high, after all, as there's so much on the chart that isn't the path. And in fact, there's no chart at all.

Gray areas

Sometimes it's not so clear what the expectations are, not even to me. Indeed, the number of clear-cut cases is relatively small; the reason we fail to be overwhelmed by the gray areas is simply that we've learned to steer clear of them. Yet they're there, lurking for us. People don't seem aware that gray is also a possible color: the advice columns are full of letters by people who seem to be unaware that it's not so odd to not know what to do. In such a case you identify the closest possible rule, and go with that. Or not: being in the smack-dab middle is possible too, and in that case we merely choose. Either one is as justifiable as the other.

A man gets to the water fountain at the gym where I'm headed to get a mouthful of water: in the gym you typically don't drink and drink—most people feel sick with too much water, so a quick gulp is the rule. The expectation is of quick in and quick out. But this man has a water bottle in his hand, and proceeds to fill the whole bottle, though he's aware of my presence. At first I stand several steps behind him until I understand what he's doing, then stay there a moment longer to send the message that someone is waiting and he's doing something outside the norm, especially in an environment where people need quick drinks after exercise and waiting is a hardship. He doesn't get it, so I abandon the project, and go over to another machine where I stretch, pretending that I don't really want to get a drink at all. Clearly he sees no reason to pay the slightest bit of attention to me. If I'd been the one with the water bottle, I'd have broken off and let the man waiting get his gulp.

How about my making a comment? Too much trouble, as clearly he wouldn't even process the point. It would lead to an argument. I could say: "Hey buddy, don't you think you're being selfish filling a whole bottle while someone is waiting, especially given that the fountain is more typically used for short drinks and people here usually need it badly when they come up for water?" But inevitably, this would lead to nastiness. If I went for low-key, as in "Hey buddy, mind if I jump in here?" he'd undoubtedly think me pushy.

In fact, this is arguably a case where neither perception would clearly win a majority of votes if a jury had to say who was in the right. There are, after all, other fountains nearby, in fact another perhaps twenty paces further. And filling bottles is arguably a legitimate function of fountains in the gym. Is this perhaps more akin to the situation in the line at the bank where you can roll your eyes mentally at the fact that someone's business is taking so long, but have no real justification for feeling miffed?

Letters to advice columnists are generally from people who sense that they are simply unable to "call" a situation, though they do not lack the capability of identifying with another person, as my daughter does. Their pathos lies in the fact that they don't see the situation objectively, as we say: either they are looking for justification of something they've already done, or simply don't know how to take the first step to solve their problem because they can't describe the state of affairs. It's the (for them) odd thought that there *are* gray areas that's stopping them. They don't know that what you do to solve your own problems is hook your gray-area situation to the closest black and white.

Here's one such letter: a friend of the writer has lived rent-free in the house since the room was offered her when she had to leave her abusive husband. Now the family needs the room, it's been a year, the roomer is showing no signs of leaving, fails to contribute in any way—what to do? The question at issue is this: At what point does generosity become masochism? The point is, we know it when it is. After a month or two there would be an area where the house-owner might want to say something and not. The period would be lengthened if the roomer showed any consciousness of the burden she was inflicting. But even daily protestations of gratitude could become hollow after a time.

We'd have to be aware of all the circumstances and factors at work here; even so there's no rule book that says, as of this day it's crossed a line. You know it, or don't know it. The pathos of advice columns is that of people apparently as at sea as the autistic, looking for a rule-book answer.

The most astonishing such letters are from people who are simply missing any objectivity about the way the rest of the world will see what they do: the writer who is expecting to be praised and instead is lambasted. One was from a sweet-sounding woman who wanted to make the gay couple who lived down the street welcome: she sent them food, complimented them on their roses, which they distributed throughout the neighborhood, and was glad to see how nicely they kept up their house. One day, however, they kissed each other goodbye on the way to work. Publicly (she spells out in her letter) as she was passing! The woman recounts how, immediately, she wrote a letter addressed to them, asking them to please for heaven's sake cease and desist with such public displays of affection; she circulated it in the neighborhood, got many signatures, and sent it to the couple.

None of this, the surprised reader learns, was the reason for her writing to the columnist. She was writing to express her surprise and anguish that all of a sudden the pleasantries from the couple had stopped, the roses were no longer shared, and the couple looked the other way when she passed, no longer saying so much as "good morning." The amazing thing about the letter was that there was no consciousness on this woman's part that she might be at fault; her only concern was that there be a happy neighborhood. What was she to do to get it back? Why were they acting so strangely?

The advice columnist let her have it, saying what to most of us is obvious: that the woman was lucky the couple had limited signs of their outrage to merely snubbing her and refusing to give her roses. She herself had—of course, the reader is thinking—acted outrageously, and there was no way she could get herself out of this one.

The people who judge a situation, as we say, wrong, are themselves in the position of the chess pieces puzzled or outraged by the actions of another chess piece. In some cases, we'd say they're wrong to say others are wrong. In some cases it's not clear (is bottle-filling in the gym kosher or not?). All are within the trees of the forest trying to figure out the way out: they can get it wrong.

Under control

Sometimes the misreadings of the situation are ones we think we have under control: students being disrespectful to me, for example, are something I usually don't worry about. Sometimes we're not in control, but there's nothing we can do about it. For example, what of people on the street who want to ask for directions or information but don't seem to be aware that their doing so is an intrusion on privacy that has to be addressed? The way are supposed to ask for directions is to prepare the person we're going to accost by looking at a watch or a map, then saying "Excuse me, but." Increasing numbers of people, especially in specific socio-economic classes, fail to note that fact of intrusion. They simply begin, "Hey, can you tell me where the mall is?" or worse, "Where's the mall?" There's no point in addressing what seems the impoliteness of the way of asking; we're alone with this person and he'll never see what's wrong with the way he's asked the question. Many times what seem misperceptions on the part of the other person are not things we can themselves address. We have to implicitly accept their view of things, respond simply by answering the question, and stifle our frustration that someone would ask the question in this manner. It's something we have to walk away from: there's no resolution possible.

Other me-against-you situations are important to us and there's equally nothing we can do about them: we think, for example, that something we've written is important. Another person doesn't. There's no argument possible, so we simply say "thank you" and head for the door. The same thing is true of a sexual relationship not quite on track. We know what we want; perhaps we can even articulate it. But if the divergence between what we want and what we get is great enough, it's not likely that divergence will ever be successfully addressed. There's no way to change the other person; once again we simply have to head to the door.

But perhaps as many human interactions fail to go correctly as do go correctly: or would, if we got out of the ruts we stay in precisely in order that we not have these to deal with. We keep to the people we know, keep to the people of our own group. Usually that ensures that difficulties are kept to a minimum. But who can say how many jolts against the world we've have if we did get out of our own world?

We have enough staying in it. Just as, for Freud, slips of the tongue, dreams, and jokes seemed like keys to the fact that things weren't as neatly ordered as we'd been told, so too all the "one chess piece thinks the other is making a mistake" situations that themselves have to be acknowledged and rectified if we're to move on (though we need not) and that become the subject matter of other interactions—make clear that we constantly put together the world at every moment. It can go horribly wrong, careen off into uncharted territory. We are most likely to articulate the structure of what is by way of explaining what went wrong: this is the use of any explanation system. When things go right, we need not get out of the rut of the moment to put things in context.

The fissures and cracks at the edges of the high road show us that human interaction, and language, are not self-enclosed systems of signs. We can never know all the things that can happen, nor can we ever list all the possible ways to deal with the unknown—and this by definition. People are always pulling articulation from the void to deal with something they weren't waiting for. As for example here:

Pool

Finished with my weight workout, I head to the pool. In half the pool the old ladies' aerobics workout is about to start. They have moved the floats out of this area to clear it out. There are three lanes over on the right. In one of them is a beach-ball shaped older man wearing on his hands black webs, so he looks like an upside-down wrong-colored duck. He has both arms extended in a sort of backstroke, and takes up the whole lane. In another lane is a young woman, obviously a real swimmer—she has a float between her legs and flips expertly at the wall. And in the far right lane two middle-aged women, one overweight, one not, sit at the other end with their feet in the water. Clearly they are about to get in, so I turn my attention again to the female real swimmer.

Usually a new arrival has to negotiate the issue of circle-swimming vs. sides. I can see that she has already opted for circle-swimming, so I figure I don't need her permission. I get in when she's at the other end and begin my laps—an add-on to the real workout in the weight room. The woman is faster than I am. It would be better if I could use the vacant lane. And after a lap or two I am aware at turn-around that the two pairs of female legs are still dangling into the water in the far lane. I wonder when they are going to get in. Ten minutes later the legs are still dangling, and I begin to get irritated—the woman has to go around me, I take a mouthful of water every time we cross: if no one is using this far lane, I could be doing so. I begin to lose my concentration so that at the turn-around I am not fast enough to make the other half of the circle swim and the young woman and I collide.

"Do you want to circle-swim or shall we do sides?" she asks quite pleasantly. I give her credit for not lambasting me. She could see as well as I that we were doing circle-swim, but it's nice of her to pretend there was simply a mix-up or an issue that had to be ironed out.

"I'm sorry," I say. "We were circle-swimming. I got distracted." And now I turn over to the two women, still dangling their legs in the pool. "Ma'am," I say—I'm more likely to say "Ma'am" when I'm irritated—"I assumed you were getting in or I'd be swimming in that lane."

"We are getting in," says the thinner one.

"But it's been ten minutes," I say. "You can't just reserve a lane like that."

"There's nobody in the next lane over," the other points out reasonably.

Sure enough, the upside-down duck man is gone. "Yes," I say, exasperated that she's right, "but there was. Otherwise I'd be in your lane."

I'd squelched the impulse to say something to these women before but my collision has made me willing to talk. And clearly they still see nothing wrong with sitting there nonchalantly dangling their legs in the lane when in fact they have no intention of using it, or plan to use it at their leisure. What did they think when they saw me come in, hesitate, and then double up with the serious woman swimmer? That I wanted to share, given the choice?

The horrible truth, I realize as I simply swim the floats and go over to the duck-man's lane, accepting for the millionth time defeat, is that they probably didn't think at all. I'm sure they're perfectly nice people, these women. Perhaps they aren't used to serious swimmers? There are after all so few at this gym, the commercial one I sometimes use. I just don't think they understood how rude they're being. And in fact fifteen minutes later there they sit, chatting away, their legs dangling in the water.

Another pool

Sometimes things wobble even more wildly on their tracks, even derailing and having to be set back upright. It was lunchtime swim at the Naval Academy pool. All the lanes had someone in them; in fact all but one had two. They were long lanes, so if I wanted to be polite I had to wait quite some time before I could flag down the person in the lane to ask, in a formulaic fashion, "Okay if we split this lane?" The person would never say "no," of course. The only thing to be negotiated was whether we could do "sides," which I prefer, rather than "circle swim."

I went to the lane with one person in it, a woman swimming in the center of the lane, on the line: I immediately noted this as impolite, as if she were trying to mark out the whole lane for herself. I did note that she was a somewhat lumbering swimmer, but this alone meant nothing in particular. I waited patiently for her to come to the end of the lap, however, given that she was hogging the lane.

She seemed singled-minded, and looked as if she was trying to ignore me: for this, she got another point taken off—she has to be aware that people will be wanting to come in, and not trying to freeze them out by pretending not to notice them. But I nonetheless yelled out, somewhat annoyed, "Do you mind if I jump in here?" "No," she shouted, before semi-submerging again and lumbering away.

So I did jump in. I was close to her, staying on my side, when I thought I heard her blubbering "No" once again—I couldn't make it make any sense.

Perhaps she thought I hadn't heard her? In any case not having me in the lane wasn't an option, so I pressed on.

When I got to the other end I saw two much fitter looking women squatting by the side of the pool. The first began to speak sharply to me. "We've got a PRT [physical readiness test, given twice yearly to midshipmen and officers] so can you move out of this lane over one?" I didn't like her tone of voice. Neither, apparently, did the other woman. "It's not your fault," she began saying as the other woman was finishing. "Look," I said, treading water and sputtering, "I asked if she minded if I shared the lane. She said no." Besides, I wanted to add, the PRT was last week. You can't expect anybody to know there's one now, especially not if there's no indication at the end where everybody gets in (this end was right next to a wall) that it's a protected area. But both women by this time had begun yelling encouragement at the lumbering swimmer, churning forward towards us. "You can do it," they yelled. "Come on. Don't mind him."

By this point the hapless swimmer was sputtering, beside herself with fury. "I said 'no' over and over," she yelled with water spewing out of her mouth. I was beginning to feel a wave of pity for this bad swimmer, obviously (now) taking a remedial test. But still I was incensed.

"You didn't listen to my question," I said. "I said 'Do you mind if I jump in?' and you said 'no.'"

She was by now hanging on to the side, shrieking: "How could I hear?" she wailed. "My head was underwater."

"It's not your fault," the second woman was saying to me.

I was furious, though now I understood the situation. "Nobody could have known this was a PRT," I said. "Your swimmer is way out of line."

I wasn't quite sure how severe to be. I couldn't tell if she was a midshipman, who should be dealt severely with, or an officer somehow inept in the water, to whom one could show mercy. In any case it was clear that she was at the end of her tether, and trying to get a test done for time. The better part of valor was simply to move. So I did. But as I swam I thought, furiously: "If they wanted to protect a lane they needed to have somebody at the end where people come in."

I looked to see if they were still there when I was done swimming, the better to give them a piece of my mind. But I didn't, because they weren't. Of course, in my mind, I was right and they were wrong: having a makeup PRT a week off the norm, with nobody to say, "I wonder if we can use this lane for just a little longer"—i.e. to acknowledge that the situation and request were abnormal—they could not expect someone to avoid their single unprotected swimmer. Even if the form of my question had not, perhaps by chance, allowed a negative answer, few people would have been able to process someone shouting "No" in such a strange fashion. Among other things, the fact of her being such a bad swimmer was anomalous for this pool: the people here tend to be serious. It took a while to sort things out and to ascribe responsibility: I think most fundamentally it lay with the two women administering the test. How could they expect people to avoid a lane with no one to protect it, or to acknowledge that protecting it was an anomaly that needed to be explained? During this time I couldn't see the pieces on the board as if from above: I was one of the pieces.

The necessity of the generic

Those who can't move up to the level of the generic are condemned to the endless strife of ignorant armies clashing by night that is the situation of being yoked to the particular. By the same token, someone who can't give up the generic for the particular can't get through life. We all move in this direction too. We dream about marrying "someone." Can we give up "someone" for a particular person? We think about the children we might have. Can we accept the particular ones we get?

Getting through life means accepting that we have to give up the dream for the reality, which here means giving up the generic for the specific. Or one plausible specific for another. We may postulate a brilliant child when we look at the baby cooing in our face; how will we deal with the reality of, for instance, a learning-disabled child who will turn into a difficult adult? We have no chance of, as the psychologists say, adapting, if we are unable simply to replace one reality with another.

Sometimes we can move to, as we might say, another level in understanding reactions. I learned long ago not to react to my daughter's mistakes the way I would if a colleague did them, trying to puzzle out the meaning I couldn't see. In her case, I know simply that they are wrong, and say so immediately, kindly but firmly, to show her. We can "re-classify" other reactions too.

Istanbul

The taxi deposits me at my hotel in Istanbul. I shower and walk up the street towards the Blue Mosque. Scarcely am I on the street between the Blue Mosque and Hagia Sophia than a young man is coming towards me, his face lighting up. "Hello," he says. "Where are you from?" I tell him. Then it comes: "I have carpets to sell," he assures me. "You want to buy a carpet?" "No," I say. He's not daunted. "Just look," he says. "Just look." "No," I say.

I go twenty paces. Another young man is making a bee-line towards me. I look away. "Where are you from?" he asks. This time I merely smile and keep going. Perhaps I don't understand English. If you don't interact with them, they can't get traction.

On the way to Hagia Sophia I am accosted at least four more times. The next time, it's not "Where are you from?," it's "What time is it?"

I'm not ready for this one, so the first time I give the time and keep walking. I must have been too fast for my questioner. The second time it happens, however, the next one isn't going to let go. He too wants to sell me carpets. I am more snappish: "You asked the time," I say. "I told you. Goodbye."

They're all using our honor against us, I think, reverting to a midshipman concept. Midshipmen are supposed to tell the truth. For this reason you can't try to trap them, ask them something you are pretty sure they'll have to lie about. It's an interesting concept, and one that makes clear that specific nature of the injunction against lying.

Someone in a foreign country where we're trying to get along, as most Westerners are—conscious as we are that they may think we're looking down at them from our rich perspective—will hesitate to brush off someone who seems friendly. These touts all use the guise of friendliness. To respond to the question "Where are you from?" as if it were not a real question requires processing it at another level, translating it not as "Where are you from?" but rather as "this person wants an excuse to stop me so he can try to sell me something."

At about the tenth insistent man, I just keep walking. "Oh," he calls out after me, "you are very angry with me." It's a last-ditch effort to engage me personally. I still keep walking.

Later I am sitting in a park. A man selling sweets comes up. I look away. He begins the usual way. "Where are you from?" Since I'm at a disadvantage, being stationary and a prisoner of my desire not to be driven away, I simply look disgusted and say, "England." (This isn't so; but it's a hollow victory.) Any answer, of course, would be just as bad: he has an answer for everything. "Manchester United," the young man tells me. "Yes," I say. Then I hear something new: "Do you have any English coins for my coin collection?" he asks. "No," I say. Still he doesn't give up. "I have coins from many countries," he insists. I make as if to leave and, surprisingly, he backs off, taking his bags of sweets to the benches on the other side of the dusty little square.

Don't they realize that this faux friendliness, to which the foreigner initially feels obligated to respond, is quickly re-processed after the second or at most third time to mean, to us: "They've seen a Westerner coming down the street and want to sell me something"? Don't they understand that such pickup lines can't be used by as many people as use them here and still retain their effectiveness? Don't they realize how self-defeating the ploy ultimate is? Or do they simply have such an inexhaustible stream of people who haven't yet figured things out—say from cruise ships docked across the Golden Horn at Beyoglu that these tactics work often enough to be worthwhile?

But the first time, I imagine everyone is taken in; everyone has the genuine desire to respond to this line as we would respond in a world where our mere appearance didn't mean we were the figure of attention we become here.

Certainly the first time I too said "USA," only to hear, "good USA, you want to buy a carpet?" And the "what time is it?" line—of course the same cheap Chinese watches are available on the streets of Istanbul as everywhere; no one need be without a watch, and those who sell carpets to tourists can probably afford the real thing, not just the Chinese fakes—only works because it's used so rarely back home. Still, the first time I thought it was what we would call a "real" question, and I answered it as such. The second time I was disgusted but not yet completely resistant, and merely pulled back my sleeve and showed my wrist. The third time I merely smiled wanly, a cross between "I don't understand" and "you surely don't think I'm going to fall for that one."

Once we have re-assigned these interactions from specific to general, we file these interactions in a different place: they come to be only the interchangeable phrases with which foreigners with money in their pockets can be approached in order to sell them something. But in the vertiginous moment between slots in the filing system, we sense the gears grinding within ourselves: something is not right.

Later the next day I am drifting, caught by the breathtaking sight of the setting sun illuminating the multifarious surfaces of the Blue Mosque. A young man breaks my reverie. "That is the Blue Mosque," he informs me. "Very famous. You can visit. I will show you." It sounds altruistic, but I know by now it isn't. Besides, I've been in Istanbul two days, visited the Blue Mosque already—breathtaking, in the dark of night with the suspended lights hovering over the carpeted floor where a few women with head scarves and their male protector walked, the famous blue-tinged tiles pulsating on the walls—and walked many times between these two great religious structures. Part of me was insulted: How dare he assume that I didn't know this was the Blue Mosque? But then I re-adjusted: this was part of the "let me explain my city to you" pose that apparently worked well enough with foreigners. For each tout, I was a fresh face. Somehow they had failed to add up the fact that on each block there were at least five, and draw the conclusion that I would be less than enthusiastic about being forthcoming after the first couple of them on the first day. Or perhaps they knew this, but knew that their chances of hitting someone who was new on his or her first day were good enough to justify any amount of annoyance on the part of those who didn't fit this bill.

The sense of annoyance, the notion that I'd paid my money and come to this place, now couldn't they leave me alone? is what I'm focusing on here. It's the moment of dissonance, where the gears clash, where things simply aren't the way they're supposed to be. Why are these people bothering me? I vahnt to be alone.

In such moments we cannot re-configure to a different level, seeing the question, "What time is it?" or "Where are you from?" not as meaning "What time is it?" but instead as meaning "This is the prelude to me asking you to buy a carpet." We're still caught in the sense of outrage: What does this person think he's doing? We react as the chess pieces we are, moving in a certain pattern that we're only aware of in many cases when it's challenged, or when other pieces don't move in the way we expect them to. Articulation only occurs when we have to re-negotiate our moves or understand something we weren't expecting. This is the reason that no amount of articulation can itself explain the world, or be primary: articulation is always a response to a specific situation, even when it's offered as the articulation of something primordial.

Chapter Eight

What's Left?

THERE ARE GOOD REASONS FOR TAKING courses in literature. Most of us find it very difficult to clear space to read things we may have always wanted to read. In a classroom situation, we're typically paying money, we have agreed to come to class several times a week, we regard it as a box to check, something we'll do because it's now officially part of our lives. The biggest problem with art, in fact, is that it doesn't typically have such a socially-defined place in our lives. The classroom gives it this place. We don't get "credit" from the world for reading Tolstoy on our own, unless we can somehow use it to gain points socially: I'm reading Tolstoy and you're not. This is also the source of the power of art: we don't have to defend ourselves against it. We needn't allow it access, and this is a very simple thing to ensure. What those who never allow art access fail to understand, therefore, is precisely the fact that it doesn't demand entry but is offered entry: if offered entry, it can change us forever.

Another reason for classes about literature is, most of us are attracted to the warmth of a social situation: if somebody expects us to read these pages, namely the professor, we'll do it. If we're trying to hold up our end of things with other people, the other students, that's another reason for doing it. Or: we're interested enough in the literature to want to read it, but perhaps not interested enough to do it without any social approbation, on our own.

Students who chafe at the fact of the social situation, the fact that what they are getting is by definition prepared food rather than groceries, will not be pleased in a classroom situation. I know: I was one of them.

Limited situation

What is an ideal professor? Someone with no axe to grind. If we offer our view of Mt. Fuji, or eliminate Mt. Fuji altogether, ramming that view down people's throats, it's not likely too many people will swallow. If we think that people have to agree with us right here, right now, we're probably not going to get many takers. Paradoxically, if we accept that we are part of a limited situation with limited access to people who themselves are at a precise and hence limited place in their lives, we can potentially do something with a bigger effect. We cease to push a bill of goods on others, accepting that what we're doing is teaching a class—nothing more and, by extension, nothing less.

What's most fundamental in the classroom is the intersection of the individual student with the work. And that's the thing that can never be codified. We can't say whether, or how, an individual reader will react to a work. This is frustrating to those who want the predictability of quasi-scientific literary "study." We can accept such an uncodifiable situation more readily if we understand that most of life is like that: we live first and articulate second.

Foucault is right

The classroom itself is just such a power podium as, influenced by Foucault, professors have for decades been telling us for decades that writing is. Most students have indelible memories of having simply to "find out what the professor wants and give it to him/her" (as company officers at the US Naval Academy, tell my students, their company members), or of having to fake it under the power of the grade.

I certainly do. My worst memory of this sort was as a college freshman in the honors program of my state university, from which I subsequently transferred. The course, a sophomore course, consisted of three separate mini-courses, each in the complete control of another teacher. One of the courses was taught by a visiting Tanzanian. The course was in social philosophy; his segment was a glowing euology of the works of his country's then-president, Julius Nyerere, whose forcing of peasants into collectivized agricultural villages is now almost universally recognized as one of the Great Leaps Backward of modern times, which further impoverished his already poor nation for decades. The texts were theories of President Nyerere, then as now respected for being an honorable man. They had some pretension to academic rigor because having been published by Oxford University Press (I can see them now, with the Oxford sign on the spine). Besides, a large proportion of the international community was behind any post-colonial attempt by locals to take charge of things; Nyerere for many years was considered a visionary, not a failed despot. Even now people sigh in regret: Oh, for what might have been! Only wasn't: the forced collectivization, it was clear even in the early 1970s, wasn't working.

What I didn't like about these texts probably it wasn't even their politics, but their lack of intellectual rigor. By comparison with what I was looking for from philosophy, this was light-weight hoo-ya polemics. Undoubtedly I said so in my paper on these texts. I failed, outright. F. Me! I remember doing the math and realizing that I would get a very low grade in the course indeed with one-third of my grade an F. So I remember embracing the inevitable, going to see the man, pleading ignorance, saying I'd somehow gotten off on the wrong foot, begging for a chance to re-write so I could "do justice to the President's work." I can't remember what I said at a distance of more than thirty years. Perhaps it wasn't this servile. All I remember was the calculated decision that I had to do whatever necessary to defuse the ticking bomb produced by this F. I must have succeeded in flattering him. I re-wrote, producing what must have been a glowing re-appraisal of the great President's works, got a B, and with my other two As for the other sections, the grade for the course as a whole I thought I deserved. So much for a rational discussion of the pros and cons of forced collectivization: President Nyerere was The Future, he insisted, and my job was merely to jump on board. This taught me early on, as similar experiences must teach countless others, that taking courses really is about grades, which means it's about finding out what the professor wants and giving it to him/her.

Grousing

Most college professors are liberal rather than conservative. And the shrillness of the marginalized has become part of the nature of professional humanistic studies. In a world where the claim is precisely that change is effected through texts, why would they have any impetus to downplay rather than play up this "get the students in line" aspect inevitable, to some degree, in any classroom situation? This, I think, is the basis of much right-wing grousing: and of course they're right.

However I just don't think the right wing has understood what feeds this. The language of the professionalization itself is what produces this effect, the fact that professionalization intrinsically means emphasizing the processing plant rather than what goes into that, and of course denying that, really, anything at all goes into it. There is nothing outside the texts (which we do in this classroom), the world consists of a vast library, and the meaning of texts is indeterminate (so all that's left is my voice filling in the void). It's not because professors are left-wing screamers that they think they can get away with spouting this stuff in the classroom. They say it because the very fact of having turned literary studies into a profession has inexorably led to this end.

Nostalgia for the "good old days" of chicken-legged bow-tied white men with wispy hair, a well-chewed pipe, and patches on their elbows is comprehensible: at least these people didn't confuse the things they did in the classroom with the world outside; nor were they encouraged by the vocabulary of their not-yet methodologized profession to think they should be teaching their views rather than trying to discuss what's in Tolstoy. If you assert there's no difference between these two ways of doing things, or no Tolstoy outside, of course your airless world has just become that much more airless. You say that something doesn't exist, so you're not bothered by the thought that it does.

No one denies that the personality of the professor plays a role in how interested the students are. The subject matter students remember decades later stays in their memory because of the transmission. So delivery, given the nature of the classroom experience, turns out to be of major importance, willy nilly. Yet a memorable theater performance can either give us the sense of having really understood the play, or of having seen a bravura technique-show on the part of the actors (the two are rarely compatible). In the same way, a class can leave us either with the sense of having looked more deeply into the essence of things, or instead of having passed a fascinating semester in the presence of an amazingly talented man or woman. The first option is better, and lasts longer.

Making Sense of Life

Where in academic literary study is the joy of personal discovery? A book meaning something to a single person? The way a work will sometimes "speak" to a reader and suddenly help him or her make sense of life? We see how odd the notion of academic literary study is to begin with by saying, with a shrug, Nowhere—of course nowhere. If you just want to read books, then read books. Why do you have to study literature to do that?

Professional literary people scorn the notion that a person alone with a book has much importance at all. That, after all, isn't study—and they're right. To become a study, it needs the trappings of a separate undertaking from anything in the world outside: a jargon, a set of "must-have-reads" that no one with a day job could hope to have read (nor want to), and most important—the focus of my consideration here—a way of approaching literature, a set of presuppositions and questions, that wasn't at all the presuppositions or questions of someone in the world outside.

Many academics in humanities, in particular in literary studies, would be happier if they'd give up on the notion that what they're aiming at is a new view of Mt. Fuji. They could get some pleasure out of their students that way—it's always fun to see new people "get" the postcard view. We're coaches: we have real people who have to be taught to be specific things so they can do other things more elegantly and with greater force. Without the players, we have no raw material: it's certainly not the books. Those we can read on our own.

We can never know enough about another person—or for that matter ourselves—to know how that person will process ideas or information about the world. How about some humility with students too? Why not reason that we do our part by giving them substantial things to think about, without having any idea what they'll do with them or ultimately use them? We do what we can, but individuals always escape our control: some people just aren't at the place in their lives where they can take on board a particular view of a work of art, or perhaps any view.

I remember, at 20, not seeing the point to *Madame Bovary*, and thinking Jane Austen boring. After I'd been around the block a bit, I "got" them. But you couldn't have told me that at 20. Back then, I couldn't read enough of the densely packed decorationist prose of a Nabokov, a Pynchon, or a Proust. Now I can't read any of them: Proust seems to me a sterile whiner, always holding on to his delusions about what life is and isn't rather than, as adults learn to do, letting them go; a profoundly immature writer, childish (bad) rather than child-like (good). Nabokov seems too clever by half: doesn't he realize there are *real problems* in the world? And Pynchon—how of his time he now seems, a real 1970s dinosaur! Yet in the 1970s, you couldn't have pulled *Gravity's Rainbow* from my hands. Now what I read for pleasure is Trollope—all the more amazing for me because at one point the Victorian three-volume novel was the very embodiment of all that the Modernists, my guides to the universe, had transcended.

If we were lucky, we at 20 met with professors who met our pig-headedness with good humor and resignation, and some degree of pleasure: it comes with being young. But are we ourselves as understanding now? Don't we remember that it's difficult to tell the young anything; they just have to figure it out on their own? That's why we have to remind ourselves that we're the coach: we take the raw material we're given, and our goal is to develop this, not transmit the same material to everyone. When they come to class, they've read the texts: all we do in class is come up with a collective version of what they've seen and what they might want to consider. They can discuss these things in class if they want and can, otherwise they can do so later. (Some won't ever do it.) If they do it now, articulately, in class and on the exam, they'll get an A: grading right here, right now is the way life works. But that's not the real goal: the goal is to give them something to help them make sense of their life. I'll never know if I succeeded, but then again, we don't know how most of our interactions with the world turn out.

What I can do for them as the coach during our two to three sessions a week when they're painfully young is articulate the general. For them, Shakespeare's *Midsummer Night's Dream* is about two couples and some fairies. For me, it's about the way attraction is incomprehensible to someone on the outside, and seems utterly arbitrary: nonetheless we're obsessed by what we're obsessed by. For them, *Madame Bovary* is about a woman in 1830s France. For me, it's about the crushing power of limits. For them, Jane Austen is about women wanting to get married. For me it's about powerlessness, something we'll all experience at some point, ultimately. Probably I hadn't at age 20. That's what I say to them: here's something to consider; file it away.

I can say these things, and do. There's still no guarantee that they'll "get" what I say—and this isn't stupidity on their part. People always fail to pay attention to generalizations, because they themselves are particular, and who knows if the general applies to them? An older person can pontificate about how we should choose a marriage partner carefully, but if we think it can't apply to us, because we *have* chosen carefully, we don't benefit from the "wisdom." Even an older person pointing out to them that they're going to die may not seem to hold much relevance for them at their age. And who's to say it should? They'll find out soon enough, when they're ready and able to take this information on board.

One big mistake of intellectuals is to think that just because something can be said, it will be processed when it's said—even: should be processed right then and there. This ignores the elements sketched earlier: of timing, the fact of who's saying it, the silence that surrounds each utterance, and whether the hearer is ready to take this on board. Sometimes the fact is that no articulation will change someone because its time hasn't come. A coach can say, and show, but if it doesn't produce results here and now, his or her job as coach is over: then it's on to another group of players. Sometimes you just have to back off. You say what you can say, do what you do. And then call it a day. You don't think you've transmitted information, because you haven't. You've interacted, using literature as a framework. We spend far too much time worrying about syllabi. We spend far too much time wondering if we've said all there is to say: by definition we never do, and who says that more is necessarily more? We've filled the hour, that's all that matters—just as we've found something to say in an interaction. We don't have to have said the perfect thing, or this thing, so long as we've said something. ·

If we're interesting, what we say will be interesting. We don't have to be interesting with respect to an objective outside world: this doesn't exist. All we have to do is create the classroom situation, not "teach the literature." What we do in class is to articulate things that are there, but that the students may have overlooked, or that may not be clear to them: we can show the patterns. What literature does for any reader is to give him or her the sense that we are not alone: things true for others, in other situations, are also true for us. Or sometimes, that not everyone is like us: this is also something we can learn from literature. We don't study literature; we read it, notice things in it, and talk about it. And then we go on to another work. We'll never read even a fraction of the works in the world before we die, but of course this is fine. That's like saying we won't eat all the food, or say all the things that can be said.

Charming

Works of literature are like verbal communication: they come to be because someone settles on a specific place in the bandwidth of the spectrum s/he is aiming at, assuming that what was aimed at is what was achieved. They're not accidents any more than it's an accident a man is (say) able to come off as competent, charming, sexy, and caring in a blind date: he's trying. (If he tries too hard, he's unlikely to achieve it.) But the particular way he achieves this is up for grabs, and it's made up in the moment, and it presupposes that things don't derail, which may or may not be within his control. Nor do we who read the work of literature have access to the controlling sensibility that was aiming in this particular direction; nor do we know how much was what that sensibility wanted and how much was what it was simply forced to accept.

In professionalized literary studies we take for granted the fact of literature. In discussions about books we don't: it's the fact of literature at all, rather than this particular piece of literature, that's emphasized. In unprofessionalized discussions about books, time spent over a book with a coach, we don't have to have "coverage" or "a sense of terrain" or "cutting-edge authors," all we have to have is authors.

But that's fine. It's only by giving up the pretense of a professionalized manifold of literary studies as our justification for doing what we do that we'll be able to re-connect the works with readers' lives. And it's only with this pretense given up that we can transcend the patchwork of knowledge and wisdom paradigms that bedevils literary studies as it's currently constituted, and focus instead on what matters: the way literature can suddenly make things make sense that didn't before in ways we can't guarantee or predict. Literature without unpredictability is toothless and faded. Which is what it's largely become in "literary studies" today. It's time to leave that world and go back to being (merely) the coach in the classroom. Because that at least might be as intense as literature itself, not as predictable and methodologically bounded as most academic study of literature today.

Football

It would be good, finally, to admit that there are some people in the world who utterly deny the unpredictable aspects of the world: these (at least in caricature, and perhaps also in reality) are the business(wo)men, the football players, the ones who peak early and then find themselves puzzled as life goes on, or become defensive grumblers about the rest of the world, unable to figure out why everybody isn't like them. These may constitute a large proportion of our students.

More generally, it's a problem with reading literature with students that most are young and just haven't figured out just how imprecise the world is, though later on they may well later figure it out. What this means, however, is that while you're reading the literature they don't see its point. It's only later, when things aren't so precise and predictable, that they'll need literature to give names to what they're feeling, to show them what's happening. Much literature, like youth itself, is wasted on the young. Among college-age students, it tends to be those slightly out of sync with the world who more immediately "get" literature, those who already feel the need to give new names to things they see. Those who are happy with the old names, let's call these people the "too well adjusted," are likely to think literature a waste of time. That's where a sympathetic coach comes in: s/he starts with the realization that what s/he is selling is alien, something the players may not even know they need. Railing at the students or pretending this itself isn't an issue is pointless, even counter-productive.

Such students are difficult for any coach. But they're not unreachable, especially if we are sympathetic to their situation of too-great consonance with the world: right now, things are going well for them. It might make them pay attention to us if we point out that no one is immune to surprises, that many marriages go awry, that many men lose their forward drive in their early 40s. Of course that's a future unimaginable to most 20-year-olds, but at least they may file away what we say.

In any case, we have to begin by acknowledging the world they know. And that means, we have to know what world they know. If we want to convince people that the sky is down rather than up, we have to begin by acknowledging that of course they have good reason to believe it up. And now we're going to show the reasons for believing it down, which we think they don't have access to. We should say: here's the world you know. Now let me show you another. This is quite different from the shrill attacks that have typified American higher education for many decades. The aggrieved marginalized won't give initial credit for the world the people they're talking to know to be the case; they are too busy proving that the world isn't this way, but another. Usually they act this way because they simply don't like those they're trying to teach, and so haven't bothered to access their point of view.

If, instead of excoriating those we teach, we can offer evidence we think those we're talking to don't have, we have a chance of connecting with them. If, on top of that, we show them that we remember having been in their place, and actually like them—as a good coach will do—we stand a chance that's probably pretty good of having them listen. This is a kind of education that might actually be effective. The world of professionalized literary studies is not, by contrast, effective education. That's yet another reason to leave its by now stifling halls.

Yes, the world is scarier outside these halls. But the air is fresher, and it's exciting knowing that what we do with students works by the same principles as the world of which they, and we, are a part. No, we can't say we're contributing to knowledge. Nor can we feel we're making them dance to our tune. Why should they? They're individuals too, people not ourselves: at least we won't be so lonely, as we'll be interacting with so many other people.

Literary studies as we've constituted it is, or should be, over. We should all get up from our seats and make for the door, if we haven't done so already. To be sure, we needn't slam the door as we leave. That would be disrespectful; literary studies provided a life to a number of people, and came to be as a natural outgrowth of human thought. We should close the door gently, but firmly, without regret: there's life beyond questions about angels on the head of a pin. It's time even literature professors were part of it again.

Endnotes

[1] Gerald Graff, *Beyond the Culture Wars: How Teaching the Conflict Can Revitalize American Education* (New York: Norton, 1993).

[2] Norman Holland, *Five Readers Reading* (New Haven: Yale University Press, 1975)

[3] M.H. Abrams, *The Mirror and the Lamp: Romantic Theory and the Critical Tradition* (New York: Oxford University Press, 1971).

[4] A methodology developed in the work of A.J. Greimas in such works as *Structural Semantics: An Attempt at a Method* (Lincoln, NE: University of Nebraska Press, 1984).

[5] J.G. Farrell, *The Siege of Krishnapur* (New York: NYRB Classics, 2004).

[6] Susan Sontag, *Against Interpretation and Other Essays*, New York: Picador, 2001, p. 7.

[7] In *Le Livre, oeuvre spirituel,* in *Oeuvres Complètes*, ed. H. Mondor (Paris: Gallimard, 1945), 378.

[8] Michel Foucault, *Language, Counter-Memory, Practice*, ed. Donald Bouchard (Ithaca, NY: Cornell University Press, 1980), 117-118.

[9] E.D. Hirsch, Jr., *Validity in Interpretation* (New Haven: Yale University Press, 1967).

[10] Jacques Derrida, *Of Grammatology*, trans. Gayatri Spivak (Baltimore Johns Hopkins University Press, 1997), 158.

[11] Emily Dickinson, poem XCIX in the *Complete Poems*, ed. Martha Dickinson Bianchi (Boston: Little, Brown, 1924).

[12] I've laid out this aesthetic theory in greater length in *A Post-Romantic Theory of Literature and What Words Can't Do and What They Can* (Lanham, MD: University Press of America, 2003).

[13] Harold Bloom, *The Anxiety of Influence: A Theory of Poetry* (New York: Oxford University Press, 1997).

[14] Richard Rorty, *The Linguistic Turn in Philosophy: Essays in Philosophical Method* (Chicago: University of Chicago Press, 1992).

[15] Lytton Strachey, *Eminent Victorians* (New York: Oxford University Press, 2003).

[16] Roman Jakobson, "Problems in the Study of Literature and Language," in *"Readings in Russian Poetics: Formalist and Structuralist View,* eds. Ladislav Matejka and Krystyna Pomorska. Cambridge, MA: MIT Press, 1971, 79-81.

[17] Roger Kimball, *Tenured Radicals: How Politics Has Corrupted Higher Education* (New York: HarperCollins, 1990); Alan Bloom, *The Closing of the American Mind* (New York: Simon and Schuster, 1988); E.D. Hirsch, Jr, *Validity in Interpretation.*

[18] David Horowitz, *Academic Bill of Rights;* widely available online but otherwise difficult to document. http://www.studentsforacademicfreedom.org/documents/1925/abor.html (accessed 25 March 2008).

[19] http://www.frontpagemag.com/Content/read.asp?ID=50) (accessed 19 June 2006).

[20] David Mamet, *Oleanna* (New York: Vintage, 1993).

[21] Bruce Fleming, *Why Liberals and Conservatives Clash* (New York: Routledge, 2006).

[22] Philip Roth, *Goodbye Columbus* (New York: Houghton, Mifflin, 1959).

[23] Laura Mulvey, "Visual Pleasure and Narrative Cinema," Screen 16.3 (Autumn 1975), 6-18.

[24] Franz Kafka, "Vor dem Gesetz" ("Before the Law"), in *The Transformation (Metamorphosis) and Other Stories* (New York: Penguin, 1995), 165-66.

[25] Randall Jarrell, *Pictures From an Institution* (Chicago: University of Chicago Press, 1986).

[26] http://www.insidehighered.com. March 28 2006.

[27] Ezra Pound and F.S. Flint, "The Imagist Manifesto," quoted in Amy *Lowell's Tendencies in Modern American Poetry* (New York: Macmillan, 1917), 235-249.

[28] Victor Shklovsky, "Art as Technique," in *Russian Formalist Criticism: Four Essays*, ed. Lee T. Lemon and Marion Reis (Lincoln, NE: University of Nebraska Press, 1965), 3-24.

[29] *Bruce Fleming, "On Technique: The Church Exhibition," Centennial Review,* 40.1 (Winter 1996): 159-169.

[30] May 22, 2006.

[31] Jean-François Lyotard, *The Postmodern Condition: A Report on Knowledge* (Minneapolis, MN: University of Minnesota Press, 1984).

[32] Suzanne K. Langer, *Philosophy in a New Key: A Study in the Symbolism of Reason, Rite, and Art* (Cambridge, MA: Harvard University Press, 1957), 18.

[33] *Chronicle of Higher Education*, Jan 19, 2003.

[34] Dec. 29, 2005.

[35] Anne Matthews, Feb 10, 199.

[36] Walter Benjamin, *The Arcades Project*, ed. Rolf Tiedemann, trans. Howard Eiland and Kevin McLaughlin (Cambridge, MA: Harvard University Press, 2002); Mikhail Bakhtin, *The Dialogic Imagination: Four Essays*, ed. Michael Holquist, trans. Caryl Emerson & Michael Holquist (Austin: University of Texas Press, 1981).

[37] Gerald Graff, *Professing Literature: An Institutional History* (Chicago: University of Chicago Press, 1989).

[38] Paul Feyerabend, *Against Method* (New York: Verso, 1993).

[39] 43. 13 (August 8, 1996), 11-15.

[40] Michel Foucault, *The Order of Things: An Archaeology of Human Sciences* (New York: Vintage, 1994).

[41] Northrop Frye, *Anatomy of Criticism: Four Essays* (New York: Atheneum:

1970).

[42] Percy Bysshe Shelley, *Defense of Poetry*, in David Perkins, ed., *English Romantic Writers* (New York: Harcourt, Brace, and World, 1967), 1073.

[43] Gertrude Stein, "Composition as Explanation," in *Selected Writings of Gertrude Stein*, ed. Carl Van Vechten (New York: Vintage, 1945), 511-522.

[44] Stated most clearly in René Wellek and Austin Warren, *Theory of Literature* (New York: Harvest, 1956).

[45] Stephen Benn and Walter Michaels, *Against Theory: Literary Theory and the New Pragmatism*, ed. W. J. T. Mitchell (Chicago: University of Chicago Press, 1985).

[46] T.S. Eliot, "Tradition and the Individual Talent," in *Selected Essays* (New York: Harcourt, 1950), 3-11.

[47] F. O. Mathiessen, *American Renaissance: Art and Expression in the Age of Emerson and Whitman* (New York: Oxford, 1968).

[48] Max Horkheimer and Theodor Adorno, *Dialectic of Enlightenment* (Stanford, CA: Stanford University Press, 2002).

[49] Joseph Gibaldi, *MLA Style Manual and Guide to Scholarly Publishing*, 2nd ed. (New York: MLA, 1998), 161-163.

[50] James Joyce, Stephen Hero (New York: New Directions, 1963), 214.

[51] William Wordsworth, "The Tables Turned: An Evening Scene Upon the Same Subject."

[52] I've considered the fact that dance lacks a text in my *Sex, Art, and Audience: Dance Essays* (New York: Peter Lang, 1994).

[53] As for example in Wolfgang Iser, *The Implied Reader: Patterns of Communication in Prose Fiction from Bunyan to Beckett* (Baltimore: Johns Hopkins University Press, 1978).

[54] Ellen Schrecker, "Worse than McCarthy," Chronicle of Higher Education Review 2/10/2006 (http://chronicle.com/weekly/v52/i23/23b02001.htm, accessed March 25, 2008), B20.

[55] Chinua Achebe, "An Image of Africa: Racism in Conrad's *Heart of Darkness*" *Massachusetts Review* 18.4 (Winter 1977): 782-94.

[56] Bernard Lewis, *Islam and the West* (New York: Oxford University Press, 1994).

[57] Andrea Dworkin, *Intercourse* (New York: Basic Books, 2006).

[58] Ferdinand de Saussure, *Course in General Linguistics* (LaSalle IL: Open Court, 1998). Ludwig Wittgenstein, *Tractatus logico-philosophicus* (London: Routledge, 2001) ; *Philosophical Investigations*, 3rd ed. (New York: Prentice-Hall, 1973).

[59] "Sketch for a Theory of Modernism: Pound and Eisenstein on the Ideogram" *Southwest Review* 84.1 (Winter 1989): 87-97.

[60] I've considered the point that life doesn't come to a halt with the abandonment of any given question in *The New Tractatus* (Lanham, MD: University Press of America, 2007), especially the propositions associated with the opening, whose number in the quasi-Wittgensteinian system is 0.

[61] John Searle, *Speech Acts: An Essay in the Philosophy of Language*

(Cambridge: Cambridge University Press, 1970).

Bibliography of Works Cited

Abrams, M.H. *The Mirror and the Lamp: Romantic Theory and the Critical Tradition.* New York: Oxford University Press, 1971.

Achebe, Chinua. "An Image of Africa: Racism in Conrad's *Heart of Darkness.*" *Massachusetts Review* 18.4 (Winter 1977): 782-94.

Bakhtin, Mikhail. *The Dialogic Imagination: Four Essays.* Ed. Michael Holquist. Trans. Caryl Emerson and Michael Holquist. Austin: University of Texas Press, 1981.

Benjamin, Walter. *The Arcades Project.* Ed. Rolf Tiedemann. Trans. Howard Eiland and Kevin McLaughlin. Cambridge, MA: Harvard University Press, 2002.

Benn, Stephen and Walter Michaels, *Against Theory: Literary Theory and the New Pragmatism.* Ed. W. J. T. Mitchell. Chicago: University of Chicago Press, 1985.

Bloom, Alan. *The Closing of the American Mind.* New York: Simon and Schuster, 1988.

Bloom, Harold. *The Anxiety of Influence: A Theory of Poetry.* New York: Oxford University Press, 1997.

Derrida, Jacques. *Of Grammatology.* Trans. Gayatri Spivak. Baltimore: Johns Hopkins University Press, 1997.

Dworkin, Andrea. *Intercourse.* New York: Basic Books, 2006.

Eliot, T. S. "Tradition and the Individual Talent." In *Selected Essays*, 3-11. New York: Harcourt, 1950.

Farrell, J.G. *The Siege of Krishnapur.* New York: NYRB Classics, 2004.

Feyerabend, Paul. *Against Method.* New York: Verso, 1993.

Fleming, Bruce. *The New Tractatus.* Lanham, MD: University Press of America, 2007.

---.*"On Technique: The Church Exhibition."* *Centennial Review*, 40.1 (Winter 1996): 159-169.

---. *A Post-Romantic Theory of Literature: Art, Artifact and the Innocent Eye.* Lewiston, NY: Mellen, 1991.

---*Sex, Art, and Audience: Dance Essays.* New York: Peter Lang, 2000.

---."Sketch for a Theory of Modernism: Pound and Eisenstein on the Ideogram" *Southwest Review* 84.1 (Winter 1989): 87-97.

---. *Why Liberals and Conservatives Clash.* New York: Routledge. 2006.

Foucault, Michel. *Language, Counter-Memory, Practice.* Ed. Donald Bouchard. Ithaca, NY: Cornell University Press, 1980.

---. *The Order of Things: An Archaeology of Human Sciences.* New York: Vintage, 1994.

Frye, Northrop. *Anatomy of Criticism: Four Essays.* New York: Atheneum: 1970.

Gibaldi, Joseph. *MLA Style Manual and Guide to Scholarly Publishing*, 2nd ed. New York: MLA, 1998.

Graff, Gerald. *Beyond the Culture Wars: How Teaching the Conflict Can Revitalize American Education.* New York: Norton, 1993.

---. *Professing Literature: An Institutional History.* Chicago: University of Chicago Press, 1989.

Hirsch, E.D. Jr. *Validity in Interpretation.* New Haven: Yale University Press, 1967.

Holland, Norman N. *Five Readers Reading.* New Haven: Yale University Press, 1975.

Horkheimer, Max and Theodor Adorno. *Dialectic of Enlightenment.* Stanford, CA: Stanford University Press, 2002.

Iser, Wolfgang. *The Implied Reader: Patterns of Communication in Prose Fiction from Bunyan to Beckett.* Baltimore: Johns Hopkins University Press, 1978.

Jakobson, Roman. "Problems in the Study of Literature and Language." In *"Readings in Russian Poetics: Formalist and Structuralist View.* Eds. Ladislav Matejka and Krystyna Pomorska, 79-81. Cambridge, MA: MIT Press, 1971.

Jarrell, Randall. *Pictures From an Institution,* Chicago: University of Chicago Press, 1986.

Kafka, Franz. "Before the Law". In *The Transformation (Metamorphosis) and Other Stories,* 165-66. New York: Penguin, 1995.

Kimball, Roger. *Tenured Radicals: How Politics Has Corrupted Higher Education.* New York: HarperCollins, 1990.

Lemon, Lee T. and Marion Reis, eds. *Russian Formalist Criticism: Four Essays.* Lincoln, NE: University of Nebraska Press, 1965.

Lentricchia, Frank. "Last Will and Testament of an Ex-Literary Critic," *Lingua Franca,* September/October 1996: 59-67.

Lewis, Bernard. *Islam and the West.* New York: Oxford University Press, 1994.

Lowell, Amy. *Tendencies in Modern American Poetry.* New York: Macmillan, 1917.

Lyotard, Jean-François. *The Postmodern Condition: A Report on Knowledge.* Minneapolis, MN: University of Minnesota Press, 1984.

Mallarmé, Stephane. *Le Livre, oeuvre spirituel.* In *Oeuvres Complètes.* Ed. H. Mondor. Paris: Gallimard-Bibliothèque de la Pléiade, 1945.

Mamet, David. *Oleanna.* New York: Vintage, 1993.

Mathiessen, F.O. *American Renaissance: Art and Expression in the Age of Emerson and Whitman.* New York: Oxford, 1968.

Mulvey, Laura. "Visual Pleasure and Narrative Cinema," *Screen* 16.3 (1975): 6-18.

Rorty, Richard. *The Linguistic Turn in Philosophy: Essays in Philosophical Method.* Chicago: University of Chicago Press, 1992.

Roth, Philip. *Goodbye Columbus.* New York: Houghton, Mifflin, 1959.

Saussure, Ferdinand de. *Course in General Linguistics.* LaSalle IL: Open Court, 1998.

Searle, John. *Speech Acts: An Essay in the Philosophy of Language.* Cambridge: Cambridge University Press, 1970.

Shelley, Percy Bysshe. *Defense of Poetry.* In *English Romantic Writers.* David Perkins, ed., 1072-1087. New York: Harcourt, Brace, and World, 1967.

Schrecker, Ellen. "Worse than McCarthy." *Chronicle of Higher Education Review.* 2 October 2006.

Sontag, Susan. *Against Interpretation and Other Essays.* New York: Picador, 2001.

Stein, Gertrude. "Composition as Explanation." In*Selected Writings of Gertrude Stein.* Ed. Carl Van Vechten, 511-522. New York: Vintage, 1945.

Strachey, Lytton. *Eminent Victorians.* New York: Oxford University Press, 2003.

Wellek, René and Austin Warren. *Theory of Literature.* New York: Harvest, 1956.

Wittgenstein, Ludwig. *Philosophical Investigations*, 3rd ed. New York: Prentice-Hal, 1973.

---. *Tractatus Logico-Philosophicus.* London: Routledge, 2001.

Index

BRUCE FLEMING GRADUATED FROM HAVERFORD College with a degree in philosophy (1974), and earned graduate degrees in Comparative Literature from the University of Chicago (1978) and Vanderbilt University (1982), with studies in Siena and Paris. While a Fulbright Scholar at the Free University Berlin, he wrote *An Essay in Post-Romantic Literary Theory* (1991), his first book, which won the Book Award in Comparative Studies of the Northeast Modern Language Association. His first published short story, "The Autobiography of Gertrude Stein," won an O. Henry Award (1990); more recently he has received the Antioch Review Award for Distinctive Prose, a career award (2005). His most recent book in aesthetics is *Art and Argument: What Words Can't Do and What They Can* (2003). Books on more far-ranging subjects include *Sexual Ethics* (2004), *Science and the Self* (2004), *Disappointment or The Light of Common Day* (2006), *Why Liberals and Conservatives Clash* (2006), and his memoir about the U.S. Naval Academy, where he has taught for more than two decades, *Annapolis Autumn: Life, Death, and Literature at the U.S. Naval Academy* (2005). The culmination of his theoretical works is *The New Tractatus: Summing Up Everything* (2007). He is also the author of a memoir, *Journey to the Middle of the Forest* (2007) and two "plays to be read," *Homage to Eugene O'Neill* and *The Thanksgiving Symposium* (2008), as well as a book of dance essays, *Sex, Art and Audience* (2000) and of the experimental novel *Twilley* (1997), which reviewers compared to works by Henry James, T.S. Eliot, Proust, Thoreau, and David Lynch.